The Era of Authoritarian Neoliberalism

Studies in Critical Social Sciences Book Series

Haymarket Books is proud to be working with Brill Academic Publishers (www.brill.nl) to republish the *Studies in Critical Social Sciences* book series in paperback editions. This peer-reviewed book series offers insights into our current reality by exploring the content and consequences of power relationships under capitalism, and by considering the spaces of opposition and resistance to these changes that have been defining our new age. Our full catalog of *SCSS* volumes can be viewed at https://www.haymarketbooks.org/series_collections/4-studies-in-critical-social-sciences.

Series Editor
David Fasenfest (York University, Canada)

Editorial Board
Eduardo Bonilla-Silva (Duke University)
Chris Chase-Dunn (University of California–Riverside)
William Carroll (University of Victoria)
Raewyn Connell (University of Sydney)
Kimberlé W. Crenshaw (University of California–LA and Columbia University)
Raju Das (York University, Canada)
Heidi Gottfried (Wayne State University)
Alfredo Saad-Filho (Queen's University Belfast)
Chizuko Ueno (University of Tokyo)
Sylvia Walby (Royal Holloway, University of London)

THE ERA OF AUTHORITARIAN NEOLIBERALISM

The Rise of Technocrats, Nationalists and Autocrats

ERNESTO GALLO

Haymarket Books
Chicago, IL

First published in 2025 by Brill Academic Publishers, The Netherlands
© 2025 Koninklijke Brill NV, Leiden, The Netherlands

Published in paperback in 2026 by
Haymarket Books
P.O. Box 180165
Chicago, IL 60618
773-583-7884
www.haymarketbooks.org

ISBN: 979-8-88890-935-5

Distributed to the trade in the US through Consortium Book Sales and Distribution (www.cbsd.com) and internationally through Ingram Publisher Services International (www.ingramcontent.com).

This book was published with the generous support of Lannan Foundation, Wallace Action Fund, and the Marguerite Casey Foundation.

Special discounts are available for bulk purchases by organizations and institutions. Please call 773-583-7884 or email info@haymarketbooks.org for more information.

Cover design by Jamie Kerry and Ragina Johnson.

Printed in the United States.

Library of Congress Cataloging-in-Publication data is available.

Contents

Acknowledgements

First of all, I would like to express my heartfelt gratitude to Alfredo Saad-Filho and David Fasenfest, without whom this book would have never been possible.

Throughout long months of reading, research, and writing, I strongly benefitted from the conversation and the encouragement of many scholars, some of whom I call friends: Andrea Lagna, Nichola Khan, Bhabani Shankar Nayak, Antonio Cerella, and of course Diego Giannone and Adriano Cozzolino from the University of Campania Luigi Vanvitelli, where I spent four weeks as a Visiting Researcher in May and June 2024. I also presented on similar topics at the SISP (Italian Political Science Association) Annual Conference 2024, in Trieste, where I benefitted from the suggestions of Adriano Cozzolino, Daniela Caterina, Aline Regina Alves Martins and Giuseppe Montalbano.

At Regent's University London I often discussed these topics with several colleagues, and I received particular encouragement and insight from Mireille Hebing, Neven Andjelic, Maria Rikitianskaia, Vanessa King and Cecile Ogufere.

I would like to also recognise the intellectual debt to some of my former colleagues in Turin, and especially Alfio Mastropaolo, Luigi Bonanate, Giancarlo Minaldi, Antonella Delbosco.

My friends, Simone Dalmasso and Janet Pinto Garces, have long kept me updated on the evolutions of neoliberalism especially in Latin America.

Thanks of course go to my mother, especially for the patience in listening to complex ideas, often on the phone.

CHAPTER 1

Introduction

Since the 1980s and especially in the 'West', neoliberalism has filled the lives of hundreds of millions of humans with empty promises, dreams of success, of ambition, of desire, ultimately dreams about personal, individualistic achievement. Initially, globalisation sounded a friendly word, one tinged with cosmopolitan tones, especially when it combined with aspirations to peace and democracy, in Europe, in the imagined worlds of the 'Third Ways', the 'New Democrats', the global humanitarian organisations, the pacific movement of humans, goods and services. Yet something happened; or, better said, neoliberalism showed its ugly face.

To be frank, this was already in the cards; it was predictable and had it been predicted. Those more attentive to the vicissitudes of developing countries had seen it before. Chile had seen it all in 1973. Neoliberalism had started in an authoritarian, repressive, violent regime, one not only supported by unelected technocrats and large multinational corporations, but also embodied by a fully-fledged dictator, one Augusto Pinochet Ugarte, a Chilean general partly enthroned by the CIA and Kissinger's sinister manoeuvres. Was that the first neoliberal government? Not necessarily, it is difficult to say; one should check every single country on Earth. Yet neoliberalism had started in developing countries, almost like an experiment, a test. More socially oriented regimes, such as Nkrumah's in Ghana or Nasser's in Egypt, had already been removed or were giving way to new forces. In the 1960s and 1970s Latin America witnessed a series of military coups, which combined the removal of communism, socialism or any other left-wing forces with support to pro-business groups, whether in Argentina, Brazil, Chile, Uruguay or Central American states. These early neoliberal regimes were benignly called cases of 'bureaucratic authoritarianism' (O'Donnell 1988), but at least some of them would end up with paramilitary violence, death squads, death flights, and, for that matter, economic failure. They were not the only ones.

In the 1980s, while the West's narrative was one of opening to democracy in the name of a fight against an 'evil empire', similar neoliberal measures extended to Africa, where, with the help of military regimes or authoritarian leaders, Washington-supported policies demolished the significant economic development achieved in countries like Ghana, Ivory Coast or Nigeria. At the same time, though formally democratic, leading Western countries such as the USA and the UK took on more authoritarian traits and adopted strong neoliberal and nationalist policies, whose real nature was recognised by few, apart from the victims. Among those few, there was a Jamaica-born British scholar, Stuart Hall (1979), who early on called Thatcher's Britain a case of 'authoritarian populism'. Meanwhile, the process of European integration was deepening, but in an economic more than a political sense. After setting aside (somewhat timid) leftist proposals from France, Italy, and other countries, the newly born European Union appeared as a largely technocratic body, little more than a firefighter against inflation, according to the rigid German doctrine of ordoliberal austerity which came to permeate its institutions and hegemonise its politics since its very beginnings in 1992. Ordoliberals, who were originally calling themselves 'neoliberals', were supporting a kind of German version of neoliberalism, with a stronger emphasis on the role of the state in maintaining competition and promoting deflationary policies. Its adoption at a both German and EU level coincided with the peak time of the 'Washington Consensus' – the cocktail of privatisations, liberalisations, austerity and deregulation proposed/imposed by the World Bank, the International Monetary Fund (IMF) and the US Treasury to many developing countries all over the world – and strongly contributed to the waves of financial collapses, economic bubbles and broader economic decline throughout the world in the 20th century's last decades.

At the same time, while the expression 'populism' had not yet become common currency, new right-wing parties, with nationalist and at times racist overtones, began gaining support: the National Front in France, the Northern League in Italy, the *Vlaams Belang* (VB; 'Flemish Interest') in the Flanders, the Freedom Party (FPÖ, *Freiheitliche Partei Österreichs*) in Austria. These forces were initially seen as slightly more than peripheral degenerations of what looked like a strong and secure path towards globalisation and democracy, also at a supranational level. Yet transnational terrorism, the Global War on Terror, the ascendancy of US neoconservatism, the surprising rise to power of an economic tycoon in Italy, Silvio Berlusconi, democracy's failure in Russia, China's incipient neoliberalisation, sub-Saharan Africa's seemingly endless decline, were already significant signals of shifts in politics' key paradigms.

The crisis which started in 2007–08 and was initially circumscribed to the West and the financial industry, spread almost everywhere (significantly, not much in China), overwhelmed both the economy and the politics of many countries, and contributed to a clear intensification of authoritarian neoliberalism in a range of directions. Technocracy became dominant in Southern Europe and, as soon as the Euro started shaking, unelected economists replaced legitimate, if flawed, governments in Greece and Italy. IMF/EU/ECB (European Central Bank) 'therapies' were imposed also to Cyprus, Ireland, Portugal, Spain.

Populism, with increasingly nationalist colours, provided a response in many countries. Sometimes, like in some Latin American and African governments, technocracy and nationalist populism went hand-in-hand. After Monti's technocratic experiment, the Italian Ministry of the Economy mostly ended in the hands of an unelected expert, including in the unusual coalition which formed the government in the wake of the 2018 elections and included right-wing and centrist populist forces. At the same time, nationalist populism, which was already existing but often far from political power, grew substantially in Central, Eastern and even Northern Europe. More traditional authoritarianism returned in the Philippines, Southeast Asia, Egypt, and of course Russia and some of its post-Soviet neighbours. This book claims that the 2007–08 'Great recession', which has never been truly addressed, was decisive in the consolidation of authoritarian neoliberalism in all its varieties.

The political field became increasingly open to any kind of adventurism and demagoguery, although demagogues obtained and maintained power with a clear sense of their purpose and full awareness of the aims of those whom they represented. 2016 is often seen as a watershed year, at least in the West. Brexit signalled to the world some dissatisfaction with Brussels' technocracy, although in many ways it had been supported by a part of the British economic establishment and signified the intention to return to some form of imperial 'nation-state'. Few months later, Donald Trump was elected to the White House in a shocking vote which empowered a nationalist, authoritarian, plutocratic representative of a new type of repressive, aggressive, protectionist neoliberalism. Yet again, most of the world was moving in a nationalist, populist, and neoliberal direction, including Japan and South Korea, India under Modi's *Hindutva*, Bolsonaro's Brazil, Kagame's Rwanda, Sisi's Egypt ... with Xi's China itself actively intensifying its policies of both nationalism and neoliberalism.

How can we make sense of all the events and changes mentioned above without avoiding conceptual overstretching? And without conflating generalisations with local and socio-historical specificities? Putting some order is of paramount importance, especially at a time of frenzied and unending convulsions, and despite promises of a more humane world in the wake of the Covid-19 pandemic. The war in Ukraine, conflicts in Gaza and Lebanon, in Yemen and Sudan, several regions in Sahelian Africa and Kashmir, all point to challenges which both the practices and ideas of the current political economy have been unable to meet.

To better address the phenomena associated with authoritarian neoliberalism, this book starts by putting some conceptual order. Chapter 2 focuses on definitions and hypotheses. First of all, it defines neoliberalism, which is here mostly understood in structural and critical terms, as a product and process of dynamics led by the upper classes and the state. The book partly relies on Harvey's theories while also critiquing some of his seminal views. Subsequently, the chapter focuses on the idea of authoritarianism, first by criticising Linz's well-known approach and then by embracing Glasius's perspective on authoritarian practices. It is claimed that democracy and authoritarianism are not polar opposites; they rather lie along a continuum. There is also a significant correlation between neoliberalism and authoritarianism, and the chapter's final part is dedicated to the emergent debates around 'authoritarian neoliberalism', which is the book's ultimate topic.

Chapter 3 is dedicated to an overview of the three varieties of authoritarian neoliberalism: technocracy, nationalism, traditional authoritarianism. They are not specifically tied to stages in economic development or geographic regions; they are often intertwined and overlapping, particularly in the cases of technocracy and populist nationalism. What is technocracy? In Political Science, the term refers to government by unelected, appointed experts. It was first somewhat popular in the 19th century, in Europe and Latin America, although mostly among intellectuals; it gained momentum in the 20th century, especially since the New Deal, and became widespread in the neoliberal era. The book claims that technocracy, far from being based in objective, neutral economic science, is deeply political and it usually serves the interests of the upper classes, especially transnational capital in the global age. The chapter follows technocracy's historical trajectory and its origins in Latin America in the tragical experiences of bureaucratic authoritarianism. It continues with its more recent evolutions in Africa, the former USSR, and the European countries the USSR controlled; in the former Soviet bloc, technocracy has often strong local roots. Lastly, the chapter concentrates on the EU experience, which has demonstrated technocracy's aggressiveness also in countries such as Greece and Italy, and on the overlaps between technocracy and populism, in Latin America as well as in Europe.

The following section focuses on nationalism, that is, the international dimension of populism. Despite the apparent contradiction between nationalism and neoliberalism, the two ideologies have often joined forces, as experiences such as those of Thatcher or Reagan demonstrate. The section discusses their elective affinities and continues by looking at prominent contemporary experiences such as Brexit, Trumpism, Orbán's Hungary, Modi's India and Abe's Japan. Chapter 3 ends with a section on authoritarianism *per se* and draws a line between the emergence of authoritarian practices, especially in the West, and fully authoritarian countries like Russia and China where nationalism and neoliberalism have merged surprisingly well, particularly for security or party elites.

The book's second half focuses on three big case studies, one for each variety. Italy, the only G7 member in which independent experts have exercised prime ministerial roles, is the representative of technocracy. In its traditionally fractious and polarised political system, technocrats, especially economists from central banking bodies, became the key players in the transition to the neoliberal era and the accession to the EU and the Eurozone in the 1990s. No other political actors could match technocrats' initial legitimacy. Yet Italy's Europeanisation also triggered the reaction of that more national fraction of the bourgeoisie which, led by the controversial billionaire, Silvio Berlusconi, since 1994 has joined the political arena and proposed more nationalist choices. Berlusconi's coalition in fact dominated the 2000s, and mostly protected its factional interests without reacting to the EU/Eurozone crisis which started in 2008 and ended Berlusconi's reign in 2011. This happened in the wake of an uproar of international capital markets and European institutions, which returned the baton of command to the economist and former EU Commissioner, Mario Monti. Ever since Italy has seen an alternation (at times a complementarity) between populist/nationalist and technocratic governments. Technocracy's peak was achieved with Draghi's executive during the Covid-19 pandemic, while nationalists, led by Giorgia Meloni, have been in power since 2022 without substantially shifting from the neoliberal/technocratic agenda.

A country in which the nationalist-neoliberal combination has been strongest is Britain, the second case-study. Such combination first emerged with Thatcher's premiership (1979–92), Hall's famous case of 'authoritarian populism' (Hall 1979), and promoted a competitive and individualistic mentality, in the relations between both citizens and countries. The New Labour hegemony (1997–2010) adopted a more internationalist agenda, but did not renounce neoliberalism at all. Neoliberalism would further relaunch under the Conservatives with their draconian austerity policies following the 'Great recession' and the 2010 elections. Migrants and the EU would then be constructed as convenient scapegoats, a fact which explains the rejection of EU membership in the controversial 2016 Brexit referendum. As we will see, Brexit has been the outcome of a nationalist, protectionist, and even imperialist attitude of the middle classes and of key fractions of Britain's (especially, England's) capital. The ensuing years have witnessed the rise and eventual decline of Boris Johnson's nationalism, but also the emergence of new and more radical forms of nationalist neoliberalism such as those embodied by Farage's various political creatures and by the new 'national conservatives'. Both have espoused strong anti-immigration policies and a competitive, aggressive form of neoliberalism. Labour's return to government (2024) has so far highlighted a shift to a more technocratic form of neoliberalism, without giving up on nationalism, which is still strong among the population, as is expressed by the popularity of Farage's latest creature, Reform UK.

The third case-study, that related to a traditional, autocratic form of authoritarianism, is exemplified by Russia. Russia never fully diverged from an authoritarian path, despite the hopes raised by President Yeltsin in the early 1990s. The neoliberal fraction within the country was quite significant, but international variables played a crucial role. The neoliberal 'shock therapy' approved by the IMF and the US Treasury in 1992 hit a tremendous economic blow, which in the short term led to a clash between Yeltsin and a more nationalist, socially oriented Parliament. While living standards collapsed, Yeltsin attempted to govern with the support of the early offspring of neoliberalisation, the oligarchs. The new state remained profoundly fractured and internationally weak, and after 1998 Yeltsin re-opened a door to the powerful faction of the security and intelligence forces (the *siloviki*), which gained the presidency with Putin's election in 2000. Initially Putin chose a neoliberal course with some, if minimal, elements of democracy. Once tensions with the West resurfaced, he slowly but surely adopted a more confrontational posture, enhanced the statist element in domestic affairs, and consolidated his own power by balancing between different factions of oligarchs, *siloviki*, liberals, nationalists and so on. After Putin's re-election in 2012, authoritarianism and tensions with the West became increasingly stronger, and the *siloviki* gradually gained more influence. At the same time, neoliberalism has hardly disappeared, and Putin's *siloviki* clique has somehow replaced the oligarchs of the Yeltsin era. The Ukraine war can be interpreted also as instrumental to the power consolidation of this specific clique. It is important to remember that Russia's modicum of prosperity is mostly due to constantly high energy prices, rather than to social policies which have all but disappeared, at least in comparison to welfarist states.

The three case-studies illustrate three important trends which, as was mentioned, are not mutually exclusive. They express different ways of catching up with neoliberalism in different contexts. Most recent evolutions seem to suggest trajectories towards new forms of authoritarianism – some silent takeover of a country the Hungarian way – as well as new and abrasive forms of nationalism; India's *Hindutva* could be an example. Technocracy itself seems to be mutating towards a form where technocrats are less and less important while data have taken centre stage, and are used by increasingly questionable conglomerates of unaccountable centres of political, economic and cultural power. Demonising Trump's return *cum* Musk would be an error. Scholarship has to first investigate and understand. Yet it has to do it fast, before the risk that an incipient dystopia might soon overwhelm us and our planet.

CHAPTER 2

Explaining the Key Terms

Soon after the inception of the 'Great recession' in late 2007, neoliberalism and anything that had to do with a 'pure' market economy were pronounced dead (Stiglitz 2009). But was that really the case? To be honest, nobody was able to find neoliberalism's corpse. Critical authors such as Smith (2008) remained cautious and doubtful; others (Crouch 2011) went further and wrote about the 'strange non-death of neoliberalism'. Or had neoliberalism morphed into a zombie (Monbiot 2016)? Despite attacks from both 'left' and 'right', critiques, denunciations, organised protests (from Occupy Wall Street to Extinction Rebellion), and the consistently precarious global conditions of planet Earth, of the global economy, of global healthcare, and so on, neoliberalism's cobweb has adapted and survived; it has consolidated and even given birth to a range of varieties and mutants. All of them seem to share a more aggressive, intoxicating, viral character: has neoliberalism become more authoritarian? Yes, it has. In fact it has always contained authoritarian seeds – clearly visible since its birth pangs in the 1930s – but they have strengthened and become more evident in recent times, especially since the beginnings of the 'Great recession' in 2007.

This chapter intends to define concepts and propose a taxonomy. Defining neoliberalism, authoritarianism and their intersection is key if we intend to theorise about the world of the early 21st century, and interpret phenomena apparently as different as the emergence of Trumpism, the rise of surveillance capitalism and the horror of pandemic politics. It is also essential to better understand a planet where the narrative of a triumphant democratic globalisation (Fukuyama 1989) in the early 1990s has quite rapidly met sharp decline.

1 Neoliberalism

The term 'neoliberalism' is largely used (especially by its critics), highly contested and deployed with a wide variety of meanings. Do we need it at all? Some commentators have rejected it and believe that neoliberalism is a useless, catch-all, simply pejorative term (Magness 2019); such noun would be mostly used by leftist critics, and rarely by pro-market (and supposedly neoliberal) politicians and authors (Boas and Gans-Morse 2009: 138). Additionally, neoliberalism has appeared in several different forms, as is illustrated by Mirowski and Plehwe (2009), since the origins during Germany's Weimar Republic (Burgin 2012) and up to the early 21st century and our days. The approach followed in this book chiefly focuses on the role played by class and state in shaping neoliberalism; other paradigms are discussed as well, since they enrich and bring to life a highly nuanced concept. This section first sheds light on the significance of the upper classes and the state to neoliberalism itself; it pays deep and specific attention to Harvey's seminal work, which is discussed and criticised together with other approaches (especially, those centred on 'neoliberalisations'), before concluding with a reflection on some of the many problems neoliberalism has brought along.

Broadly following Springer (2012) and England and Ward (2007), in the first-place neoliberalism can be defined with reference to market-oriented policies (privatisation, deregulation, liberalisation, fiscal discipline, austerity, etc), which have been usually promoted by international organisations since the 1970s in developing countries. This is the neoliberalism of the Washington Consensus (Peet and Hartwick 2009: 84–94) and the IMF/World Bank conditionality programmes. It is the neoliberalism of the structural adjustment reforms and their highly controversial and often brutal effects, especially in Latin America, South Asia, sub-Saharan Africa, the former Soviet Union, and later the European Union (EU). These policies have been heavily criticised, usually because of their destructive impact on the environment, people's well-being and health, traditional social institutions, local cultures and economies, employment patterns, working classes' conditions, and more. But where do such policies originate? Who are their supporters and proponents? What are their objectives? Focusing on the policies tends to overlook bigger issues related to their roots and structural origins; in other words, it neglects the dimension of the 'politics' of neoliberalism. Replacing policies with more 'benevolent', generous ones, overlooks the reality that policies are embedded within specific political systems and ideologies, which influence the policy choices. Changing the latter requires understanding and transforming the former.

Drawing on a critical political economy which dates to Karl Marx (1818–83), this book claims that neoliberalism's most important agents are the upper classes and the state. Neoliberalism is not a specific economic theory; it is a political theory, an ideology, at times even a doctrine. More precisely, the male-dominated upper classes in wealthy countries (usually former colonial metropoles and their neighbours), their emerging counterparts in the developing world, and rich, powerful states have been neoliberalism's key instigators. Neoliberalism itself is a political theory and at the same time a political initiative; it is a worldview, as Thatcher claimed when she famously remarked

"Economics are the method: The object is to change the soul" (1981, in Albertson and Stepney 2020: 320). Broadly speaking, the core aim of the various forms of neoliberalism is to increase the upper classes' profits and power; wider and deeper markets are usually the key means to that objective. In this sense, a major contribution to the debate on neoliberalism is that of the British Marxist geographer, David Harvey (2003; 2004; 2005; 2006; 2016), and like-minded scholars such as the French economists, Gérard Duménil and Dominic Lévy (2004).

An anthropologist and interpreter of 'The Capital', Harvey reads neoliberalism as an upper-class project, which has been adopted and implemented by states throughout most world regions. In his view, it emerged as the new leading bourgeois ideology after the 1960s and 1970s, when in the West (especially the USA and Britain) profits had declined as a result of the working class's gains in the age of welfare, protests and rising salaries. Moreover, since the 1960s new leftist movements (pacifist, ecologist, feminist, anti-racist, socialist, etc) and parties (nationalist, socialist and communist, in Latin America, Africa, Southern Europe, the Middle East, etc) had gained visibility in many continents and were challenging capitalist domination. Following Harvey, neoliberalism became the expression of the ideas and interests of the bourgeoisie and rapidly spread all over the world, sometimes pushed by US imperialism (especially in Latin America), sometimes in a more autonomous and culturally specific way (in China or India or Eastern Europe). According to the capitalist logic of 'accumulation by dispossession' (Harvey 2004: 73–6), neoliberalism has taken the shape of privatisations, financialisation, crisis management (especially in developing countries, with the active intervention of the IMF and the World Bank) and redistributions in favour of the wealthy (Harvey 2004). This has led to worldwide deprivation, inequality, feelings of injustice, and outright poverty. An example of the key role of financial capital in neoliberalism's early stages is illustrated by the neoliberal takeover of New York City in 1975 (Harvey 2006: 150), when the bankers, together with the Republican Party and the 'moral majority' the latter had captured, strongly contributed to the collapse of social policies in the USA's economic heartland. In developing and emerging countries financialisation's effects have been even more traumatic. Saad-Filho (2011) highlights how financial capital has not only damaged the working class and (to a lesser extent) productive capital. It has also weakened developing countries' states, since they have been forced to open up markets, cut welfare programmes and co-exist with worldwide financial turbulences, while financialisation has strengthened US (and Western) imperialism and power worldwide.

Together with the upper bourgeoisie, the other key agent and promoter of neoliberalism has been the state, especially in the world's most affluent regions.

This is recognised by Harvey (2005), who points to the contradictions between neoliberal theory (where governments and markets are often pitted against each other, especially in the American tradition of the University of Chicago) and neoliberal practices, by which the state has been a key gatekeeper to capital and one of its main promoters. *This book argues that in reality there are no such contradictions.* The neoliberal state has taken upon itself the role of creator and guardian of markets, a task which in fact is also acknowledged in neoliberal theory. For instance, Konings (2012) illustrates how US state power has paved the way to the rise of financial capital and the upper class's success by resorting to Mann's (1984) concept of 'infrastructural power'. In other words, the neoliberal state, far from being a victim of financial markets, has penetrated and reshaped them, especially by adopting monetarist policies and creating new regulations, and has later rescued massive financial institutions under the rhetoric of the 'too-big-to-fail' (Konings 2012: 93–6). The state has created markets, empowered financial capital, dispossessed the poor, and become ever more business-like, up to morphing into a neoliberal player – a business entity – itself, since the era of the 'New Public Management'. The bailout of banks and other financial institutions in the USA, Britain and elsewhere after 2007 is a key example of these practices. After all, such practices are fully aligned with some neoliberal theoretical traditions like German ordoliberalism. Ordoliberal thinkers in the Weimar Republic (on this see Foucault 2008) first used the expression 'neoliberalism' in 1938 (Boas and Gans-Morse 2009) and emphasised the importance of a strong and active state, which would have been pivotal to the continental European experience.

Ordoliberalism laid the intellectual foundations of the more socially oriented 'social market economy' and the German economic miracle (*Wirtschaftswunder*) after World War Two; additionally, it stressed the importance of an active, interventionist state able to maintain order and protect the market and competition, even to the detriment of democracy. Ordoliberal economists such as Walter Eucken and Alexander Rüstow cared about the state and economic freedom more than about democracy (Foucault 2008). Ordoliberal theory might also better explain the authoritarian shift of the latest decades and unearth neoliberalism's early authoritarian leanings. Harvey (2005) refers extensively to neoliberalism's authoritarian shift, for instance in the Chilean, Chinese and Russian experiences, but without mentioning the ordoliberal tradition (sometimes known as 'German neoliberalism'), which had a strong impact on the redefinition of the state in continental Western Europe after 1945 and on the EU after 1992. Ordoliberalism placed strong emphasis on the necessity to maintain competition and on the role of technocrats, although some ordoliberals later embraced more welfarist policies and contributed to the progressive aspects of the social market economy (*Sozialmarktwirtschaft*; Boas and Gans-Morse 2009). Despite overlooking ordoliberalism, Harvey discussed in depth the question of neoliberalism's variety (2005). More than following a well-defined trajectory, neoliberalism has in fact moved through a multiplicity of forms. In recent decades neoliberal states have often assumed stronger nationalist and authoritarian characteristics. Following Harvey, we have seen combinations of neoliberalism and nationalism in the age of Reagan and Thatcher, let alone Pinochet's dictatorship in Chile (1973–90); we have seen a neoliberal-neoconservative blend in Reagan's and Bush Jr's militarism and occasional protectionism; we have seen the rise of neoliberal-populist and neoliberal-authoritarian hybrids (including in China, India, and Russia), all aspects which are linked with this book's core theme.

On other aspects, Harvey's work is less convincing. A questionable aspect of his theory is the view of neoliberalism as a political 'project'. The expression 'project' sounds too strong and overarching; it implies a well-defined rational will which does not give justice to the complexities and varieties of the neoliberal phenomenon. Perhaps other terms ('movement' or 'initiative'?) would be more fitting. Moreover, while Harvey's work focuses mostly on social classes and states, other players and relations are important as well. What are they exactly?

An alternative (or complementary) position on neoliberalism rotates around the processes and the micro-players, which would interact with states, international organisations, and other 'big' actors. In this sense, following and even going beyond Foucault (2008), neoliberalism would also be an everyday practice, a governmentality, which develops in microsites and interstices. The stress here is on circumscribed phenomena and on processes. Instead of 'neoliberalism', the expression 'neoliberalisation', often in the plural, would better capture the essence of variegated phenomena (Larner 2003; Peck 2004; Brenner, Peck and Theodore 2010), which cross states, corporations and large institutions and embody a diffused, shared mentality of power and control, government and domination. Both 'big N' and 'small n' neoliberalism deserve full scholarly attention (Ong 2007).

Brenner, Peck and Theodore (2010) have explained the advantages of focusing on neoliberalisation rather than neoliberalism by highlighting the limitations of some of the main approaches to the latter. For example, the 'Varieties of Capitalism' (VoC) paradigm tends to lock neoliberalism within states, which would act as 'containers', and sees it as a mainly Anglo-American product, which is later reproduced in other countries (Brenner, Peck and Theodore 2010: 191). According to Brenner and his co-authors (2010: 197), historical materialist approaches would mostly concentrate on the global and supranational dimensions and overlook the local. Foucauldian and governmentality approaches, by contrast, would focus on the local and contingent. Brenner and his collaborators prefer emphasising a more variegated, spatially uneven, and hybrid set of processes which have taken place in a historically varied manner since the origins of the word 'neoliberal' in Weimar Germany.

The concept of neoliberalisation possesses significant strengths. It provides a flexible, plural, historically situated view of social and economic change in the direction of a stronger market. It gives account of the continuities as well as the differences between many 'neoliberalisms' in theory and practice, at a macro- and micro-level. At the same time, however, the emphasis on class, state and other long-standing structures is less pronounced. The key supporters and actors of neoliberalism are not clearly identified; in particular, the proponents of the 'neoliberalisation' paradigm could have expanded on the relations between neoliberalism and the state, which is deemed so crucial in this work and, far from being a mere 'container', is one of neoliberalism's main enablers, actors and players.

Neoliberalism has been attacked and criticised on many grounds. From a purely quantitative viewpoint, since the 1970s economic inequalities have risen in many leading countries such as the USA, China, Germany, Britain, France (The World Bank n.d. a and b; Harvey 2006: 148–49); growth has slowed down and unemployment (or underemployment) has risen, also because of massive crises partly caused by neoliberalism – such as the 'Great recession' and the Covid-19 pandemic. Many regional crises, often with worldwide effects, have then burst out since the 1980s' turbulences in Latin America and Central/Eastern Europe. Neoliberalism has also ossified gender inequalities, by forcing the survival of traditional production relationships, in developed and in many developing countries (Federici 2012). Even more than the quantitative effects, however, the qualitative impact of neoliberalism has been devastating. In some relatively strong economies, neoliberal reforms have contributed to collapse in public health: in the mid-1990s Russia's life expectancy precipitated to 58 years for men and 68 for women (Standing 1998). Climate crisis and pandemics are the tips of the iceberg of a series of traumatic consequences. Emphasis on marketisation and self-entrepreneurship has often led to the emergence of underclasses of deluded working poors. The commodification of states, whole industries (healthcare, culture, education, the media, hospitality among others) and entire sets of social relations has engendered loss of quality, disaffection, poor morale, and alienation. Standardisation rather than quality has often become the norm, as had been early envisaged by Ritzer (1993). Rules and bureaucracy have returned centre stage, according to Weber's prescient predictions and in line with what, after all, markets require if we want them to 'function' properly. The domination of instrumental rationality has accompanied the emergence of a form of accumulation which appears quintessentially capitalistic along the lines famously written by Marx and Engels (1848: 15–6):

> [The bourgeoisie] ... has drowned the most heavenly ecstasies of religious fervour, of chivalrous enthusiasm, of philistine sentimentalism, into the icy water of egotistical calculation. [...] In one word, for exploitation, veiled by religious and political illusions, it has substituted naked, shameless, direct, brutal exploitation.

But when and how has neoliberalism turned authoritarian? In a sense, both its theory and practice have contained many authoritarian elements since the beginnings. While the 'Great recession' seems to represent a kind of watershed (Ryan 2019), the authoritarian turn had started earlier. The authoritarian elements have become dominant and neoliberalism has started mutating in at least three main directions. First, it is though important to clarify what we mean by authoritarianism.

2 Authoritarianism

'Authoritarianism' is a quite recent term. It gained prominence in the 20th century's final decades (Przeworski 2019: 17), and often replaced older terms such as 'dictatorship'. It is usually associated with either a non-democratic political form – a type of government or regime (Linz 1964; 1978; 2000) – or a psychological type, a personality with some well-defined traits (Adorno et al 1950).

This work concentrates on the former and contends that, more than a clear-cut divide, there is a continuum (Schedler 1998), a spectrum, between authoritarianism and liberal democracy. Liberal, consolidated democracy can fully mutate into 'traditional' authoritarianism or, under some structural conditions, simply take on some authoritarian 'practices' (Glasius 2018a), which *de facto* limit the quality and at times even the nature of democracy itself. This section first analyses and critiques the classical interpretations of authoritarianism (especially, that proposed by Linz) and later explores and critiques the concept of 'authoritarian practice'; finally, it introduces the key theme of the nexus between authoritarianism and neoliberal capitalism.

Juan J. Linz started his classical works on authoritarianism (1964; 1978; 2000) by focusing on his Francoist Spain, which he studied both in Spain and from the USA, as a Professor at Yale University. His scholarship has been much debated and criticised, especially because of the allegedly static, descriptive nature of his ideal types and particularly in Spain, where debates on Franco's regime have been extremely heated and intense (Miley 2011). Despite their limits and rather dry contours, Linz's categories, based in vast historical knowledge, capture some aspects of authoritarianism, but especially outside Spain and in more contemporary times. Famously, Linz saw in authoritarianism four key characteristics. Two of them refer to the institutions, that is, 'limited pluralism' and a strong executive. Formal institutions were, after all, among Linz's core scientific interests. The point on 'limited pluralism' remains though tremendously contentious. What kind of pluralism, if limited, was possible in Francoist Spain, where children, women, political opponents, homosexuals, and others were killed in the hundreds of thousands in concentration camps also after the civil war's end? In a regime where experiments were carried out on humans to find the 'red gene' (Preston 2006: 303–20)? There was a chilling kind of pluralism indeed, within the ruling class, between the leader, the *Falange*, the Church, and other players; this, to a large extent, was also true for fascist and usually called 'totalitarian' Italy and in fact other non-democratic states all over the world.

The other two characteristics that Linz singled out attempted to encapsulate the regime's deep nature. Authoritarianism, unlike totalitarianism, would draw on a mentality, not a fully-fledged ideology. This element points to its contingency, pragmatism, reliance on emotions, as well as to difficulties in mobilising both the masses – other than for temporary reasons (economic crises, national unity and security issues, coping with more-or-less imagined threats, and so on) – and intellectuals, who would not feel attracted by authoritarianism's poverty (and ultimately barbarity) of vision. Finally, authoritarianism would rely on rather passive obedience and submission, in contrast with totalitarianism's constant mobilisation towards a utopian (or in fact dystopian) national future. The focus on mentality and passivity has been lively debated, notably by Spanish authors. Franco's Spain was far less static, much more ideological (often in different directions: nationalist, fascist, Catholic), violent, and authoritarian than what Linz probably assumed; Linz's study of Francoism has been accused of being too benign, and Linz himself of being even an 'organic intellectual' of Franco's regime (Miley 2011: 41). Abstracting from Spain, however, Linz captured dimensions (some degrees of pragmatism and apathy) which would characterise authoritarian regimes at a later stage, particularly after the end of the Cold war and its ideological divides. He (1978: 14–15) also pointed to authoritarianism's relative weakness vis-à-vis both democracy and totalitarianism, which have tended to attract the interests and ideological debates of the 'Great Powers', from the USA, the USSR and Britain after World War Two to China later. None of them is, or has been, simply and only authoritarian.

Linz's work has been criticised also because he provided a 'negative' definition of authoritarianism, that is, a definition of what authoritarianism is NOT; in particular, it would be neither democracy nor totalitarianism (Glasius 2018a: 519). Authoritarianism would therefore be a kind of residual category; additionally, Linz located its origins in the political and institutional dimensions, rather than in the more comprehensive social and structural sphere, as Marxist authors did. These critiques hold value, but we must not forget that, soon after the Second World War, scholarly and media attention focused more on either US-style liberal democracy or Soviet communism, and not much attention was paid to other regimes. As a matter of fact, many authoritarian regimes came into being later, especially after 1989 and in a rather pragmatic way. Linz's concept of authoritarianism provides a framework to understand some aspects of political realities such as 21st century China and Russia, other ex-Soviet republics (Kazakhstan, Uzbekistan, Azerbaijan, Belarus, etc), some states in Africa and Asia (Egypt, Rwanda, Qatar, Myanmar, Vietnam, etc), and so on.

Different authors, including Linz, have also distinguished between different types of authoritarian regimes (Gasiorowski 2006; Geddes, Wright and Frantz 2014). Some types are quite old. Among them, for example, we find traditional military regimes (such as Pakistan and South Korea before democratising) and those labelled 'bureaucratic-authoritarian', which were more typical of Latin America in the 1960s/70s (for instance, in Argentina and Brazil), claimed to aim at development and included coalitions of military officers and economic technocrats (O'Donnell 1988). Scholars have also studied traditional monarchies (for example, those in the Gulf region such as Saudi Arabia; Al-Rasheed 2018), racist regimes (South Africa under apartheid), single-party or dominant-party states (Mexico under the PRI, *Partido Revolucionario Institucional*, as well as communist countries) and personalist regimes, in Africa (such as Mobutu's Zaire or Mugabe's Zimbabwe), Latin America (Chile under Pinochet), the former USSR (Aliyev family's Azerbaijan and Turkmenistan above all; on changes see Anceschi 2021). Since the 1980s we have also learnt about 'post-totalitarian' (Thompson 2002) states in the former Communist bloc; this is a very complex umbrella term which in turn applies to a range of cases and types. Especially in the 21st century we have then witnessed the rise of new and complex regimes such as those in large countries like China and Russia, where single party rule has given way to more personalistic forms, which have steered economic and military growth also as a response to the dangers and uncertainties created by neoliberal globalisation and worldwide competition.

While the literature on authoritarianism has often concentrated on the absence of democracy or totalitarianism more than on the nature of authoritarianism itself, the early 21st century in fact provides the possibility to reflect on the significance of the links between perceived global economic and security threats and authoritarian systems. In some cases, authoritarianism has taken on developmental traits and simultaneously resorted to neoliberal strategies to catch up with the neoliberal West; these are, at least in part, the examples of China since 1978, post-Soviet Russia, Kazakhstan, Singapore. In others, it has combined traditional authoritarian characteristics with a stronger statist/developmental drive (for example, in Ethiopia and Rwanda since the 1990s).

Authoritarianism has in some cases been called 'electoral' (Schedler 2006; yet what is a regime with an electoral façade other than pure authoritarianism?) and in others 'competitive' (Diamond 1999; Levitsky and Way 2002), which would include some democratic elements and thus classify as 'hybrid'. However, even hybridity points to an authoritarian core, to a backslide, a flight from democracy. What leads to such a backslide? Again, the literature tends to neglect structural aspects, while more light is shed on institutions and the role of political factions, especially among the elites, whose actions while in power, however, cannot alone explain authoritarianism's rise and survival.

With exceptions, not enough has been written about the international (or transnational) links between authoritarianisms either. Does authoritarianism spread? If yes, in what ways? Are some countries (China? Russia?) favouring or promoting it (Ambrosio 2010 and 2012; von Soest 2015)? Is there such thing as a kind of 'international authoritarian cartel'?

Finally, studying authoritarianism requires attention to history, cultures, and specificity. Catch-all labels do not do justice to the differences experienced by different countries, regions, even continents. A political macroregion such as the former 'Soviet space' includes a wide variety of cases, from rather solid democracies in the Baltic states to a form of 'sultanism' 2.0 in Niyazov's and Berdimuhamedov family's Turkmenistan.

Authors such as Glasius (2018b) have recently proposed the concept of 'authoritarian practices' with the aim of explaining realities which have become increasingly common in both (formally) authoritarian and democratic countries. Following Adler and Pouliot (2011), Glasius defines 'practices' as "patterned actions that are embedded in particular organized contexts" (2018b: 523). Practices are social, that is, they rely on set rules and shared understandings. Sometimes they depend on states and their regimes; sometimes they are linked to single leaders and individuals (Trump, Orbán, Modi, etc); other times they are expressions of bureaucracies, corporations, traditions. Practices, according to Glasius (2018b: 527), become authoritarian when they 'sabotage accountability', that is, when the authorities disable access to information (see the CIA rendition flights or the US surveillance measures after 9/11, which remained fully secret for a long time) or voice itself (as in the control over the media exercised in several contemporary states, from Berlusconi's Italy to Orbán's Hungary). Glasius distinguishes these practices from those she prefers calling 'illiberal', which directly infringe on rights and persons, their "dignity" and "autonomy" (530–31). Illiberal practices give birth to 'illiberal democracies' (Zakaria 1997) and directly challenge liberalism. Authoritarian practices, by jeopardising accountability, defy and hamper democracy itself. Generally, authoritarian and illiberal elements go together, as Orbán's Hungary or Erdogan's Turkey demonstrate.

Formal democracies often make use of authoritarian practices – Glasius and Michaelsen (2018) refer to cases such as US National Security Agency (NSA)'s surveillance (more illiberal than authoritarian) and CIA rendition flights. The digital industry has broadened the possibility of such practices. Controlling diasporas has become another area for authoritarian policies and repression, especially in formally authoritarian states. The latter in fact govern their migrants in at least three ways. Following Glasius (2018a), in the first place they use technologies of repression such as surveillance, threats, withdrawing nationality, expulsion, and even assassination; these are, for example, practices used by governments such as Iran's or Assad's Syria's. Other countries, in the second place, attempt to mobilise fellow citizens, who would then become either 'patriots' or 'traitors' (2018a: 188); still other countries attempt to buy the support of nationals overseas by using clientelistic methods (for example, Kazakhstan with some of its study abroad students; Glasius 2018a). That said, Maerz et al (2020) demonstrate how the Covid-19 pandemic has engendered further authoritarian practices, especially in terms of executive power abuses, disinformation, misinformation, discriminations, etc, in democracies as well.

The idea of 'authoritarian practices' is not immune to critiques. To start with, it risks overstretching (Sartori 1970), and being used to define many different practices in very different contexts. Furthermore, the links with authoritarianism as a regime should be clarified. What is the impact of such practices on the form of government and vice versa? In a sense, they already are an authoritarian element, a kind of spreading virus, also in formal democracies. They are seeds of authoritarianism, which in turn nurtures them. How do they evolve? Do they contribute to strengthen authoritarianism, both in mainly democratic states and in traditional authoritarian ones? How can we separate such practices from the nature of a regime? It seems insightful to look at democracy and authoritarianism along a spectrum, and to see these practices as signs of authoritarianism, which can co-exist with formal democratic institutions but at some stage can also overthrow them. Additionally, it is important to connect authoritarian practices with structural elements; more specifically, it is key to give account of the role of socio-economic aspects such as the rise of capitalism, which in the modern age has been the most common mode of production and has strong links with both authoritarianism and its practices.

In this sense, according to scholars such as Piketty (2017), capitalism showed its real and authoritarian face before and after the exceptional age of the post-World War Two welfare state, that of the *trente glorieuses* ('the glorious thirty'). Drawing on vast empirical evidence (both quantitative and qualitative) since the 19th century, Piketty demonstrates how capitalism tends to enhance long-term inequalities and therefore fosters instability. Additionally, in his view it would lead to concentration of wealth and income and the emergence of oligopolies and oligarchies, with detrimental effects on democracy. Capitalism, if left unchecked, would pave the way to authoritarianism.

Piketty's theory is empirically sound and strongly supported by data. However, he does not unpack what is authoritarian in capitalism itself, especially in its neoliberal version. Capitalism is rather seen as a path to authoritarianism. Going beyond Piketty, we can further appreciate the authoritarian nature of neoliberalism and their toxic combinations in the early 21st century. Bloom (2016) theorises that the discourses of capitalism and authoritarianism meet in that they both share essentialist, ideologically closed, 'no-alternative' narratives. This is especially evident in the neoliberal age, in which states are supposed to be 'forced' to catch up with globalisation. The authoritarian-capitalist nexus manifests itself in a range of experiences: from those of China and Russia to various cases of 'soft authoritarianism' (Roy 1994), from the authoritarianism of the 'Global War On Terror' and the 'War on Drugs' (Bloom 2016: 12–3) to that of Western-dominated and unaccountable international economic organisations (the IMF and the World Bank with their reform diktats), emerging powers (Brazil, India, Turkey), let alone Trump's politics and its European counterparts. It is therefore no surprise that, drawing on these premises, an increasing number of authors has started using and exploring notions such as that of 'authoritarian neoliberalism'. It is to this concept that we now turn our attention.

3 Authoritarian Neoliberalism

The affinities between authoritarianism and neoliberalism had been noticed, although only at the margins of mainstream social sciences, as early as the 1970s. Nikos Poulantzas, a prematurely disappeared Greek-French Marxist scholar, introduced the key concept of 'authoritarian statism' in the late 1970s (Poulantzas 1978). Poulantzas understood the state as a battlefield among classes and their fractions; in the context of the bourgeoisie's crisis and the impoverishment of the middle classes since the late 1960s, he foresaw an authoritarian torsion, which would materialise in the 1980s in Thatcher's Britain, Reagan's USA, and was in fact already a reality in Pinochet's Chile. Stronger executives and authoritarian practices would have restored bourgeois hegemony and repressed or divided the working classes. In Britain, Stuart Hall lived through Thatcher's experience which he interpreted as 'authoritarian populism' (Hall 1979: 15), a movement towards an "exceptional form of the capitalist state", which still relies on formal democratic institutions, but in a substantially corrupt and authoritarian way. Hall detected the rise of a new politics, which was adopted by the Conservatives and valued individualism, law, order, the 'people', and the nation (sometimes also with racist tones) against the 'state' which was associated with Old Labour policies, bureaucracy, and stagnation. In later writings, Hall (2011) reconstructed the trajectory of neoliberalism, from Thatcher to New Labour, and its intersections with populist, nationalist, and authoritarian ideas.

Very early on, Poulantzas's and Hall's writings pointed to a combination between (neoliberal) capitalism and authoritarianism, especially in a nationalist, populist mode. At the very beginning of neoliberal politics, Chile under Pinochet, infamously supported by the USA and guided by the monetarist doctrines of the 'Chicago boys', was a fully-fledged and brutal dictatorship open to markets and foreign capital. In a sense, neoliberalism was born authoritarian and in the developing world, as a kind of experiment to be later reproduced in core Western states. However, at least in the West's economic heartland and in Japan, the era of deep neoliberal reforms (1980s–2000s) was marked by the preservation of formal democratic rules. The 'Great recession' which started in 2007 has though represented a kind of watershed in global power relations. New economic powers have risen: China above all, the Chinese-led BRICS+ group (with Brazil, Russia, India, South Africa, and a growing number of new members), Turkey, Indonesia, Mexico, Saudi Arabia, Malaysia, and still others. In many cases – though to different degrees – they have been guided by strongmen (Xi Jinping, Bolsonaro, Putin, Modi, Erdogan, and so on) or different types of oligarchies. At the same time, the 'Western' or economically hegemonic part of the world has witnessed the emergence of populist and nationalist leaders and movements, sometimes even with fascist overtones (Trump, Le Pen, Orbán, etc), while the EU has increasingly morphed into a technocratic structure and imposed fiscal austerity on its member states, particularly those in its South and East and after the impact of the financial crisis onto sovereign debts in 2011. Austerity and financial stability have become synonyms with the Eurozone's highly controversial 'Maastricht parameters'.

All the above-mentioned events have triggered a windfall of debates and publications, on capitalism, its varieties, sustainability, alternatives, as well as on its compatibility with democracy. Keynes and Marx have re-obtained a degree of intellectual purchase. A new literature on 'authoritarian neoliberalism' has started to emerge (Bruff 2012 and 2014; Bruff and Tansel 2019). Bruff has specifically highlighted the qualitative shift towards a less democratic state, aimed at preserving neoliberalism by using legal and constitutional means, as the EU experience illustrates in a clear and powerful way. Neoliberal measures and aims – such as a balanced budget – have even made their way into national constitutions within the EU. The concept of authoritarian neoliberalism should then also be used to encompass a variety of experiences in a variety of world regions, including in developing countries (Bruff and Tansel 2019).

The literature on worldwide authoritarian neoliberalism has grown indeed. Jessop (2019) has focused mostly on theoretical aspects and the West; Clua-Losada and Ribera-Almandoz (2017) on Spain; Stubbs and Lendvai-Bainton have analysed authoritarian neoliberalism in Central and Eastern Europe (2020); Tansel has consistently studied Turkey, especially in relation to urban landscapes (2019). Harrison (2019) has then researched African countries; Springer (2017), the case of Cambodia. Mexico (Jenss 2019) and Brazil (Saad-Filho and Boffo 2021) have been studied within this framework, too. Harvey (2005), among others, had already explained the nationalist and authoritarian torsion in Latin America, Russia and China, especially since the demise of communism.

As to the USA, the critical pedagogist, Henri A. Giroux, has illustrated the toxic and haunting connections between neoliberalism and neo-fascism, as embodied by the figure of Donald Trump (Giroux 2017 and 2018). Looking at politics from the angle of critical pedagogy and psychology, Giroux argues that neoliberalism, by commodifying everything (including education, the media, diplomacy, and so on), has produced an atomised, terrorised population, overwhelmed with feelings of loneliness and uselessness, and reduced to ignorance also by a flawed capitalistic education. This state of affairs would open the gates to authoritarianism and even fascism, which in the USA relies on a history of white suprematism, racism, Christian fundamentalism, and individualistic,

Darwinian morals. In Giroux's insightful view, Trump is an American phenomenon in an age of unbridled neoliberalism, which is producing and reproducing other 'monsters', e.g., Bolsonarism in Brazil or Milei's success in Argentina.

The links between capitalism's general, 'organic' crises and authoritarianism had been discussed by Gramsci long ago. In his prescient words (1971: 210),

> At a certain point in their historical lives, social classes become detached from their traditional parties. In other words, the traditional parties in that particular organisational form, with the particular men who constitute, represent, and lead them, are no longer recognised by their class (or fraction of class) as its expression. When such crises occur, the immediate situation becomes delicate and dangerous, because the field is open for violent solutions, for the activities of unknown forces, represented by charismatic "men of destiny".

The 'organic crisis' of capitalism, a kind of general economic, political, and ideological crisis, would awaken new forces such as demagogues and party bureaucracies. Hegemony would show its coercive, authoritarian side. Gramsci was reflecting on the rise of 19th century Bonapartism and of course on that of fascism which had put him in jail. Yet his reflections are more relevant than ever in the contemporary world. Approximately since the 1980s, we have in fact seen the emergence of 'populist', or 'radical right'/'far right' groups, movements and parties, which have gained traction in a vast number of countries and are usually led by charismatic leaders (Kiely and Saull 2017; Saull et al 2014; Eatwell and Goodwin 2018; Müller 2016). How are these populist right-wing movements linked to neoliberalism? What role has the latter played in generating them? How do they express a 'variety of (authoritarian) neoliberalism'?

'Populism' is an extremely complex term, which has been interpreted and understood in countless different ways, sometimes fully misunderstood, and sometimes rejected straightaway. "Populisms are diverse and the concept appears elusive" (Patomäki 2020: 110). While populism has historically resurfaced since the 1980s, its geographic distribution is so vast and across all continents that providing a comprehensive definition is very problematic. There are clear historical specificities; populism has taken roots in both very wealthy (Denmark, Sweden, Austria, Switzerland, and others) and developing countries; there is a left-wing populism (for example, in Mexico and Venezuela) and a right-wing one, which is more important in this context (Mudde and Rovira Kaltwasser 2018). Populism's key element here is in fact nationalism, which often borders with xenophobia and fascism. Scholars have also used the expression 'nativism' (Mudde 2007), which refers to natives, but does not necessarily have ethnic connotations; however, this book's preferred choice remains nationalism, which resonates well in an inter-national context, too. The Finnish scholar, Heikki Patomäki (2020: 110–11), highlights how both authoritarianism, often expressed by simple, radical, and anti-intellectual slogans, and nationalism are key characteristics of this new, right-wing populism.

Yet this book contends that populist nationalism is only one of the three faces of authoritarian neoliberalism in the late 20th and early 21st century. The other faces – or 'varieties' – are the sometimes more reassuring technocracy and the traditional form of authoritarianism.

All three varieties are authoritarian, though in different ways. By definition, this is true for traditional authoritarianisms. Technocrats, for their part, are usually unelected and appointed, very often by authorities from above, who select them among 'international' experts. They rarely enjoy democratic legitimacy; one exception might be the Indian economist and Prime Minister, Manmohan Singh (2004–14), who was an Indian National Congress (INC) member. Additionally, 'technical knowledge' or expertise is often supposed to be a kind of 'truth', beyond democratic accountability and requiring unconditional obedience. The economist (or the jurist, the diplomat, the engineer) knows better. In a sense, this is also valid for populism, which is not only nationalist and therefore potentially exclusive, but also authoritarian. Populists, in other words, tend to claim that what the people (but who are the people?) think and want is a 'truth', usually in opposition to the elite (Mudde 2007): *vox populi, vox dei* ("The voice of the people is the voice of God"). Ultimately, populism and technocracy share a belief in a form of 'superior' knowledge, be it from the top down or a popular 'common sense'; a knowledge which is somewhere above a democratic, representative, liberal dialogue and beyond democratic decision-making. In this sense, both have core inner authoritarian aspects. But how are they connected to neoliberalism?

Technocracy, populism, and traditional authoritarianism are in fact much older than neoliberalism. Technocracy can be traced to at least 19th century positivism (for example, in authors such as Saint-Simon and Comte) and the 20th century experiences of the New Deal and the European Communities. Populism has deep historical roots in the Americas and Russia. Modern authoritarianism appeared mostly after World War One. The three political systems did not *cause* neoliberalism. However, it is reasonable to believe that they contributed to it, together with other factors, which this book will analyse in depth (Patomäki 2020). Moreover, the combination between them and neoliberalism occurred because they share important traits with the neoliberal vision and practice, as Chapter 3 will explain.

In many ways, after the benign and sometimes paternalistic experience of 'Keynesian' welfarism (roughly 1945–75), capitalism has returned to show its more concealed but real face of brutal exploitation and authoritarianism. This face has manifested itself in neoliberalism and its varieties, especially since neoliberalism's crises have become more recurrent. But how is each variety linked to neoliberalism? And what are the connections among the three of them? As the following chapters will illustrate, there are significant overlaps among the three types.

Authoritarian rulers often resort to populist measures and use technocrats to legitimise their choices or promote economic development (this was the case, for instance, in Franco's Spain, with the Opus Dei's economic experts in the 1960s). Similarly, combinations between technocracy and nationalist populism do exist (Bickerton and Invernizzi Accetti 2018); one remarkable and current case is Orbán's Hungary, while others have long taken roots in Latin America (for instance in neoliberal Mexico since the 1980s).

While each variety contains elements of the other two, in each case one emerges as dominant (Gallo 2021: 3). This book aims at understanding how the varieties have emerged and how they combine and co-exist, rather than whether and why different varieties correspond to different states or even stages of economic development (provided that such stages exist, which remains highly questionable). After all, the world's biggest economy, especially under Donald Trump, is coming close to combine all three varieties. There certainly are some broad trends; for instance, more peripheral or semi-peripheral economies look rather inclined to move in a fully authoritarian direction. However, rather than formulating quantitative correlations, this work intends to comprehend and explain some key case-studies, one for each variety.

First, light will be shed on Italy's case. A core market economy, a G7 member and a consolidated democracy, Italy has almost become the epitome of technocracy, especially since the 1980s. In the Cold war's final decade Italy started the long march towards joining and supporting the European single currency, while scores of technocrats, usually economists from its central bank (the Banca d'Italia), have occupied key ministerial armchairs and even that of Prime Minister. Within the European Monetary Union (EMU), the trend has continued, with personalities such as Mario Monti and Mario Draghi and repeated interventions of the European Central Bank (ECB). At the same time, Italy has witnessed rapid alternations, and sometimes even combinations, between technocracy and populism, as represented, among others, by the right-wing League party and Berlusconi's various political forces. It is a kind of laboratory for political experiments and a highly significant case-study of neoliberalism's authoritarian versions.

The second case, almost a symbol of populist nationalism, is that of Britain. The UKIP, Brexit, the Vote Leave campaign and Johnson's erratic governments have filled the political landscape of one of the West's traditional core economies, with a strong emphasis on financial services and a dominant position in the capitalistic heartland since Thatcher's governments in the 1980s. How strong is the link between neoliberalism and populism? Which factors are contributing to the latter? How authoritarian has Britain become? Is there any room for technocracy, which has usually not crossed the Channel? Why would that be the case?

The third case is that of a traditional, and increasingly authoritarian, regime: Putin's post-Soviet Russia. What are the relations between authoritarianism and neoliberalism in a giant country which has suffered the effects of the post-Cold war collapse? How far has Putin rejected neoliberalism and how much has he embraced it in a special, Russian form? What are the links between the Western neoliberal offensive in the 1990s and Putin's subsequent authoritarian turn?

Before analysing the three case-studies, however, the book will clarify and explain the historical roots, current relevance, significance, and evolutions of the three varieties (technocracy, populism, and traditional authoritarianism) and how they have co-developed with neoliberalism. This is in fact next chapter's core theme.

CHAPTER 3

Three Varieties of Authoritarian Neoliberalism

1 Comparing Socio-historical Types

Comparing social and political actors is always a complex exercise. More specifically, states cannot be conceived as 'containers' or 'boxes', especially in a modern age in which global forces and dynamics flow above and below, and ultimately cut across, them. Therefore, the paradigm centred on 'neoliberalisations', as we have seen, remains important. At the same time, far from being interpreted as a passive spectator, the state is here explored as one of the key agents of neoliberalism. States are still powerful actors and can be fruitfully compared, particularly when the events under scrutiny are contemporary and the focus is mainly on 'how' questions (Yin 2018: 43–44).

Additionally, comparisons are 'incorporated', that is, they are used to give account of the worldwide and regional flows of processes and historical events which intersect the entities to be compared, states in this case (McMichael 1990; Gallo 2022: 557). Many social forces are at play, a fact which also explains the intertwining of different varieties such as that between technocracy and populism, or 'techno-populism'. That said, it is first necessary to comprehend the faces of authoritarian neoliberalism one-by-one, with the help of empirical examples.

2 Technocracy

In a broad sense, technocracy refers to the dominating role that technique and especially technology have been playing over the ecology, human beings, and nature in the modern age. This momentous theme has been studied by authors with different worldviews and sensibilities such as Heidegger (1953), Anders (1956), and Ellul (1954), among others. Analysing these scholars' reflections goes beyond the scope of this work, and none of them wrote on neoliberalism specifically, but one concern is common to all three and relevant to the neoliberal age. In their views, instrumental rationality and efficiency have become the defining criteria of the modern era, and the market has emerged as the leading model of efficiency, in the economic sphere and beyond. In this sense, these authors' ideas tie up with the criticism of the neoliberal interpretation of the market as a paramount expression and technology of efficiency. In the neoliberal view, in the name of efficiency, market-led politics is generally technocratic, and driven by measures of productivity, rationality, transparency, accountability and by a host of metric variables which have become increasingly powerful in everyday life (Giannone 2010).

In a narrower sense, closer to the criteria of Political Science, a government is technocratic (McDonnell and Valbruzzi 2014) when it is led by non-elected, independent officers, who are usually appointed with the support of international or supranational organisations (especially the EU, in the three latest decades, but also the IMF or the World Bank, that is, the traditional Bretton Woods world financial institutions). Sometimes the technocratic dimension is limited to one or few ministries, usually those associated with the economy, finance or technology (occasionally, justice or home affairs). Technocrats usually work in cooperation with *tecnici* ('technicians'; Giannone and Cozzolino 2023: 27), that is, lower-rank experts who help technocratic leaders run increasingly complex administrative machines. In the recurrent Eurocentric narrative, technocracy is linked with industrialisation, economic and technological development, and Western countries. Reality, as we will see, is far more complex. Technocracy is in fact rooted and has developed in non-Western and developing countries as well. Certainly, technocracy's importance has risen faster in the neoliberal age, in both developing and developed economies (notably in the EU) and has morphed into a government by experts in economics and similar subjects. Technocrats usually serve the interests of transnational capital and large multinational corporations, even if they often express some variety of political and economic views. In this sense, as this section will clarify, there is nothing apolitical in technocracy; technocracy itself is a form of politics by other means. There is also a great variety of historical experiences. Let us start with some general ideas on technocracy's history and development, followed by an overview of its most relevant contemporary cases across a range of world regions, from Latin America to Africa, the former Soviet bloc and Europe.

Technocracy has often been traced back in time to ancient or early modern thinkers such as Plato with his vision of rule by 'philosopher-kings' and Thomas More (1478–1535) with his *Utopia*. In reality, technocracy is a modern phenomenon, with significant roots also in developing countries. Saint-Simon's call for industrial planning and Comte's positivism, for instance, had vast resonance in 19th century's newly independent Latin American states. Brazilian intellectuals promoted Comte's ideas in the late 19th century; the French philosopher's motto, 'Order and Progress' (*ordre et progrès*), even became Brazil's official slogan and still appears on the national flag. In Chile, progress, rationality and economic development were promoted by liberal and positivist intellectuals such as Valentin Letelier (1852–1919). Interestingly, Mexico's proponents of technical progress, also known as *científicos*, sided with Porfirio Diaz's 'developmental' dictatorship (1876–1911) and even embraced racist ideas (Priego 2016; Skidmore, Smith and Green 2014: 403), to which some strands of positivism, with their social Darwinist leanings, were not immune.

In the 20th century, technocracy gained popularity in the New Deal's USA, with the science-driven 'technocracy movement' (Akin 1977), in Europe, particularly in the early stages of the European Communities, in which functionalist experts played major roles, and in communist countries – the USSR and China, in both of which scientists and technologists often enjoyed important political positions.

In absolute terms, we cannot fully associate technocracy with any specific and traditional ideology on the left-right spectrum. Experts collaborated with both right-wing autocrats (like in Mexico and South America) and communist party hierarchies. At the same time, a quick look at figures across all continents demonstrates the importance of neoliberalism to technocracy's thriving since the late 20th century. Just in the EU, according to McDonnell and Valbruzzi (2014), 87.5% (that is, 21 out of 24) of its technocratic governments have emerged in the neoliberal age and with the objective of implementing policies of pro-market reform and restructuring. Before the adoption of the Eurozone's Maastricht parameters, however, countries in Africa, Latin America, Asia, the post-Soviet space, and still other regions, had been the object of the IMF/World Bank's neoliberal attentions; they had been pushed to neoliberalise by the often-unwelcome therapies proposed by supporters of the Washington Consensus. In many cases, technocracy and neoliberalism had local roots as well. An overview of key examples across world regions will help better frame technocracy's main experiences.

In Latin America, to begin with, technocracy has often arrived from overseas (especially from the USA and Western Europe), even if in the neoliberal era it has found fertile ground in the economic interests of the ruling classes and in the intellectual inclinations of some of their members.

Mexico is probably Latin America's most spectacular case of a top-down neoliberalising experience; since the early 1980s it has witnessed a meteoric political rise of economic experts, usually with an affiliation to the once omni-present PRI (*Partido Revolucionario Institucional*), the dominant party in the post-revolutionary age. Mexico is a clear example of a combination of technocracy and authoritarianism, especially in the final years of PRI hegemony. Miguel de La Madrid, President in the years 1982–88 and the first neoliberal reformer, was a Harvard-educated economist with experience in central banking and the oil industry. Technocrats played key roles under his successors Carlos Salinas de Gortari (1988–94) and Ernesto Zedillo (1994–2000), who themselves were highly trained economists with postgraduate studies in the USA and experience in Mexican public administration. Even under the subsequent PAN (*Partido Acción Nacional*, conservative) and MORENA (*Movimiento Regeneracción Nacional*, leftist) presidencies, key ministries – Finance, the Economy, Treasury – have been assigned to academic economists, bankers, entrepreneurs, usually with postgraduate backgrounds in the USA. After all, their task was to align the interests of global and especially US capitalism with those of Mexico's. Results have been problematic. Formal democratic institutions have remained in place (if tremendously challenged), but massive privatisations, accession to NAFTA (North American Free Trade Agreement, 1994, revised as USMCA by Trump and his Canadian and Mexican counterparts in 2019) and bank bailouts (Marois 2011) have brought about terrible consequences, in terms of inequality, poverty, an endless and ferocious war on drugs, and ultimately 'destruction of society' (Laurell 2015). All such initiatives have been taken with the support of international institutions as well as Mexican and US capital and to the detriment of the working class in both Mexico and the USA. Remarkably, at the roots of Mexico's long-lasting problems, we find highly educated economists, who have persistently and corruptly centralised wealth and power (Centeno 1993; 2010).

Between the late 1960s and the 1980s, meanwhile, several South American countries (among them, Argentina, Brazil, Chile and Uruguay) underwent an unusual experiment, with clear evidence of US support. Economic technocrats started working in conjunction with professional armed forces in a solution famously called 'bureaucratic authoritarianism' by the Argentine political scientist, Guillermo O'Donnell (O'Donnell 1988). In this book, Argentina is highly relevant since the new government after the 1966 military coup included both nationalists (or "paternalists", according to O'Donnell 1988: 72) and liberals. What united them was the aim of curtailing the power of trade unions, left-wing parties and workers' organisations, which had grown in 1960s' Argentina as well as in the rest of the world. Among the liberals, a key role was played by a technocrat, Adalbert Krieger Vasena, a Minister of the Economy, Labour and Finance, who was very well-connected with international organisations and transnational corporations and strived to promote foreign investments. His early neoliberal measures – the freezing of salaries and anti-labour provisions, would though exacerbate class conflict in the country (O'Donnell 1988). Krieger Vasena would later become a World Bank executive, in line with his neoliberal views and his Washington connections.

Argentine neoliberalism returned with a vengeance on at least three other occasions, in all cases with a strong technocratic presence. First, the economist and businessman, José A. Martinez de Hoz, became Minister of the Economy

(1976–81) of the hideous military junta initially led by Videla. Strongly connected with US banks and companies, Martinez adopted radical measures of deregulation, wage freezes, trade and financial liberalisations, which in few years led to increasing inequality and extreme financial volatility, without resolving the country's chronical inflation issues (Dornbusch 1984 provides a moderate and rather generous evaluation). Second, Harvard-educated Domingo Cavallo became Minister of the Economy (1991–96) during the flamboyant Menem presidency (1989–99), which enacted a massive plan of stabilisation and liberalisation (*Plan de convertibilidad*) and, after some apparent success in the 1990s, led the country to bankruptcy in 2001. Cavallo himself defended his autonomous role and Argentina's domestic reformist impulse, but also indirectly recognised the country's dependence on US and IMF support (Cavallo 2004). Interestingly, Cavallo was a technocrat in a democratic regime, which was though including authoritarian traits in the way Menem was enforcing reforms rapidly, forcefully, and under international financial pressure. The third and controversial case of technocratic neoliberalism started with the presidential election of the vociferous and populist economist, Javier Milei, in December 2023. Measures of austerity and deregulation have been met with massive protests of trade unions and students, and Argentina's future remains once again highly uncertain (Forti 2024).

Argentina's giant Northern neighbour, Brazil, has witnessed neoliberalism in different forms since at least the 1980s (Saad-Filho 2020) and with a prominent role for technocrats, who have usually secured the position of Minister of Finance. Austerity and a boost to foreign investment, together with strong pro-business policies, had started under the military dictatorship (1964–85), which often entrusted the job to internationally connected economists such as Antonio Delfim Netto, in charge of Finance between 1967 and 1974, and resembled Argentina's 'bureaucratic authoritarian' regime. The Berkeley PhD and former central banker, Pedro Malan, adopted the *Plano Real* during the democratic and fully neoliberal presidency of Fernando H. Cardoso (1995–2003). Brazil then experienced a brief phase of 'inclusive neoliberalism' and a longer one of 'developmental neoliberalism' under Lula and Dilma Rousseff (2003–16; Saad-Filho 2020), during which accommodating diverse domestic and international interests became increasingly difficult. Technocrats returned in full control of the economy under the truly authoritarian neoliberal phase inaugurated by Bolsonaro in 2018 (Webber 2020). The ultra-neoliberal, Paulo Guedes, a 'Chicago boy' and a former collaborator of the Chilean dictatorship, became his Minister of the Economy. With Lula's return in 2022, the post has been assigned to Fernando Haddad, a politician and former Mayor of São Paulo but also a scholar in economics and political science.

Chile is perhaps the most discussed South American instance of a collaboration between a dictatorship, that of General Augusto Pinochet (1973–90), and neoliberal technocrats, the infamous 'Chicago boys', usually trained in Chicago within the school of Friedman and Hayek but also at the Catholic University of Santiago (Valdés 1995). Many of them enacted sweeping reforms aimed at eliminating any working-class right, in sectors such as social security, healthcare, free trade, and so on. Supported by the USA, the Chicago boys acted as a true 'revolutionary vanguard' of authoritarian neoliberalism (Clark 2017) and aimed at creating a "market society" (Clark 2017: 1354), going far beyond 'technical' economic changes and anticipating Thatcherism's policies and mentality. Their ambitions to give birth to a 'market society' also overlapped with those of the 'Gremialists', representatives of Chile's Catholic right and proponents of a long-term strategy (Huneeus 2000: 462). By contrast with common places, Chile's economic indicators for the Pinochet era are far from brilliant, and generally better only than those dating to the US-sabotaged Allende presidency (1970–73; Huneeus 2000). Not really earning 'richly deserved glory' (*sic!* Becker 1997), the Chicago boys operated in a context of torture, forced disappearances, and massive human rights violations. That context was supported or at least accepted by major Western countries – the USA and Britain were among them.

Translating neoliberalism into Africa was initially more difficult. This may be due to many factors. At least until the 1970s the Washington Consensus institutions dedicated less attention to Africa, in part because of the scarcity of bastions of neoliberal knowledge on the continent and in part because of the stronger role played by traditional politicians. Among the postcolonial founders, 'African socialists' such as Nkrumah, Nyerere or Senghor were far more popular than any technocrats (Mkandawire 2014). In the global age, however, neoliberal technocrats have gained significant ground, especially in some large countries and often with the aim of countering China's sustained economic expansion throughout the continent. Nigeria embarked on a neoliberal path during the military rule which started in 1983 (and reminds us of Latin America's bureaucratic authoritarianism) and continued in an even more brutal way throughout the 1990s under Abacha's leadership. Privatisations and neoliberalism went hand-in-hand in the more democratic context which followed Obasanjo's election in 1999. Economic technocrats then entered the stage. This was the case, for instance, of the current WTO Director and former Minister of Finance (2003–06 and 2011–15), the MIT-educated economist, Ngozi Okonjo-Iweala, who expresses a less radical view of neoliberalism than her Latin American counterparts (Okonjo-Iweala 2012). Another economist, Zainab Ahmed, and the banker, Wale Edun, have served as Ministers of

Finance (respectively, 2018–23 and 2023–) in the more recent administrations of Buhari and Tinubu. Nigeria (Thurston 2018), Ghana since the 1980s and several other countries have also witnessed the emergence of neoliberal technocrats in the context of the structural adjustment reforms which have swept the continent since Reagan's times. The combination of traditional authoritarianism, if only to some extent, and resort to technocratic experts has also characterised the more recent experiences of Kagame's Rwanda and 21st century Ethiopia (Behuria 2018), two cases in which elements of Asian-inspired developmentalism and elements of pro-market ideology have so far co-existed in an often-complex way.

The former Soviet space, from Central Europe to Vladivostok, has experienced yet other vicissitudes. Before the bloc's collapse, it was already home to technocrats, who had often been educated in Economics during the communist era and had played roles in the single party's ranks as well as in dedicated research institutions. They, together with the party leadership and 'humanistic intellectuals' (King 2002), were among the crucial players in the neoliberal transition. In some countries (notably, Poland) their alliance with intellectuals against the top echelons of the party bureaucracy led to a more efficient, if highly dependent, form of capitalism (King 2002). In Russia and other ex-Soviet countries, by contrast, the party bureaucrats maintained control and gave birth to a highly patrimonial, oligarchic capitalism. Other forces mattered as well. In Russia, Uzbekistan and to a lesser extent Kazakhstan the legacy of security apparatuses has remained strong and has partly contributed to selective adaptations to neoliberalism (Gallo 2021). Additionally, the impact of global neoliberal politics has been significant. Well-known experts such as Jeffrey Sachs, who worked with the IMF, proposed 'shock therapies' (in simple words, packages of neoliberal policies to be adopted all at the same time) in the forms of privatisations, market liberalisations, and austerity measures. While it is correct that in Poland these policies were rather accepted, especially soon after 1989, their long-term outcomes, in terms of inequality, unemployment and dependency, would be significant and detrimental. Russia is a complex case, and Sachs's common places about the country ("to move from 1,000 years of authoritarian rule to democracy ... [...] ... from empire to nation state"; 1994: 282) seem to express a global top-down approach towards neoliberal reforms with little interest in historical specificity. Specificity has usually been downplayed by technocrats, who have tended to envisage similar solutions to highly different problems and contexts.

A key feature of technocracy in the former Soviet bloc is the fact that it often had national or local roots and was represented by experienced and highly trained economists. In Poland, a major role in the neoliberalisation process was played by the economist and long-time Minister of Finance, Leszek Balcerowicz (1947–). An academic at the Warsaw School of Economics (WSE), which during the Cold war had been an incubator of open-minded scholars, including all Ministers of Finance between 1988 and 1997, Balcerowicz was also an economic advisor to the Solidarity union and movement, which catalysed millions of workers, intellectuals, and technocrats and handed a decisive blow to communism in the 1980s (King 2002). He later became the main proponent of the Balcerowicz Plan, which was supported by the IMF and established shock therapy measures in Poland. Its negative effects were mitigated in later years and the country would follow a path of relative prosperity, though it has remained mostly dependent on foreign investments and trade. Other important scholars of the WSE who became prominent in Polish neoliberalisation processes have been Grzegorz Kolodko, who would negotiate Poland's accession to the EU, and Pawel Wojciechowski, one of the privatisations' main architects.

A similar role to Poland's WSE was played in Hungary by the Financial Research Institute (FRI, within the Ministry of Finance), which supported neoliberal reforms after the 1970s. Its document 'Turnabout and Reform' became a blueprint for the transition (Fabry 2018 and 2019; Gallo 2022) and some of its proponents adopted Hungary's reforms after 1989, before and in some cases during Orbán's long and continuing reign. Both Poland and Hungary demonstrate the persistent complementarity of technocracy and populist nationalism. Similarly, the national and local roots of technocratic neoliberalism are confirmed by the case of Romania, where the Academy of Economic Studies in Bucharest has formed leading post-1989 reformers such as Nicolae Vacaroiu (Prime Minister 1992–96) and Mugur Isarescu, who has been at the helm of Romania's central bank almost without interruption since 1990 (Ban 2016).

In the former USSR republics, where technocrats started from a weaker position vis-à-vis the single party leadership (King 2002), problems have been much amplified. In Russia or Kazakhstan, Communist Party leaders managed to lead the transition and included technocrats in a subordinate role, which made their coordination with the IMF/US Treasury more problematic. As we will see in Chapter 6, Russian economists such as Yegor Gaidar, Minister of Finance (1991–92) and proponent of early liberalisations, or Anatoly Chubais, who continued the process with Yeltsin until 1999, had to face the challenge of powerful interest groups (Gel'man 2018), not to mention the collapse in living conditions from the 1990s onwards (Stuckler et al 2009). Russia's neoliberalisations were proposed by global technocrats such as Sachs, but also by local experts especially in the 1990s (Huskey 2010). So long as relations between Russia and the West remained in broadly cooperative terms (roughly, until Putin's re-election in 2012), the Russian Ministry of Finance stayed in the hands of an experienced neoliberal technocrat, Alexey Kudrin (2000–11). Interestingly, technocrats enjoyed important positions also in the highly authoritarian context of Kazakhstan, the former USSR's second biggest country, where they added to the regime a touch of fashionable neoliberal competence, contributed to many privatisations from above and maintained links with Western capitals and financial hubs. One example is Kairat Kelimbetov, a graduate of Georgetown University, former Minister and civil servant, and Governor of the Astana International Financial Centre until 2022 (AIFC; Peyrouse 2012).

The local (or 'national') roots of neoliberalism can be seen also in Western Europe, where technocrats have more recently (since the 1990s and the Treaty of Maastricht) become the transmission belt of capital from core European countries to some of the Eurozone's financially more vulnerable members. The Eurozone itself has been labelled a case of 'transnational authoritarian statism' (Schneider and Sandbeck 2019). The EU's technocratic apparatus has often exchanged personnel with specialised agencies in nation-states. Italy, the subject of Chapter 4, is a big case in point. Since the 1980s the 'cosmopolitan' elite of the central bank (the Bank of Italy) has significantly intervened in politics and provided to governments experts who have helped the country join the Eurozone. Former Bank of Italy's Governor Carlo Azeglio Ciampi and former Director-General Lamberto Dini became Prime Ministers in largely technocratic executives between 1993 and 1996. The economist, Mario Monti, a former EU Commissioner, led an all-technical cabinet in 2011–13 (Culpepper 2014), while the MIT-educated, former Bank of Italy's Governor and former European Central Bank's President, Mario Draghi, was premier in 2021–22. With Draghi's leadership, the connections between national, European and global neoliberalism fully came to the fore. Monti's 2011 cabinet in Italy was paralleled by the imposition of a technocratic government in Greece, headed by the economist and Central European banker, Lucas Papademos. In Greece, however, Papademos led a party government, while on several other occasions key Greek ministries have been entrusted to economists within party ranks (Verney and Bosco 2013).

The EU itself has been interpreted as the quintessential expression of technocracy (Majone 1996), sometimes in opposition, sometimes in combination with populism. The contrast has been made explicit by authors such as Offe and Schmidt (in Bickerton and Invernizzi Accetti 2017: 187–88), as a tension between the EU as a producer, a subject of policies, and national populisms, as the loci of current mass politics, in a case of 'policy/politics' dualism.

As explained by Bickerton and Invernizzi Accetti (2017; 2018), however, relations between technocracy and populism can be much more complex and multifaceted, including in the EU. The EU itself would be 'technocratic' but also increasingly 'politicised', considering the input of what Radaelli calls 'politics of expertise' (1999; 2017), and the significant expansion of its powers, for instance on monetary and economic matters. Such a tension has been increasingly illustrated by several authors (Sánchez-Cuenca 2017).

We argue that, in the EU as elsewhere, technocracy has in fact little or nothing to do with depoliticisation. While it is a rejection of parties and traditional democratic processes (Jessop 2014), technocracy is in fact also *politicisation by other means*. More precisely, we can argue that technocracy is *neoliberal politicisation by other means*. In a technocracy, experts, officers and economists pursue policies of austerity, price stabilisation, market liberalisation, privatisations and so on, using knowledge of the market economy (and its supposed benefits) as a universal ideology. Sometimes they appeal to European rigour and order, sometimes to price stability, other times to the importance of attracting foreign capital to achieve growth, etc. In all cases, technocrats are political instruments or actors, even when they do not pursue typical neoliberal agendas. They work with capital and political parties to achieve political transformation in a kind of passive revolution. Their political role becomes even more clear when technocracy merges with what is often considered its opposite (Caramani 2017), that is, populism.

Populism and technocracy share more than one feature. Both claim to aim at what is good for the country, which is understood as 'the people' by populists and 'the elite' by technocrats. Sometimes they even join forces and give birth to what has been labelled 'technocratic populism' or 'techno populism' (de la Torre 2013; Bickerton and Invernizzi Accetti 2018). The elite would cooperate with 'the people' in finding a direction for the whole country. This experience has roots in Latin America, for example in the rise of Vargas, Perón or Peru's Aprism, when protectionism and corporativism were seen as ways to arguably defend both capital and the working class, and has resurfaced in more recent times, both against neoliberalism (see Morales's Bolivia, Correa's Ecuador and Chávez's Venezuela; de la Torre 2013) or in favour of it (Barrenechea and Dargent 2020; see Fujimori's Peru). The case of Argentina's current President, Javier Milei, seems to embody a tragically grotesque example of a combination of nationalist, populist and technocratic elements (being Milei himself an academic economist, if with a rather unimpressive curriculum; Guidi 2024). In recent times, technocratic populism has also been associated with experiences in Italy and Spain (Bickerton and Invernizzi Accetti 2018) as well as in Central and Eastern Europe and President Macron's France (Perottino and Guasti 2020); there is even a growing body of literature on 'Varieties of Technocratic Populism' (Guasti and Buštíková 2020; Deseriis 2017).

While populism and technocracy have indeed combined in different ways, the paradigms and works on 'technocratic populism' tend to underestimate the root causes of such combination, that is, the structural power of neoliberalism and the perceived necessity to control its effects by mixing elitist and populist ideologies and policies. Technocracy, populism, and their intertwining have clear structural roots and tend towards a clear direction, as the case of Italy, which will be studied in Chapter 4, demonstrates.

As we will see, neoliberal politics is agile and plastic enough to merge with other political forms, from populism to classical authoritarianism. It is to populist nationalism that now this work turns its attention.

3 Nationalism

'Populism' is here mostly interpreted through the lens of nationalism. As a concept, nationalism is broader than populism; while populist forces and movements are usually nationalist, there is also a statist, non-populist type of nationalism (Joppke 2021); in any case, the connections and overlaps between the two are definitively strong (Brubaker 2019). This nexus was evident in Thatcher's Britain (Hall 1979; 2011) and Reagan's USA (Gamble 2021), not to mention some populist experiences in Latin America (such as Fujimori's Peru; Roberts 1995; Weyland 1999) and more recent populist nationalisms in the Indo-Pacific region (from India to the Philippines, South Korea and Japan; Jayasuriya 2018) and postcolonial contexts (Kaul 2019). In very broad terms, populists claim to value and represent 'the people', who, from a more international angle and in a world of nation-states, can be seen as 'the nation', and oppose 'the elite', which populists usually depict as uprooted, cosmopolitan, socially liberal and collusive with incarnations of the 'Other' like immigrants (Mudde 2007; Albertazzi and McDonnell 2008).

The links between nationalism and neoliberalism, for their part, may at first sight look rather counterintuitive. Isn't neoliberalism usually associated with global markets, open trade, digital finance, transnational corporations, international organisations and institutions, and the fading away of national borders and identities? Blyth (2013) and Blyth and Hopkin (2018) claim that populist parties were already gaining importance in the 1990s and at any rate before the 'Great recession' and that their political platforms would reject economic liberalism; this claim would be corroborated by evidence from an analysis of the parties' manifestos (Blyth and Hopkin 2018: 12–5). However, the two variables (society, from 'progressive' to 'conservative'; the economy, with either 'more state' or 'more market') which Blyth and Hopkin used to study the manifestos are not independent from each other; they are rather intertwined as usually the economy, politics, culture and society are. A more progressive society in fact tends to be associated with 'more state' and egalitarianism. Additionally, state and market are not necessarily alternatives; in a neoliberal perspective, more state often means more market, which is engineered by the state itself. As to Crouch's work (2017), it is as unpersuasive as Blyth's and Hopkin's are. In his view (Crouch 2017: 228), neoliberalism and conservatism (of which nationalism is a key component) would be like "two horses going in divergent directions". Yet, experiences such as those of Thatcher and Reagan (not to mention plenty of cases in developing countries) clearly and early illustrated that the two horses often move in the same direction. How do markets and national identities converge? When did such a convergence begin?

We can distinguish circumstances when nationalism and neoliberalism combine because they reflect a similar ethos from circumstances, more common in recent times, when nationalist forces, while still promoting a somewhat similar ethos to neoliberalism, embrace protectionism and reject globalisation in a more instrumental way. The latter can also be interpreted as a move towards a 'neoliberalism in one nation' or 'one country' and towards a 'mutation' (Callison and Manfredi 2020; Scheiring 2022) in which nationalism has a significant instrumental value; the nation-state becomes the servant of capitalism, or at least of fractions of it. That said, in all cases there are some structural, instrumental and ethical overlaps between the two; after all, both nationalism and neoliberalism espouse competitive and eventually antagonistic visions of society. Additionally, it is striking to notice how nationalism has mixed with neoliberalism in a wide variety of countries, from highly dependent economies to those we usually associate with the world capitalistic core (the USA, Britain, France, Japan, and many others).

In some cases and aspects, nationalism and neoliberalism co-constitute each other (Joppke 2021: 966–69); they somehow merge. This is clear in the experience of Thatcher's Britain, whose policies enjoyed a significant degree of domestic consent (Da Costa Vieira 2023) and relied on a powerful and toxic ethics of competitive individualism as well as on a nationalist vision of a strong Britain as its world champion. The nationalist-neoliberal fusion fully manifested itself on the occasion of the Falklands War (1982) as well as in the British diplomatic manoeuvres of the 1980s and 1990s to limit the powers of the European Communities. A political Europe was seen as an opponent of both nationalism and neoliberalism, especially when it was embodied by a (very moderate) socialist, Jacques Delors. Thatcher's politics reflected a competitive, hierarchical, tendentially essentialist, authoritarian and socially Darwinian view of the world and of relations among citizens as well as among nation-states and political communities. As a matter of fact, according to Fekete (2016: 17),

> Authoritarian solutions are also hardwired into neoliberalism and there is much in its practice (as opposed to its superficial ideology) that nationalists can build on. Power over and punishment of the weak and vulnerable are as intrinsic to neoliberalism as they are to authoritarian nationalism.

Those who do not comply with the logic of the market are usually constructed as weak and vulnerable and end up 'isolated'; they find themselves marginalised and in similar conditions to those non-conformists (or dissidents) who do not follow the logic of nationalist communities or authoritarian governments. Who is in fact more isolated than the immigrant, who is Otherised on a daily basis, treated as a 'source of problems', a scapegoat, within a process which eventually sidelines those who do not even possess the actual instruments to challenge the system? The marginalisation of the migrant parallels the marginalisation of market opponents; and the role of isolation in nationalist neoliberalism is clear from the words and deeds of Thatcher, according to whom, while "There is no such thing as society" (Hall 2011: 11), there is no such thing as a society or community of countries and peoples either. There are individual nation-states, with historical, cultural and ethnic differences. There is division, even a gap, between the nation of the hard-working property owners who compete on the market and those who live off the state, sometimes receive welfare benefits and reject, or are unable to comply with, the dominant economic model; the latter are often immigrants. This is apparent in the neoliberal vision of both the domestic and the 'international' society – or rather, 'sphere', considering Thatcher's disdain for the word 'society' itself.

The neoliberal-nationalist combination appears even more strongly in the traditionalist approach of the US 'New Right' (de Orellana and Michelsen 2019). Its main tenets, which would powerfully reappear during the Trump administration, are summarised in Gingrich's famous 'Contract with America' (1994). Tax and regulation cuts combine with strong 'law and order' proposals, and emphasis on national security. Neoliberal economics is promoted as a form of American nationalism, together with reference to traditional US values, also in conservative religious terms. The ties with Reagan's experience (Cannon 2000) are strong; the same is valid for the links between the 'New Right' and Christian fundamentalism. As to economic policies, the Reagan and Bush Sr. administrations adopted protectionist measures, especially towards

Japan and the European Communities, and in industries such as steel making. On this there is clear continuity between these Republican administrations and Bush Jr.'s and Trump's later presidencies (Slobodian 2021: 54–57; Wraight 2019).

The nationalist dimension has become far stronger with the worldwide emergence of 'populism' (which was already a part of Thatcher's discourse) since the Cold war's end. Some commentators and politicians have even talked about the decline or demise of neoliberalism (Stiglitz 2019) or at least of its more 'progressive' face (Fraser 2017 and 2019), in part expressed by Clinton's New Democrats, Blair's Third Way and Germany's *Neue Mitte* (Busch and Manow 2001). Neoliberalism would have been rejected because of a renewed emphasis on national values, traditional norms and economic protectionism, in a kind of backlash from below (Inglehart and Norris 2016 and 2019). Global uncertainties and the way populists have instrumentally demonised globalisation would have led to nationalism's rise, sometimes with strong racist and xenophobic connotations. However, nationalism was already there (Slobodian and Plehwe 2020) and neoliberalism has not been rejected by populist nationalists in any way, shape or form. What has emerged in countries such as Trump's USA, post-Brexit Britain, Orbán's Hungary, or with leaders like Le Pen in France, Salvini and Meloni in Italy, Wilders in The Netherlands, Modi in India, is something more akin to a 'neoliberalism in one country', with emphasis on economic protectionism and national identity, but also on a continuation (in fact an intensification) of neoliberal policies in a more authoritarian and aggressive fashion. Such policies aim at strengthening the position of fractions of the national bourgeoisie (for example, the steel and defence industries in the USA; some specific sectors in British manufacturing, trade and finance; Feldmann and Morgan 2021b). At the same time, while in some cases the nationalist-neoliberal combination has become more instrumental, in others the two aspects have remained fully symbiotic; their ethics are largely consistent. The nation-state, for its part, has returned to the fore as the key neoliberal player, and the leading provider of pro-business policies, which have been further directed towards and in fact against large majorities of poor and dispossessed citizens. Trump's politics has indeed combined a protectionist, neo-mercantilist approach to trade under the hawkish Director of Trade and Manufacturing, Peter Navarro (Slobodian 2021: 59–62; Navarro and Autry 2011) with severe welfare cuts, the dismantling of Obamacare, tax reductions for the wealthy and corporations, neglect of sectors such as housing, education, infrastructure (despite campaign promises) and healthcare, and a renewed expansion of defence, security and police expenditures (Cozzolino 2018). Not only does Trumpism represent an incarnation of neoliberalism (Dardot and

Laval 2019; Fraser 2019; Hart 2020; Konings 2018); its core politics largely draws on those of previous Republican administrations, at least since Reagan's. Trump himself can be seen as an embodiment of neoliberalism (Fuchs 2017); his narcissistic personality, possessive individualism, limitless ambitions, reckless behaviours truly speak to a neoliberal audience of would-be self-entrepreneurs. Of course, Trumpism and the nationalist-neoliberal nexus are far more than one person and one, if vast, country.

Brexit is another example of neoliberalism in one country, as we will better see in Chapter 5. Many Brexiters share with Trump's supporters a narrative of rejection of international organisations and commitments (in this case, the main target is the EU), anti-immigration attitudes and rejection of diversities, conservative nationalism and support of an independent, 'global' Britain in a neoliberal world. Watkins (2016) and Watkins and Urbina-Montana (2022) have stressed the contradictions between neoliberalism and nationalism, but also how the two have combined in the dominant British political discourse from Thatcherism to Brexit and through the New Labour phase. "British nationalist-neoliberalism" is defined as "a project which appeals towards a consensual project of national harmony and renewal, but which is premised on a coercive project of exclusion and destruction" (Watkins 2016: n.p.). Migrants and international institutions are treated as 'dispensables', unlike the practices of a market-driven society. Additionally, a significant fraction of Britain's business elite has either supported Brexit or at least remained cautious. While the financial community expressed itself for Remain (Feldmann and Morgan 2021b: 121), even if without a strong, well-defined position (perhaps also because of its increasing fragmentation), other industries' representatives thought otherwise (see also Chapter 5). For example, "The large supermarket chains... [...] ...had never successfully implanted themselves in the European Union" (Feldmann and Morgan 2021b: 121) and their orientations were far from clear (Hellier, Inman and Butler 2016), but certainly not in a straightforward pro-EU direction. Moreover, manufacturers such as Dyson or the Murdoch-dominated media industry openly endorsed Brexit, also because of their limited interests in the European market. While no UK business rejected neoliberalism as such, the main choice became whether to prefer a regulator in London or one in Brussels, and several companies and sectors opted for the former. The choice of a nationalist state has persisted with the promises to strengthen policing, defence, and the armed forces, as is clear in the post-Brexit Conservative Party Manifesto of 2019 (Conservative Party Manifesto 2019). The same is valid for the rise of anti-immigration positions in 2022–23, the heated debates in their wake, in Britain and the EU (Rankin 2023), and the riots in Summer 2024 (Safdar 2024).

Similar recombinations of nationalism and neoliberalism have been at play in other Western countries, from France and Italy to Austria with the Freedom Party, Germany's *Alternative für Deutschland* (Slobodian 2018) and Sweden's *Sverigedemokraterna* (Swedish Democrats, SD). Outside of the core Western (and developed) economies, the nationalist-neoliberal marriage has manifested itself, especially since the 1990s, in countries which are often associated with capitalism's semiperiphery (or are anyway dependent on foreign capital; Madariaga 2020; Scheiring 2022). Among them we find some post-1989 new market economies in Central and Eastern Europe such as Romania, Hungary (Ban, Scheiring and Vasile 2023) and Poland, in all of which neoliberalism has taken on a more authoritarian and nationalist character (Stubbs and Lendvai-Bainton 2020; Lendvai-Bainton and Szelewa 2021). Orbán's Hungary, in particular, has become one of the symbols and almost the epitome of populist nationalism. Even if Viktor Orbán (Prime Minister 1998–2002 and since 2010) has embraced the rhetoric of 'illiberal' democracy (Zakaria 1997) and has strongly repressed the media, the judiciary, parliament and civil rights, in the economic sphere his policies have been fully neoliberal indeed (see the indicators used by Scheiring 2022: 1601–2). Mostly aiming at promoting a national bourgeoisie, Orbán has enacted very limited welfare programmes for 'ethnic' Hungarians and repressed everyone else, especially by 'othering' migrants and the Roma community, under a strict neoliberal regime (Fabry 2019; Gallo 2022: 566). Flat taxes (16%), subsidies to national and international companies, workfare programmes and welfare cuts have mixed with the promotion of FDI, particularly in the carmaking sector, which is largely dominated by German corporations. The nationalist mutation of neoliberalism owes also to a compromise between national and transnational capital, the political class and nationalist technocrats, in which populism is used as a legitimising strategy (Scheiring 2022: 1614–20). Far from being a generic 'mafia state' (Magyar 2016), Hungary incarnates a sophisticated balance of hegemonic forces which use nationalism to perpetuate their power in the country and in the EU.

Hungary's nationalist-neoliberal combination is not unique among 'dependent' economies. Post-communist Poland has also notoriously become home to a coexistence of xenophobic nationalism, populism, and neoliberalism (Shields 2015). Moreover, such combination has characterised several developing countries since neoliberalism's beginnings in the 1970s; this reality is often overshadowed by the mostly Western-centric mainstream approaches to neoliberalism (Connell and Dados 2014).

Some large emerging economies (among them, Turkey, Indonesia, and India; Chacko 2018) have also been drifting towards authoritarianism, using nationalism as a legitimation strategy (Chacko 2019); other ones have remained in a kind of hybrid 'grey zone' and have accepted nationalist ideas and practices.

Brazil, which never really abandoned neoliberalism even during the supposedly progressive PT (*Partido dos Trabalhadores*) administrations (2003–16), shifted to its authoritarian version in the wake of Rousseff's impeachment (2016) and especially after Bolsonaro's election in 2018 (Saad-Filho 2020). A strong nationalist conservatism, supported by Brazil's most reactionary forces (the armed forces, the agrarian business, evangelical groups), characterised its politics at least until Lula's narrow election win in late 2022 (Kenkel 2022). In a similar way to Hungary's Orbán, Bolsonaro relied on the perceptions of corruption which had tarnished the image of the left, and especially the PT; he also embodied "a racialized form of nationalism" (Saad-Filho and Boffo 2021: 304), mostly directed at natives and Afro-Brazilians, and drawing on a significant history of Brazilian far-right nationalism (Iamamoto, Kubík Mano and Summa 2021). He also capitalised on the economic crisis of the middle classes and deployed a nationalist, chauvinistic, sexist, homophobic rhetoric which played into the hands of those Brazilians, mainly in the middle classes, who were disaffected with the PT's policies. At the same time, Bolsonaro's economic choices were in line with a neoliberal trajectory, starting with the cuts to pensions and trade unions' powers (Saad-Filho and Boffo 2021) operated by the already mentioned Economy Secretary (2018–22), Paulo Guedes.

Another economic giant-in-the making, Mexico, has not witnessed any significant change since the election (2018) of left-wing President Andrés Manuel Lopez Obradór (AMLO), who had been greeted as the herald of a new and progressive era for the country. Not only has AMLO stuck to Mexico's long-term neoliberal regime; he has also persisted in resource nationalism, which was a hallmark of the PRI hegemony especially in the oil industry (Wattnem 2023). How Mexico will evolve under the more recently elected (September 2023) leftist President, Claudia Sheinbaum, remains yet to be seen.

The case of India, as of 2025 the world's fourth-largest economy (IMF 2025) and a BRICS founding member like Brazil, illustrates even more powerfully the links between neoliberalism and nationalism. While both pre-dated Modi's first election win (2014), the combination between an emerging and aggressive national fraction of capitalism and a radical-right version of Hindu nationalism, which draws on *Hindutva* and organisations such as the Bharatiya Janata Party (BJP) and the Rashtriya Swayamsevak Sangh (RSS), led to the rise and persistence in power of Modi's ultra-nationalist form of neoliberalism (Siddiqui 2017), which is often compared to outright fascism (Bhatty and Sundar 2020). In India, too, the BJP is relying on the perceptions of corruption linked to the governments of the National Congress Party and to the disaffection engendered by the neoliberal policies of the Congress's former Prime Minister, Manmohan Singh (2004–14).

While some African countries have also been experiencing the toxic combination of nationalism and neoliberalism (Harrison 2010; 2019), Japan is arguably the leading non-dependent and economically developed economy in East Asia which underwent similar transformations, without morphing into a fully authoritarian polity.

Japan's nationalist-neoliberal moment gained prominence during the premiership of the late Shinzo Abe (2006–07 and especially 2012–20). Highly controversial because of his negationist views of the Japanese past, Abe won elections at a moment of national decline, especially in the economic performance, and in the aftermath of the Fukushima tragedy of 2011. His programme of economic revitalisation (often dubbed 'Abenomics') contained clear neoliberal elements and aimed at the "most drastic reforms since the end of World War II" (Abe 2015: n.p.). As he put it in a famous speech in 2015, "In the face of an ever-more globalized economy, any company that cannot be internationally competitive cannot hope to survive" (Abe 2015: n.p.). Once again, we find a socially Darwinian rhetoric. At the same time, Abe championed a nationalist foreign policy, particularly in dealings with traditional opponents such as China and South Korea (Dobson 2017). He persisted in venerating the fallen at the Yasukuni Shrine, never addressed the tragical issue of 'comfort women' in World War Two, a matter of controversy especially with South Korea, and insisted on revising the peace clauses in the Japanese Constitution. He took an assertive posture in both domestic and international affairs and advocated a stronger Japanese role in world politics. In many ways, there are similarities between Modi's India and Abe's Japan in both foreign and economic/social policies.

Nationalism and neoliberalism are on converging terms. This phenomenon has taken place all over the world, often in dependent economies but also in the capitalist core. Sometimes the convergence can be framed in terms of a common ethos, sometimes the most nationally oriented fraction of the bourgeoisie has been attempting to rebuild neoliberalism within one country in a more pragmatic and instrumental way. There are also other reasons; among them we can mention expediency and the way neoliberals and conservatives have increasingly embraced nationalism as a reaction to social democratic cosmopolitanism (Harmes 2012), even if since the 1990s centre-left parties have never truly endorsed supranationalism and have, by contrast, usually claimed strong elements of neoliberalism.

While both nationalism and neoliberalism contain authoritarian aspects, a fully authoritarian mutation has occurred only in some countries. The next section will explore this issue.

4 Authoritarianism

As Chapter 2 illustrates, the literature on authoritarianism has developed in Political Science at least since Linz's well-known contributions (1964, 1978, 2000).

However, as we have seen, the categories used by Linz and many scholars in the Comparative Politics tradition (Cheibub, Gandhi and Vreeland 2010; Geddes, Wright and Frantz 2014; Levitsky and Way 2010; Schedler 2006) are not entirely convincing. While there have been several attempts to create typologies of authoritarianisms ('electoral', 'competitive', and so on), the concept of authoritarianism is not really defined or explained: it is rather interpreted as a negation of democracy or a political system in-between democracy and totalitarianism, somewhat more similar to the latter. Glasius (2018b) has correctly proposed to refocus on the concept of 'authoritarian practice', which she interprets as a way to limit accountability; such practices would occur also in formally democratic systems (see also Chapter 2). But what is then the link between authoritarian 'systems' and authoritarian 'practices'? And between 'illiberal practices' (which tend to limit fundamental rights) and authoritarianism (Glasius 2018a)?

As we have seen, this book maintains that the difference between democracy and authoritarianism is not clear-cut; both are expressions of modern capitalistic societies and their borders are rather blurred; the two types locate themselves along a spectrum or continuum more than being antithetical opposites. Additionally, authoritarian and illiberal practices are here interpreted as aspects and elements of authoritarianism. Even in a formal democracy they can be seen as *loci* of authoritarianism; they can evolve in a more autocratic direction and transform the whole system, subside or remain somehow latent and persist over time.

Authoritarian practices – or 'aspects' – can in fact emerge in many democratic states, especially in conjunction with neoliberalism. This section's first part deals with the growth of authoritarianism within liberal democracy, which, as we have seen, can already occur within a nationalist-neoliberal shell. This has taken place in several Western and non-Western countries, from the USA to Britain, Brazil to India, Japan to Turkey.

The section's second half focuses on two cases, Russia and China, where neoliberalism has coincided with the strengthening of 'traditional' authoritarian states, with very limited accountability and significant repression of fundamental rights. Authoritarianism is here supported by a combination of rather widespread acceptance and some ideological influences. What is the relationship between authoritarianism and neoliberalism in these two large countries and powerful states? How influential have they been as models or promoters of authoritarianism in relation to other states such as those in neighbouring Central and Southeast Asia?

In the latest decades democracy has sometimes been seen as 'ending' (Runciman 2018), 'dying' (Levitsky and Ziblatt 2018) or 'backsliding' (Bermeo 2016), with an emphasis on its erosion or demise; but what about the rise of some new and different political forms, that is, authoritarian ones? What about the emergence of a new type of authoritarianism, a neo- or in fact 'new' authoritarianism (Wiatr 2019)?

Although Wiatr (2019) locates the origins of 'new authoritarianism' in the more 'fragile' democracies of Central and Eastern Europe (such as Hungary and Poland) or in countries like Russia and Turkey, some of its characteristics can also be seen in states traditionally associated with the 'liberal democratic' West.

A 'new authoritarianism', following Wiatr (2019: 173), would maintain elections (despite occasional manipulation) and a degree of pluralism; the use of force would be quite limited. Its authoritarian dimension would derive mostly from the subjugation of the judiciary (Wiatr 2019: 176) and the control over the media, from the printed press to the digital and the social media. These processes, which are certainly more visible in Hungary, Russia or Turkey (but also in India and some African countries, from Ethiopia to Rwanda), have been occurring in some of the leading economies as well. What role has neoliberalism played in authoritarianism's rise? Certainly, 'massive frustration among those who have not been able to join the ranks of the beneficiaries of the capitalist system' (Wiatr 2019: 177) has been a key factor, chiefly as a consequence of neoliberalism's impact on equality, income, and social justice.

Together with the disillusionment of the lower-middle classes, another (and in fact more decisive) key factor of neoliberal authoritarianisation has been the impulse of those sectors of the bourgeoisie which feel damaged or penalised by the globalisation of the economy and politics that started emerging in the 1970s. This more 'national' bourgeois fraction has often supported opportunistic political entrepreneurs who have then promoted its own projects. In some cases, as we have seen, this has led to stronger emphasis on nationalism as a tool of ideological legitimacy. Where democratic institutions did not have strong roots, the slope towards authoritarianism has been more slippery.

Yet, also in more consolidated market democracies, aspects of authoritarianism have emerged. This is evident in the USA, as is demonstrated even by the 2025 US-based Freedom House report on the USA, 'Freedom in the World', the product of an institution which has often and correctly been criticised as pro-Western and in fact neoliberal (Giannone 2010). The tensions around the 2020 elections, which culminated with the Capitol Hill events on 6 January 2021, add up to structural problems of lobbying, media partisanship, racism and exclusion, and severe issues of social and economic inequality. All these elements have led to significant erosion of the US democratic fabric in recent years (Freedom House 2024b and 2025). Neoliberalism has clearly contributed to democratic decline, by marginalising both workers and some national industries, exacerbating inequality, and paving the way for authoritarian political entrepreneurs like Donald J. Trump. The US authoritarian torsion has been documented by several scholars and commentators (Fuchs 2017; Giroux 2017 and 2019) and in the long-term can be explained by the nature of US capitalism as well as by the legacy of historically authoritarian dimensions (McCarthyism and racial inequalities are just two examples). Project 2025, the massive 920-page collective book which appears to provide a blueprint for Trump's second mandate, goes even further (Project 2025). Prepared by the conservative Heritage Foundation, it sets sweeping proposals on presidential powers and a reshaping of US society, in the name of a new and belligerent American nationalism. The Commander-in-Chief would make political appointments and take control of commissions and departments, including the Department of Justice and the FBI. Gender and Critical Race Theory would disappear, and Christian nationalism, become hegemonic. Economically, there would be a minimal state, consistent with the idea of free banking and the possible elimination of the Federal Reserve. Immigration and China would be treated as dangerous threats. While some of these ideas and policies had already appeared under previous administrations, especially in the name of a 'unitary presidency' under Bush Jr, the key difference now would be the attempt to 'institutionalize Trumpism' (Garcia-Navarro 2024).

The United Kingdom is a more complex case. Even by relying on a source – Freedom House – which often understands liberty in a formalistic and neoliberal way, aspects of Britain's democratic backsliding have become apparent. The reports on Britain for 2022 and 2023 highlight several problematic aspects: issues of corruption (Freedland 2021) and integrity linked to Johnson's government's management of the pandemic and the related contracts; issues of academic freedom and surveillance; racial bias and rise in hate crimes; in other words, all traits which illustrate Britain's authoritarian involution and add to the 2023 immigration mismanagement (Taylor 2023). Additionally, under Johnson and the other Tory governments (2010–24) the British executive has become even more centralised, a fact which in part is a legacy of an already centralised type of government and in part owes to changes instigated by neoliberalism (Ward and Ward 2021).

Other Western countries, including France, Italy, Spain, Germany and The Netherlands, have witnessed the rise in power and sometimes to government of political forces which are usually identified with the far right and possess authoritarian traits. Jordan Bardella, the latest heir to the lepenist tradition, has long-time links with Italy's League's Salvini (Berteloot 2018; on the League see Chapter 4 in this book) and incarnates a legacy (that of the National Rally) of anti-immigration and authoritarian policies.

No state such as Russia, however, has come to epitomise what in the 21st century is usually considered an 'authoritarian' regime, and well before the 2022 Ukraine war (Freedom House 2023a). How important has neoliberalism been to Russia's authoritarian involution? How distinctive is the Russian type of 'authoritarian neoliberalism'? And where can its origins be located, rather domestically or internationally? Chapter 6 will answer some of these questions but, considering Russia's importance as a political model, also to some Western European countries' far-right groups, some key points are anticipated here.

Despite the promises of Gorbachev's reformism, Yeltsin's new and independent Russia never evolved along the lines of a traditional liberal democracy. As was somehow predictable in a vast country which needed to adopt momentous reforms in a limited span of time, its trajectory started with a phase of "phony democracy" (Sakwa 2010: 186) or 'regime democracy' (Sakwa 1997), which was soon characterised by institutional fragility, personalism, defective rule of law and informality.

Enter neoliberalism. In parallel with other formerly socialist states, Russia had its own intellectual neoliberal tradition, with its own ideological apparatus, and its own political faction of supporters. Among the latter, the contribution of "liberal-technocrats" (Sakwa 2010: 186) was particularly significant. Yegor Gaidar (Minister of Finance, 1991–92; Prime Minister, 1992; First Deputy Prime Minister, 1992–94; see also the section on technocracy) was the Russian architect of the 'shock therapy', while the economist, Anatoly Chubais, led the privatisation effort (Rutland 2013). The "liberal bloc" (Sakwa 2021: 228) also included other prominent figures such as the pro-Western Minister of Foreign Affairs Andrei Kozyrev (1990–96) and the energy industry reformer and Deputy Prime Minister, Boris Nemtsov (1998), who would be assassinated with his partner in 2015 in the surroundings of the Kremlin (Nemtsov 2000).

Neoliberalism, in other words, had some important Russian roots, but its policies and especially the 'shock therapy' adopted on 2 January 1992 (Ghodsee and Orenstein 2021), have been perceived as proposed and imposed over the Russian people by foreign powers, especially the US Treasury, the IMF and the World Bank (Harvey 2005; Dale 2011). Whether neoliberalism came from Russian ideas and policies, or from choices formulated in DC or some Western Economics departments, the immediate results were terrible and led to further metamorphoses of Russia's type of statehood. In few years, life expectancy dropped, inflation skyrocketed to four digits figures, while the poverty rate reached at least 40% (Milanovic 1998). The implementation of neoliberal measures was not always corresponding to theoretical prescriptions (Rutland 2013), but it was sufficient to generate economic collapse, social unrest, and political deadlock between parliament and president, as became clear in the tragical confrontation in 1993. Russia morphed even more into a 'dual state' (Sakwa 2010), a conglomeration of a formal, constitutional democratic structure and an informal, personalistic and pragmatic 'administrative state', in part democratic and in part authoritarian.

This duality would combine with the emergence of a fragmented, heterarchical model of government (Sakwa 2021), in which different power blocs compete for power and influence the leaders, who depend on their support to maintain their positions. Even when Yeltsin was succeeded (2000) by the ex-KGB officer, Vladimir Putin, duality and heterarchy remained in place. The new president was able to downsize the power of the Yeltsin-related oligarchs (among them, Boris Berezovsky and Mikhail Khodorkovsky), and rely more strongly on the *siloviki* (the security apparatus officers, the 'guardians' of Russia; Sakwa 2021) without disregarding technocrats and liberal economists such as the Minister of Finance, Alexei Kudrin (2000–11). In many ways, during the first two Putin mandates Russia remained a 'hybrid' state, with a combination of democratic and authoritarian elements, strong economic growth (higher than 7% per year), and a societal balance between all the power pyramids (Hale 2015) of whom Putin was the supreme arbiter. Such pragmatic model was not far from a neoliberal state, one which drew on high energy prices but also on slow but significant reforms on capital freedoms, flat tax rates, labor code changes, and a modicum of privatisations (Rutland 2013). Putin's early presidencies signalled a commitment to integration into the world economy and neoliberalism, which was pushed forward by a stronger state hand.

Two and partly connected game-changers were the decline in hydrocarbon prices in the early 2010s and the growing tensions with the West after Putin's return to the Kremlin in 2012. Perceived threats, at home but especially abroad (the tensions over Ukraine and Syria, the subsequent sanctions, talks about new NATO enlargements, and so on), further shifted Russia's political system towards what has been called 'competitive' and later 'electoral' authoritarianism (on the former, Levitsky and Way 2010; on the latter, Schedler 2015).

Electoral authoritarianism, as Chapter 2 illustrates, is *de facto* authoritarianism. The Russian state has to some extent remained dual and heterarchical (Sakwa 2021), and in fact new power blocs, such as various groups of traditionalists and the 'Eurasianists', have gained leverage (Sakwa 2021: 228–29). Some moderate liberals, at least until the Ukraine war, have also maintained power positions; among them, one can recall the Prime Minister (since January 2020), Mikhail Mishustin, a technocrat and expert on digitisation, and Herman Gref, a long-time ally of Putin's and now at the helm of Sberbank, Russia's largest bank.

At the same time, the *siloviki* have progressively gained power and influence; the fear of a Western threat has propelled them to ever more important positions in government and business, while the democratic element has slowly faded and given rise to a repressive authoritarian system. A series of reactionary laws on free speech, executive powers, repression of any fundamental rights, including LGBTQIA+ rights, has transformed the state into a truly authoritarian regime.

Yet Russia has not ceased to be neoliberal. It has become a case of authoritarian neoliberalism, in which an interesting phenomenon is the 'neoliberalisation of the *siloviki*'. The old oligarchy still exists, while the guardians of order have become new corporate oligarchs, often linked to the criminal underworld (Galeotti 2018) and sometimes referred to as 'silovarchs' (Treisman 2008). For example, Putin's old aide Sergey Chemezov is at the helm of Rostec, the military-industrial giant, while other former collaborators, Alexei Miller and the much-discussed, Igor Sechin, preside over Gazprom and Rosneft, the gas and oil majors (Sakwa 2021: 231). At the same time, *siloviki* and oligarchs, Eurasianists and technocrats, corporate managers and neofascists often combine their forces in supporting a regime which has certainly become more authoritarian, but is also rhizomatic (Sakwa 2021) and can evolve into more than one direction.

China's political reality is more complex and multifaceted, also because of its unique civilisational legacy and historically problematic relations with the West. Few scholars would doubt the authoritarian nature of its regime, even if some have also highlighted the existence of limited democratic aspects, especially at a local level (Bell 2015); China's authoritarianism is also often qualified. For example, it was seen as 'fragmented' before Xi Jinping's second presidential term (Lieberthal and Lampton, eds., 1992) but has been read as more personalistic and centralised since Xi Jinping's policy changes and his 'third revolution' (Economy 2018). Given the strictly collectivistic traits of China's political economy under Mao (1949–76) and especially during the cultural revolution (Naughton 2007), it is difficult to envisage in it any neoliberal elements until at least the late 1970s and Deng Xiaoping's 'opening and reform' policies.

Deng's reforms introduced aspects of a ('socialist') market economy, but reflected pragmatic choices, rather than ideological ones (Shirk 1993). In the early 1980s China was poor and internationally weak, and Deng attempted to intervene and restore the country's past economic and political standing (Weber 2018). Facilitating FDI in Special Economic Zones (SEZs) and introducing marketizing reforms (e.g., that of the rural households) were moderate, step-by-step, ways to enhance living standards rather than a fully-fledged neoliberalisation. In fact China set out to pursue its own route to 'modernity', rather than being inspired or influenced by the neoliberalising West. Price liberalisations such as those invoked by the Czech dissident economist, Ota Šik, were in the end not accepted (Weber 2018) and the liberalising Secretary-general of the CCP (Chinese Communist Party), Zhao Ziyang (1987–89), ended up under house arrest. Even the growing emphasis on *suzhi* ("human quality"; Kipnis 2007: 388) cannot be fully understood within a neoliberal framework (Kipnis 2007). Under Deng's rule major privatisations did not take place either. However, a door remained open to further and incremental reforms.

In relation to the reforms of the 1980s, Harvey (2005) has written about a 'neoliberalism with Chinese characteristics.' There has been a vast debate on the nature, whether neoliberal or not, of contemporary China's political economy. We may or may not agree with Harvey, but certainly China has taken on neoliberal aspects, which have grown over time and have even 'globalised', from the country's early accession to the WTO (2001) to the construction of the giant BRI (Belt and Road Initiative; Huang 2016; Callahan 2016) and the recent rise in the financial and digital industries. Despite Beijing's confrontational posture towards the West and the USA and its avowed support for an alternative model (Breslin 2011), China has in fact rather adapted to the Washington Consensus and adopted some of its policies, also relying on the experience of the developmental (and neoliberal) states in East Asia (Japan, South Korea, Singapore; Horesh and Fan Lim 2017). A part of the urban elites has clearly embraced the narrative of consumerism and its production of desire (Rofel 2007), even if this does not apply to the country as a whole (Nonini 2008). Neoliberalism has also manifested itself in the erosion of social expenditure programmes (Duckett 2020) and in the emergence of forms of welfare which have created further inequality (including the management of migrations from the countryside to cities; Zhang 2018). China's Gini coefficient has risen tremendously and reached levels up to 0.55 (Mazzocco 2022).

As to the financial industry, which has often been described as repressed (Lardy 2008) and could therefore be seen as an example of China's isolation from neoliberalism, significant changes have been under way with the rise of AI and fintech. Algorithmic governance has become a powerful reality in China, too (Gruin 2019).

In summary, while the debate on China's neoliberalism carries on, it seems fair to locate the country into the realm of 'authoritarian neoliberalism.' Neoliberal reforms, if in a more tentative and pragmatic way, have occurred, and Xi has centralised power in the hands of the single party and the state. Paradoxically, the largest socialist state ever might be a clear example of a model neoliberal state, which directs and regulates the market and enforces its governmentality mechanisms in many domains. Such model, which crucially relies on digital technology, has also an export potential.

While the Chinese government has consistently referred to its history's uniqueness, and has not promoted any specific template abroad, China has been influencing countries in Southeast Asia both by showcasing a successful economic example and by more-or-less directly supporting authoritarian governments, especially in Cambodia, Myanmar, and to some extent Thailand (Einzenberger and Schaffar 2018: 7–8). Yet some states (certainly, Malaysia, which has for decades been steered by Mahathir's astute leadership) have maintained strong agency and have followed their own paths to both authoritarianism and neoliberalism. This is true also for Central Asia, where Russia's and China's influences are strong, but states such as Kazakhstan and Uzbekistan have protected their autonomy (Gallo 2021) and re-elaborated both neoliberalism and authoritarianism in a post-Soviet context.

Liberal democracy and authoritarianism share some aspects and can be seen as fluid and moving along a continuum. To different extents and in different guises, the adoption of neoliberal politics has led to constraints on both accountability and rights and to the establishment of truly 'authoritarian neoliberal' states in several countries. Such states represent the response of parts of the bourgeoisie, fractions of the ruling classes, or the dominant party, to the tensions, inequalities and perceived injustices generated by neoliberal reform.

The book's empirical part will now focus on an analysis of the first authoritarian neoliberal variety, that is, technocracy, and use Italy as a case-study. Once again, it is important to bear in mind that technocracy often combines with both nationalism and traditional authoritarianism, as the experiences of Russia and China neatly illustrate.

CHAPTER 4

Italy and Its Technocrats

Among the wealthier developed economies, both in the 'West' and the G7/G20, Italy is by far the one in which technocratic experts (especially economists and jurists) have played the most important role. In fact, since the Cold war's end, Italy has had at least four *governi tecnici* ('technocratic governments'; on the distinction between *tecnico* and *tecnocrate* see Giannone and Cozzolino 2023: 26–9), those headed by Carlo A. Ciampi (1993–94) and Lamberto Dini (1995–96), two central bankers; Mario Monti (2011–13), an economist and former EU commissioner, and Mario Draghi (2021–22), an economist and former EU central banker. In the Dini's and Monti's governments there were only independent experts, especially in areas such as the economy, home affairs, and diplomacy; in this sense, they were 'pure' technocratic governments. Italian technocracy and neoliberalism have been usually associated with the EU technostructure (Galbraith 1967) and its stringent fiscal constraints, but it is fair to say that Italy has its own and significant, if often overlooked, neoliberal and technocratic traditions (Masini 2019). While in previous times Italian neoliberals were often marginalised, they have become more influential since at least the 1970s, just before the emergence of the imperatives dictated by EU parameters and criteria – especially in the Eurozone.

This chapter begins with a history of neoliberal ideas in Italy, also in the attempt to trace their potential links with authoritarianism. Before moving on to the technocratisation of the Italian state since the 1990s (and the ambiguous flirtations between technocracy and populist nationalism), the chapter also explores the economic and political changes which slowly turned Italy's political system towards authoritarian neoliberalism from the 1970s onwards. In the final part the chapter assesses the implications for technocracy as a general political form and its relations with 21st century neoliberalism as an idea and a practice.

1 Neoliberal Traditions

Italy has a strong tradition in liberal thinking as well as in classical and neoclassical economics. The Sicilian scholar, Francesco Ferrara (1810–1900), and especially the well-known marginalist economist, Vilfredo Pareto (1848–1923), are just two among the many authors who would exercise a significant influence on the discipline in the country and in Europe (Schumpeter 1986).

Further into the twentieth century an important liberal school emerged in the field of public finance (Masini 2019: 332–35). The seminal contributions of authors such as Gustavo Del Vecchio (1883–1972) and Antonio De Viti De Marco (1858–1943) have been acknowledged by one of US neoliberalism's intellectual leaders, James M. Buchanan (1960) from the Virginia School of Economics.

Even more interestingly, in the early twentieth century there emerged a new Italian school of Economics, the 'pure economics' (*economia pura*), whose intellectual leader, Maffeo Pantaleoni (1857–1924), became a top advisor to Alberto De Stefani. De Stefani, himself a liberal economist, was a follower of Pantaleoni's and became the first Minister of Treasury under fascism (1922–25; Mattei 2017 and 2022a). De Stefani adopted strict, intransigent austerity reforms: in the name of a supposedly objective economic science, he drastically cut public expenditures and investments (especially public works), dismissed 65,000 employees in the public administration, privatised railways and the telephone industry (Mattei 2017; Bel 2011) and helped Italy achieve a balanced budget in 1926, amidst vast national and international praise (including from *The Times*, *The Economist*, the British Embassy to Italy, etc; Mattei 2022b). In simple words, De Stefani combined authoritarianism (notably, fascism; he had been a member of the Fascist National Party since 1921) and liberalism (in the form of neoclassical economics); his work as a politician as well as his theoretical writings can be seen as an early 'marriage' between neoliberalism and authoritarianism. As a matter of fact, he served the interests of the Northern Italian bourgeoisie and used a strong state hand to achieve his (and Mussolini's) aims, especially in fascism's early years, when the regime needed international legitimacy in Britain and the USA. Interestingly, De Stefani would remain loyal to fascism until the very end of the regime in the night of 24 July 1943 (Mattei 2017).

This early Italian encounter between authoritarianism and liberalism was a kind of warning. Perhaps the most famous Italian liberal economist, Luigi Einaudi (1874–1961), who had praised De Stefani's austerity policies and was among the first members of the Mont Pélerin Society, would later position himself on the anti-fascist front (Faucci 2012).

Not a dogmatic thinker, Einaudi was generally close to classical liberalism, and to its values of individual initiative, entrepreneurship, fight against private and public monopolies, and protection of private property. Crucially, Einaudi saw private property and economic liberties as the foundations of all other liberties (Einaudi and Croce 1988). Despite Einaudi's outstanding intellectual prestige and political achievements (in 1945 he was appointed Governor of the

Banca d'Italia, the Bank of Italy, henceforth BoI; in 1948 he became President of the Republic), his ideas never became dominant in the country, with the partial exception of the early post-World War Two governments, when Italy successfully attempted to gain international credibility by resorting to policies of monetary stability and austerity.

Einaudi's perspective was arguably closer to the ordoliberals than to Hayek's neoliberalism; like Röpke, he was also a promoter of European integration and in fact one of the founders of European federalism (Einaudi 1986). While a strong emphasis on ethics, economics, and common European values is shared by both Einaudi and ordoliberals, post-World War Two Italian liberalism mainly drew on the legacy of the well-known philosopher, Benedetto Croce (1866–1952), who rather minimised the role of economic and material aspects.

A highly renowned philosopher and historian, an idealist in the tradition of Hegel, Croce (Galasso 2002) embodied a different type of liberalism, one which emphasises the foundational role of values, ethics, and ideas, which he saw as more important than economic and structural factors (Croce 1970). It is Croce who separated the concepts of *liberismo*, which has mostly economic connotations, from *liberalismo*, which refers to liberal thinking as a whole; this distinction remains specific to the Italian language. Croce's influence remained significant in Italian post-war politics and, together with Einaudi's proximity to ordoliberalism, it contributed to maintain Italian neoliberalism somewhat distant from its Anglo-American versions.

At the same time, the presence in the country of the strongest Communist Party in Western Europe, the PCI (*Partito Comunista Italiano*, Italian Communist Party), founded by Gramsci in 1920, urged the pro-Western coalitions led by the DC (*Democrazia Cristiana*, Christian Democracy) to turn to the left and adopt more state-driven and welfarist economic policies, if in a fragmented, often inconsistent and usually clientelistic way. These policies would strongly characterise Italy's experience until the mid-1970s (Zamagni 1993; Ginsborg 2003a).

Especially in the 1960s and also as an effect of the stormy industrial growth of the previous decade (the 'Italian economic miracle'), a part of the DC started exploring the possibility of an 'opening to the left' (*apertura a sinistra*) to form governments with the support of the rather moderate Socialist Party (*Partito Socialista Italiano*, PSI), a choice which was also a way to separate the Socialists from the PCI. The new 'centre-left' governments were inaugurated in 1963 and immediately took stronger social measures. Electric energy was nationalised, and more inclusive reforms were adopted in both education and agriculture, if in a somewhat erratic way (Ginsborg 2003a, Chapter 8).

One of the few typically neoliberal voices in Italy throughout the post-war period was that of Bruno Leoni (1913–67). Tragically killed in 1967, Leoni had been far more popular abroad than in Italy. His neoliberalism was probably the closest to Hayek's body of political, economic and philosophical thinking (Leoni 1961), at least in Italy. Italy's history, however, was still distant from Leoni's individualistic aspirations.

After all, the country had always been deeply divided; both before the 'unification' in the *Risorgimento* (1861) and after, with profound cleavages (Pezzino 2002) such as those between North and South, (Roman Catholic) believers and non-believers, fascists and anti-fascists, pro-Western camp and communist camp (De Felice 1999). The Italian bourgeoisie had traditionally been rather weak, concentrated in the Northern cities (especially Genoa, Milan and Turin), dominated by few families, and ultimately unable to exercise any lasting hegemony, as was famously explained by Gramsci (1971).

The social changes and upheavals of the late 1960s led to further reforms such as the adoption of the *Statuto dei lavoratori* (1970), a kind of code of laws protecting labour rights. At the same time, like in most of the Western world, in the 1960s profits started shrinking, while the PCI remained unable to reach government positions and adopt more robust policies to support a growing number of millions of unionised factory workers.

In the mid-1970s, between high social tensions and heated class conflict, neoliberalism started emerging. In Italy it was moving more slowly than in other countries; yet in some circles and contexts it began gaining momentum as well.

2 Changes since the 1970s

While Italy's political system was prisoner of political infighting (but also cooperation and collusion) between parties (the *partitocrazia*, or 'rule by parties'; Calise 1994) and their factions, on economic matters the practices of the BoI already demonstrated some autonomy. As is argued by Quaglia (2004: 1098), in economics and foreign policy ideas can matter. The BoI, which since the Second World War had been relatively independent from political pressures (Quaglia 2005: 555), was not indifferent to the transnational circulation of ideas, among which neoliberalism was becoming more vocal; according to Quaglia (2005: 552): "Neo-liberal ideas gained international currency and spread across countries in the late 1970s. Central bankers and monetary experts constitute epistemic communities". As a matter of fact, neoliberal ideas, in their different versions, were already spreading in the *early* 1970s. Pro-market positions, if not in radical forms, were becoming more influential at the BoI as well. The BoI itself was part of an important epistemic community. MIT-educated economists such as Tommaso Padoa-Schioppa joined the

BoI's Research Department in 1970 (Ciampi 2011), while the post-Keynesian Nobel Prize winner, Italian American Franco Modigliani, was already working on Italy's monetary policy and its models in the late 1960s (Rossi 2007: 16–7). In a famous article, Modigliani and Padoa-Schioppa criticised Italy's wage policies and their indexation mechanisms (1978), which were seen as potential inflation-triggers. While the influential BoI's Governor, Guido Carli (1960–75), had usually combined classical liberal influences with attention to planning and even forms of technocracy (Gigliobianco 2006: 262–307), his successor, Paolo Baffi, was already more familiar with newer neoliberal ideas (Gigliobianco 2006: 307–34).

Outside of the BoI, a new generation of 'modernising' intellectuals with stronger liberal views was emerging in an increasingly less ideological PSI. Some of them such as the jurist, Giuliano Amato, would have played important political roles in Italy and Europe (Gervasoni 2004). Even in moderate parties like the DC or the centrist PRI (*Partito Repubblicano Italiano*, Italian Republican Party), new and more market-oriented views started gaining prominence; one key moderniser was the economist, Beniamino Andreatta, who would have played an important role in shaping Italian economic policies since acting as an economic advisor to Prime Minister Moro in the 1970s (Salsano 2014).

Four key episodes between the late 1970s and the early 1980s marked important changes (Cesaratto and Zezza 2018: 13–6). The first was the kidnapping and ensuing murder (9 May 1978) of Aldo Moro, the President of the DC and a former Prime Minister (Craveri 2012). Moro was the chief architect of the so-called 'historic compromise' (*compromesso storico*) between the DC and the PCI, which would have allowed the Communists to participate in Italy's governments. Italy might have moved closer to a social democratic model. His killing's circumstances remain clouded with obscurity, but one undeniable effect was the end of the negotiations between the DC and the Communists. Such negotiations may have dragged Italy away from strong US influence and possibly neoliberalism.

A second, important moment was Italy's decision to join the European Monetary System (EMS) of adjustable exchange rates in 1978. Given the country's difficult fiscal position and deteriorating public accounts, let alone the weakness of the *lira*, such choice would have entailed severe sacrifices and austerity. Paolo Baffi, the Governor of the BoI, opposed it (Quaglia 2004: 1100), thinking that in the first place the country required long-needed social adjustments. Yet political considerations, especially in terms of 'foreign policy beliefs' (Quaglia 2004: 1098), prevailed. Italy wanted to remain in the group of 'core' European countries, whatever the socio-economic costs. The majority of the citizens seemed satisfied with the governments' pro-European choices.

This highlights the interesting paradox that most Italians accepted austerity in the name of European norms, values or simply longer-term interests.

A third moment was the so-called 'march of the 40,000' FIAT employees (Cesaratto and Zezza 2018: 14), which put an end to the era of protests, strikes and trade union activism which had started in the late 1960s. A large number of FIAT employees and cadres (FIAT, the carmaker from Turin, was Italy's largest private employer) rejected strikes and embraced negotiations with employers. Companies felt now legitimised to dismiss workers, something that would happen in the early 1980s on a massive scale.

A fourth, and decisive, episode was the separation between the BoI and the Treasury. Until 1981 the BoI had the task of buying those State bonds unsold at auctions. In Spring 1981, with a rapid exchange of letters and without parliamentary oversight, the BoI's new Governor, Carlo A. Ciampi, and the Treasury's Secretary, the reformist DC economist, Beniamino Andreatta, decided to sever the relationship between the BoI and Italy's unsold public debt (Ventresca 2023). The episode demonstrates the strong links between the BoI's technocracy and key parts of the country's governing class, which used the Bank's expertise as a way to legitimise potentially unpopular choices. Italy's fiscal and monetary policies became now much more dependent on markets; the Treasury could no longer avail itself of the safety valve represented by the BoI purchases.

The so-called 'divorce' between the BoI and the Treasury led to two parallel experiences during the 1980s. Interest rates rose, a fact which pushed in an anti-inflationary direction and confirmed the BoI's renewed orientation towards price and exchange rate stability, within the limits of what Ciampi called *discrezione* ('tact' or 'discernment'; Ciampi 1992). With a tighter monetary policy, the inflation rate went down from more than 20% in 1980 to some 5% in 1987 (Ventresca 2023: 198). At the same time, governments' fiscal policies continued to be deflationary and expansive, but up to some point. The new five-party executives (*pentapartito*) in which the PSI, and especially its ambitious leader, Bettino Craxi, played a significant role, adopted measures to cut the *scala mobile* ('sliding wage scale') by which wages were automatically catching up with rises in prices; the cuts (Balcet 1997: 77) took place with the San Valentino Decrees (14 February 1984). State bonds' markets became more diversified and new products were offered, also with the aim of fencing off Italy's rising public debt (Lagna 2016: 172).

Throughout the 1980s the *lira*'s exchange rate remained relatively stable and the same is true for inflation. However, public accounts and especially public debt continued deteriorating, also because of higher interest rates (Balcet 1997: 78). This was not a good omen when Italy had to face its European commitments.

In the last Andreotti governments (1989–91 and 1991–92), the BoI gained even more prominence: Guido Carli was appointed Budget Minister to coordinate the long 'march towards Maastricht' between the government, the Bank itself, and their European partners. Italy signed the Treaty on 7 February 1992, but in the meantime social and political problems, in part linked to the Cold war's end (the start of inquiries on massive bribing scandals, *Tangentopoli*, and a series of ferocious mafia attacks on the judiciary in 1992) hit tremendously hard. A 'core executive' of technocrats, embedded in the BoI and the Treasury (among whom there was Carli himself), pushed the country towards stronger European integration, which after all was also one of the key normative goals of Italy's leading politicians (Dyson and Featherstone 1996), including Andreotti and Craxi. Together with Carli, Ciampi and Padoa-Schioppa from the BoI played crucial roles in the Maastricht negotiations, while the Treasury was chiefly represented by its Director-Generals: Mario Sarcinelli and later, Mario Draghi (Dyson and Featherstone 1996: 278). This group of economists and experts constructed the *vincolo esterno* (the 'external constraint') as a symbol of the necessity to join the EU (and especially the EMU, European Monetary Union, or Eurozone) and as a challenge Italy had to win at any rate. It was a synonym of modernisation, fiscal discipline, reliability as an international partner and eventually of a full 'Europeanisation.' Following Dyson and Featherstone (1996: 280), "The government's approach to the institution-building required for EMU was dominated by the beliefs of the Banca d'Italia on EC monetary cooperation." While the negotiations' outcomes were mixed, the Italian negotiators were able to tie the state to the EMU and create a strong, overarching technostructure which would have brought about not just fiscal discipline, but also massive doses of neoliberal adjustment and austerity. Accession to the EU/EMU was mostly achieved by technocratic experts, who had never been elected, and operated in the corridors between the BoI and the Treasury. What would their legacy be – for the majority of Italians? Some answers would come in the 1990s.

3 The 1990s: from Amato to Amato, from the Lira to the Euro

The 1990s, the 'golden age' of globalisation and neoliberalism, are for Italy a decade of massive political earthquakes, slow economic growth and recurrent social instability. During the decade several technocrats obtain government positions and even become Prime Ministers. Interestingly, the pro-EU and austerity agenda is promoted by an unusual convergence between technocrats and a 'new left', briefly represented by the PSI and later by the PDS

(*Partito Democratico della Sinistra*, 'Democratic Party of the Left'), which after 1991 becomes the main heir to the PCI on the left of Italy's political spectrum (Ginsborg 2003b: 159–62).

The dramatic challenge represented by the accession to the EMU mobilised the 'core executive', which increasingly included several technocrats from the BoI, experts from political parties and from the Treasury, and other fractions of the public sector (Elgie 2011). A core executive (Elgie 2011) is usually transnational, that is, it acts in connection and with the support of transnational ruling elites (in business, finance, international institutions, politics, the media, the academia, etc) and generally promotes neoliberal, pro-market policies. In Italy's case, its members, whom we can aptly characterise as 'cosmopolitan intellectuals', according to Gramsci's (1971) definition, and would be typical of a lately unified country like Italy, mainly acted as heralds and promoters of ideas of European integration and unity. They interpreted it in various ways according to their personalities and individual agencies; nevertheless, the ideal of European unity, which has been powerful throughout the whole of modern Italian history, demonstrates the importance of values in foreign policy and economics epistemic communities. An example of a European epistemic community in action was the Delors Committee, which paved the way to the EMU and included Padoa-Schioppa as a rapporteur (Verdun 1999).

In the middle of the storm generated by the tremendous corruption scandal usually known as *Tangentopoli* ('Bribesville'), which started in early 1992 and decimated Italy's Parliament and parties (Koff 2002), Giuliano Amato was appointed Prime Minister (28 June 1992). A sophisticated scholar of constitutional law more than a professional politician, Amato was nonetheless an experienced member of the PSI and represented a key link between party politics and technocracy, also because in his government there were three independent experts with specific competences in public finance, criminal law and cultural policies (Paolo Baratta, Giovanni Conso, and Alberto Ronchey). Also known as 'the subtle doctor' of Italian politics, Amato nevertheless adopted two draconian austerity measures. In July he decreed a forced levy of .6% on a range of deposits and bank accounts; in September he approved a budget of 93,000 billion liras, in order to stave off the continuous deterioration of public and foreign accounts. It was not enough. Because of rampant speculations, Italy had to rapidly leave the European Monetary System (together with Britain), while technocrats rapidly started stepping in (Bufacchi and Burgess 1997).

In April 1993, in the context of deteriorating public accounts and the collapse of political parties, Ciampi left the helm of the BoI and was appointed Prime Minister by the President of the Republic, Oscar L. Scalfaro. Interestingly, since the inception of the neoliberal era and in a global context of growing executive powers (Poguntke and Webb, eds., 2005), the role of the President of the Italian Republic, which according to the Constitution should be rather ceremonial, has increased in visibility and political power. Successive Presidents would have become crucial players in promoting European integration and Italy's role in it (Giannone and Cozzolino 2023: 60–1). As to Ciampi, his was the first largely technocratic government in Italy's republican history, and it included ten independent experts. Ciampi was a strongly pro-European banker and an intellectual committed to the European project. His executive had a clear "double task: to draft a rigorous budgetary law and to oversee and accompany the writing of a new electoral law" (Pasquino and Valbruzzi 2012: 619). This meant proposing electoral reforms to enhance the country's governance quality and efficiency as well as kicking off processes of privatisations and adopting austerity measures. Both objectives were achieved. In less than a year Italy had a more majoritarian electoral law; processes of reform of a plethoric public administration and privatisations of major state companies had launched (Ginsborg 2003b: 276–78). Ciampi left further decisions to the electors in early 1994. In the meantime, the country's political and party systems were disgregating and mutating. Ciampi's government is usually considered the last of the so-called 'First Republic' (Bobbio 1997), although from another angle its neoliberal and technocratic spirit could qualify it as the first of the 'Second Republic' (Giannone and Cozzolino 2023: 57).

The political right meanwhile regained life faster than the left. In the wealthier regions of the Italian North, a separatist, regionalist, populist and openly pro-business party, the *Lega Nord* (Northern League; Albertazzi, McDonnell and Newell 2011), allied with the newly founded party, *Forza Italia*, the brainchild of a much talked and rampant media billionaire, Silvio Berlusconi, who was also popular as the owner of the successful football team, AC Milan. In Southern Italy, Berlusconi's party made a pact with the nationalist and post-fascist, *Alleanza Nazionale* (AN, National Alliance). The new and unexpected coalition, supported by Berlusconi's mediatic power and appealing to disaffected citizens, proved decisive in defeating the centre-left, which in the Spring 1994 elections was let down by the uncertainties of the PDS and the decline of its other forces. The left was deeply divided between a part which was anchored to its traditional socialist ideals, and other fractions which were embracing globalisation. Yet Berlusconi's first government was not to last. Its internal divisions, lack of experience and feeble commitment to European integration led to rapid demise and replacement with yet another technocratic executive, led by Lamberto Dini, a former Director-General of the BoI and Treasury Minister as an independent under Berlusconi himself (Caciagli and Kertzer, eds., 1996). Again, President Scalfaro played a key role in handing the government over to a committed pro-EU technocrat and getting rid of somewhat Eurosceptic Berlusconi.

Dini's executive was the first all-technocrat government in Italian history; the only minister with a party affiliation was the Foreign Affairs Minister, Susanna Agnelli (PRI), the first Italian woman in that role and a representative of the famous Turin-based 'dynasty' of carmakers. The government steamed ahead with several reforms, including a comprehensive revision of the pension system, which was partly transformed into a contributory one with the left's support (Fifi 2023: 1449–50), and paved the way to the rise of a centre-left coalition, *L'Ulivo* ('The olive tree'), led by the economist and former DC cadre, Romano Prodi, a student of Andreatta's. Yet Prodi's executive, whose origins were the outcome of the 1996 elections (when *L'Ulivo* obtained a clear majority; Eligendo 1996a and 1996b), more than being a fully-fledged centre-left government, embodied a strong continuity with its technocratic predecessors. Many ministers were experts in their own fields and two previous premiers were handed key positions: Ciampi in the role of 'Super' Minister of the Economy, so-called because his new portfolio replaced the previous division between the Budget and Treasury Ministries; Dini as Minister of Foreign Affairs. Other economists such as Andreatta, Fantozzi and Vincenzo Visco from the PDS were also appointed ministers. Prodi's mandate was clear: Italy had to take all necessary measures to re-enter the EMS and join the first group of countries forming the Eurozone (Ginsborg 2003b: 302–09).

Prodi's experience (1996–98) demonstrated the continuity between pro-European technocratic experts, especially from the BoI, moderate centrist economists (such as Prodi himself) and centre-left modernisers with a vision of Europe as the ideal *locus* of Italian politics. Thanks to further and tight budgetary laws and job market reforms (the *pacchetto Treu*, named after the Labour Minister, Tiziano Treu, introduced temporary jobs in 1997; Gualmini and Hopkin 2012), Italy was able to re-enter the EMS and meet some of the criteria (or demonstrate improvements, if modest) which were necessary to join the first nucleus of countries forming the Eurozone in May 1998. After all, Germany itself was facing economic difficulties and financial markets were betting in favour of Italy, while France, with a new Socialist government, became more favourable to Italy's immediate accession to the Eurozone (Lagna 2016: 175–77). Once the aim of joining it was achieved, it seemed as if Italy was again ready for 'the return of (traditional) politics', and the emergence of a possible alternation between a Berlusconi-led centre-right and a new centre-left, inspired by some form of progressive neoliberalism (Fifi 2023). The centre-left was led by the ambitious PDS (later DS, *Democratici di Sinistra*, Left Democrats; then

PD, *Partito Democratico*, Democratic Party) Secretary, Massimo D'Alema, who became premier in October 1998 (Hine and Vassallo, eds., 1998) after toppling Prodi's more centrist executive.

Yet D'Alema's government, which relied on a limited majority and a wide variety of political forces (from former Christian Democrats to former Communists), did not bring about a shift to a much-coveted 'normality', a favourite expression of its leader (D'Alema 1995). Ciampi and then Amato remained in charge of the Economy Ministry. Joining the Euro entailed continuing with constraining fiscal policies (Quaglia 2004: 1103–08). 'Europe' had become the key idea driving both the economic and foreign policy elites and it seemed to persuade Italian voters to accept austerity, sacrifices and deflationary policies (Della Sala 2002). D'Alema pursued a vision of a 'normal country' (Gilbert 1998: 310 in Gallo 2022: 564) which owed more to neoliberalism than to his supposedly social-democratic credentials:

> A country with an efficient state that is the citizen's friend and that might not be a producer of milk or steel, but does know how to provide European levels of education, scientific research and essential services. A country that guarantees a social safety net able to offer support, hope and opportunity to society's weakest members and which does not leak away resources in the thousand different channels provided by clientelism.

To summarise, Prodi and D'Alema mostly promoted policies to support corporate interests, without addressing chronic and structural problems such as the exclusion of the youth, of women, and of millions of Southern Italians other than trying to resolve such problems in purely neoliberal terms (Blim 2000; Amable, Guillaud and Palombarini 2011). They resorted to introducing temporary job contracts or largely ineffective attempts to attract foreign investments, in a globalising planet where cheap and qualified workforce had become available all over the world.

The 1990s were also the decade of privatisations, in a massive exercise which was second only to Conservative Britain and one of the world's leading cases of large-scale privatisations. Between 1995 and 1999 Italy was every year the OECD's largest privatiser (Goldstein 2003). The 1999 privatisation of ENEL, the electricity utility, was at the time the world's largest IPO (Initial Public Offering) ever (Goldstein 2003: 4). It has been demonstrated that large-scale privatisations tend to lead to corruption (Peña Miguel and Cuadrado-Ballesteros 2019: 72–4), and that would be Italy's case as well, at least to some extent.

As a matter of fact, up to the 1990s large parts of the Italian economy and most of its banking system ("about 90 per cent of total financial investment and 80 per cent of total deposits in 1991"; Goldstein 2003: 5) were owned by the state, including the largest banks such as Banca Commerciale Italiana and Credito Italiano. The colossal sales of the 1992–2000 era meant the privatisation of most of the Italian economy, as represented by the IRI (*Istituto per la Ricostruzione Industriale*, 'Institute for the Industrial Reconstruction'), whose activities had stretched from banking to food processing and carmaking, by other giant companies such as ENI and ENEL, the major energy corporations, by most of the banking system (Napoleoni 2014) and still more. Some of the operations were made in haste and with a short-term orientation. Although companies such as ENEL (2023) and ENI (2025) are now listed and globally profitable, the Italian state maintains major controlling shares (as of 31 December 2023, 23.6% of ENEL; as of 13 March 2025, 31.8% of ENI) and their top executives are usually chosen among managers with extensive experience in the public sector. Paolo Scaroni has been at the helm of both ENEL and ENI (ENI 2009), while Fulvio Conti (Aon 2023) has moved between Telecom Italia and ENEL, just to name two significant cases of leading managers. In Leonardo, probably the major Italian high-tech group, which has its origins in IRI, the public share is still 30.2% (2024). While international investors gained relatively little, groups close to the various governments – for example, the Benetton family (Del Corno 2020) – became important shareholders. In general, ownership concentration and public involvement remained significant (Goldstein 2023). Moreover, despite privatisations, Italy set out not to avail itself of a new industrial plan (Cavazzuti, in Artoni, ed., 2014). In other words, while Italian privatisations were half-hearted and mostly driven by the aspiration to 'remain in Europe's core', no significant policy directions aiming at creating stronger, better, and inclusive development were proposed and implemented. Prodi's and D'Alema's Italy followed Blair's and Clinton's 'Third Way' and its Eurozone version as expressed by Maastricht's convergence criteria.

The decade of technocrats, privatisations, incipient financialisation (Lagna 2016) and the march towards the Euro ends with a new and partly technocratic government, again headed by Giuliano Amato, this time as an independent (April 2000). In 2000, Italy is in the Eurozone and its economic performance has gradually improved. Yet austerity has taken a toll and many Italians are dissatisfied with the policies adopted by the centre-left, which they see as too 'centrist' and not enough 'leftist'. A part of the Italian business class, fearing the leftist wing of the centre-left coalitions, is turning to the right and to populist/nationalist parties such as the Northern League and Berlusconi's forces. Berlusconi's coalitions were seen as potentially more stable and hegemonic.

For their part, the technocrats of the 1990s – Ciampi and Dini, Amato and Andreatta, Grilli (an economist in charge of privatisations at the Treasury) and Padoa-Schioppa, Prodi himself – are sophisticated diplomats and politicians, engaged intellectuals, subtle negotiators. Despite different standpoints, either closer to American neoliberalism or to German ordoliberalism, or other schools of thought (including socialism and Christian social thought), they share a commitment to make Italy financially more viable, more 'modern', more efficient and especially, more 'European'. Europe stands as a signifier of modernisation, peace (especially for Ciampi, who had memories of the Second World War; Signorini 2018), institutional integrity and quiet strength, for example in Padoa-Schioppa's view (2001) of Europe as a 'gentle force'. While they interpret the interests and views of the corporate world, and call for adapting to, and adopting neoliberal measures, they do so in a specifically Italian way, and promoting interests which are in the first place Italian and European. The fact itself that large state companies such as ENI or ENEL remain under partial state control and do not become public companies, testifies to a degree of 'social' or 'institutional' element in their visions.

Yet the country's relative impoverishment and the attraction of Berlusconi's charismatic leadership (together with his ability to capture the aspirations of millions of Italians; Ricolfi 2001) led to the centre-right's clear victory in the 2001 elections. What would Berlusconi's coalition's attitude towards neoliberalism be?

4 The Decade of Silvio Berlusconi (2001–11)

Apart from the years 2006–08, when Prodi's centre-left coalition returned to government after winning the elections (19 April 2006) by a narrow margin of less than 25,000 votes (La Repubblica 2006), the new millennium's first decade was dominated by Silvio Berlusconi's embarrassing persona and riotous coalitions (2001–11).

Seven years after the first and brief appearance as a Prime Minister in 1994, Berlusconi and his controversial allies, the regionalist Northern League and the post-fascist AN, were handed over a clear mandate to govern the country, with strong majorities of 93 seats in the House and 49 in the Senate (Eligendo 2001a and 2001b). Berlusconi's victory was not only, and not particularly, due to his Fininvest-Mediaset media empire or to the center-left's chronic internal and ideological infighting (Ricolfi 2001). The Berlusconi-phenomenon is also much more than a case of patrimonial capitalism or, worse, a symbol of supposedly 'Italian vices' (individualism, corruption, antipolitics, etc), as per some "conventional wisdom" (Mancini 2011: 3). Unfortunately, Berlusconi's rise to political power, with its dismal parade of sexist remarks, sexual scandals, homophobic jokes, xenophobic positions (especially in allied parties such as the League; Lewis 2008), conflicts of interests between political and business roles, corruption, and the like, has largely to do with identification with a lifestyle, an "aesthetic politics" (Mancini 2011: 16), a form of consumerism and clear political choices, which Berlusconi concisely expressed in the TV-launched *Contratto con gli Italiani* ('Contract with the Italians', 8 May 2001; Ricolfi 2005 and 2006). Certainly, Berlusconi's rise and story (including the idea of the 'contract', which had been put forward in the USA by Newt Gingrich) smells of neoliberalism, and so do the contract's main ideas: simplifying and reducing taxation; enhancing local security and enforcing local police; raising minimum pensions (a kind of counterweight to the cuts with the aim of maintaining consent among an ageing Italian population). Yet those who expected of Berlusconi a 'neoliberal' or even a 'neoconservative' revolution, somewhat similar to Thatcher's or Reagan's experiences, would remain disappointed.

From the angle of political economy, there are differences but also continuities between the technocratic governments of the 1990s and Berlusconi's populism (Biorcio 2015; Tarchi 2018). In many ways Berlusconi was in fact a representative of a 'technocratic populism' (Castaldo and Verzichelli 2020), in light of his professional know how as an entrepreneur and a businessman, and his attempt, especially in the early stages of his premiership, to govern Italy as a firm (Castaldo and Verzichelli 2020: 489; for a Czech version of technocratic populism, see Buštíková and Guasti 2018). Furthermore, in his governments Berlusconi often appointed independent experts (7 in the long second government; among them, the former Director-General of the WTO, Renato Ruggiero, as Minister of Foreign Affairs, who would soon resign because of divergencies over Europe; the economist, Domenico Siniscalco, as Minister of the Economy between 2004 and 2005; the entrepreneur, Letizia Moratti, as Minister of Education). Other experts had a more political profile; among them there was Giulio Tremonti, the Minister of the Economy before and after Siniscalco, a member of Berlusconi's *Forza Italia* party and an often-criticised economist and politician, especially due to his heterodox and sometimes protectionist economic choices (Tremonti 2023). A classical neoliberal in the Chicago school sense was Antonio Martino, Minister of Defence, professor of Economics and a former student of Friedman's at Chicago (Martino 2005). In other words, aware of the necessity to maintain a dialogue with the EU, if at times a confrontational one, Berlusconi took onboard several scholars and practitioners, who often expressed divergent opinions. The Prime Minister, the *Cavaliere*, would have the final and decisive word on most topics.

As a matter of fact, Berlusconi's politics was quite far from any neoliberal orthodoxy. From an international standpoint, it was in fact somewhat protectionist, in the spirit of Tremonti (2008). Like Orbán in Hungary and Trump in the USA, and before them, Berlusconi embodied the interests of that significant fraction of capitalism which was mostly 'national' in outlook and fragile when exposed to international competition, while itself often having limited activities overseas; Fininvest-Mediaset was an example. These companies were large, but not enough to resist global or European competitive pressures, and had been rather marginalised by the centre-left governments, which had promoted State-managed conglomerates and the historically largest private businesses (the FIAT Group, Assicurazioni Generali, Pirelli, etc). The latter had been usually rotating around the international industrial capital of FIAT and its satellites and had been controlled by Mediobanca, the secretive Milanese investment bank which was at the heart of Italy's 'good salon' of business (Amyot 2003: 79–80; Tognini 2023); Mediobanca aimed at preserving the *status quo* against national (such as Berlusconi) and international disruptors. Berlusconi and his coalition found therefore 'natural' allies in other 'marginalised' large- and mid-size companies and in the plethora of small- and medium-size firms of Lombardy, the Veneto and parts of Central Italy (Amyot 2003). An outsider to the FIAT-Mediobanca galaxy, Berlusconi was also expression of a new capitalism, centred in services, the media, advertising, and distant from the assembly lines of Italy's strong industrial history.

Many of the characteristics illustrated above – the technocratic dimension, protectionist tendencies, the efforts to gain control of a changing Italian political economy – would become visible during Berlusconi's governments. What would hardly materialise is the much avowed (by many of Berlusconi's supporters) 'liberal revolution'.

To start with, Berlusconi's relative reformist inertia was in part due to recurrent coalition infighting. The League had an economically liberal and often anti-EU agenda, while AN proposed a more statist and moderately pro-European course (Blondel and Segatti 2004). Additionally, as early as 2001 clashes emerged between ministers, and especially between Tremonti and the strongly pro-EU Minister of Foreign Affairs, Ruggiero, who would eventually resign in January 2002 (Blondel and Segatti 2004). Tensions would continue especially in the Economy Ministry, where Tremonti was replaced by the more liberal Economics professor, Domenico Siniscalco, between July 2004 and

September 2005 (The Economist 2005a). More broadly, there often seemed to be a lack of a clear sense of direction, or a lack of interest in crucial economic reforms. It appeared as if (Mascitelli and Zucchi 2007: 134):

> The objective of Berlusconi's term in government seemed more to pass laws which favoured his private empire rather than to put in place real economic reforms. The barrage of judicial investigations into Berlusconi's business affairs… […] … were a distraction to the centre-right government.

After all, Berlusconi's government was avoiding significant reforms precisely because it was defending the interests of an emerging but embattled 'national' fraction of the bourgeoisie, of which the *Cavaliere*'s companies were fully representative. The same is true for other prominent businesspeople who have often been associated with Berlusconi's interests, though to different extents and in different ways. A 'national bourgeoisie' is mostly oriented to the domestic market (Avci 2022: 82) and faces strong international and domestic competition, also (though not only) because of smaller size in comparison with vastly transnational and more diversified businesses. Notwithstanding fast growth in production and sales in several markets, the Parma-based pasta producer, Barilla, is a case in point. Guido Barilla, its chairman and major shareholder, despite denying any potential political involvement with Berlusconi (Reuters Staff 2013), has often been seen as close to him in personal and professional terms. A leading banker and powerbroker often associated with Berlusconi has then been Cesare Geronzi, a discreet, crafty and power-driven executive who accumulated resources as President of the Banca di Roma and Capitalia in the 1990s and early 2000s. Geronzi is rumoured to have financially supported Mediaset before Berlusconi's 'descent' into politics. His synergies with the *Cavaliere* continued (Giannini 2010) and were to some extent understandable. Geronzi, too, represented a mostly Italian-based financial company, dependent on political support even more than on creating value for shareholders. Another businessman with a mostly 'national' company and personally close to Berlusconi was Urbano Cairo, the founder and owner of 50.101% of Cairo Communication, which also includes RCS (Rizzoli Corriere della Sera), the largest Italian publisher of daily newspapers. Cairo had strong personal ties with Berlusconi, is the owner of a Serie A (Italian football's first tier) football team (Torino FC) and was Berlusconi's personal assistant in his twenties (Cazzullo 2023), before starting a significant career in Mediaset. What unifies such a variety of companies and businesspeople (with Geronzi's exception) is also the fact that they mainly represent patrimonialistic and patriarchal family businesses, in which property and governance are largely in the hands of the (male) leaders. Additionally, businesses in the national fraction of capital tend to rely more on the support of the state, which works as a bulwark against national and international competition. In a sense, the necessity to resort to the state might also explain Berlusconi's decision to enter the political arena.

The only areas where the Berlusconi governments II and III (2001–06) acted in a decisively neoliberal way are in truth those related to the job market. The Biagi Law of 2003 introduced more flexibility and more types of temporary contracts (Mascitelli and Zucchi 2007: 136). Apart from creating just modest opportunities for women, this law would bring limited benefits in terms of unemployment or underemployment, while increasing the precarious dimensions of a significant fraction of the job market. While unemployment declined slightly, up to 2004 economic growth was almost non-existent (Mascitelli and Zucchi 2007: 135). In 2005 Italy's GDP grew by a modest .8%, followed by a 1.8% in 2006 (The World Bank 2023). Furthermore, and despite promises, fiscal pressure decreased just slightly, from 42.2% (2001) to 41.7% in 2006 (Mascitelli and Zucchi 2007: 137). Productivity, competitiveness and expenditure on research in science and technology declined. Siniscalco, a rather orthodox neoliberal, resigned while complaining about the government's "absolute immobility" (Mascitelli and Zucchi 2007: 140). Following *The Economist* (Mascitelli and Zucchi 2007: 143), "Mr. Berlusconi himself is not a true believer in free markets. ... His own business success was built on the creation of near-monopolies." To put it better, Berlusconi was a believer in free markets only when they suited his own commercial interests. A similar logic would later apply to Donald Trump's experience.

Berlusconi's inaction was interrupted by a second Prodi government (2006–08), which started under the extreme uncertainty of the 2006 elections (in which Berlusconi's coalition won more votes, while Prodi's obtained a narrow majority of seats; La Repubblica 2006) and continued in very challenging circumstances, due to Prodi's tiny majority of two seats in the Senate. Interestingly, Prodi's government returned to liberalisations, especially with the two Bersani decrees (2006 and 2007), which liberalised aspects of the markets of professions, energy, and local public services. The return to government of Prodi and Amato (as Minister of the Interior) was complemented by the choice of the well-known Banca d'Italia economist, Tommaso Padoa-Schioppa, as Minister of the Economy. Yet the shift towards a more pro-European direction would not last, also because of Prodi's constant parliamentary troubles and coalition fragility. The vote of April 2008, in which the *Cavaliere* faced the rather neoliberal PD Secretary, Walter Veltroni, would once again (and for the last time) reward Berlusconi's coalition with a sound victory, expressed by 46.8% of the Chamber and 47.3% of the Senate votes (Eligendo 2008a and 2008b).

The last Berlusconi government before the financial and economic crisis of 2011 would not really change track, especially in its early stages. There were several and long-term constraints: Italy's massive public debt (in contrast with its banks' rather limited exposure to the subprime crisis); the EMU's stringent parameters; the country's relative economic decline, which had been entrenched for at least a decade (Rovelli 2009). The executive attempted to make some changes. With Tremonti back at the helm of the economy, the government intervened with (limited) tax cuts, plans for infrastructure spending, bonuses and social cards for low incomes (Rovelli 2009: 230–31) and a controversial fiscal shield for "previously undeclared foreign investments" (Rovelli 2009: 232). However, the effects were not sufficient (Jones 2018: 4). At the same time, Italy adopted a significant series of measures on education and the university (the 'Gelmini reform'), which brought about cuts and uncertainty, and included elements of privatisation (Ichino, Terlizzese and Regini 2012).

It is correct to say that the last Berlusconi government maintained a cautious line and followed the conservative position of the previous centre-right executives, while it respected EU fiscal constraints, too. Before July 2011 Italy's financial and economic conditions were on the whole seen as acceptable, whereas the storm of the markets was damaging those Eurozone countries more exposed to the global financial crisis such as Cyprus, Greece, Ireland, Portugal and Spain. In July 2011, however, Italy quite suddenly entered the eye of the speculative tempest. In a few days the difference (or 'spread') of the interest rates between Germany's and Italy's bonds started rising steeply. The potential explanations are many: Berlusconi's scandals and his tensions with Tremonti, close to the Northern League and increasingly averse to globalisation; rumours of Deutsche Bank's or Anglo-American financial speculation; French manoeuvres at the European Central Bank, whose President was a Frenchman, Jean-Claude Trichet (Ricolfi 2018). While a combination of them might better explain the crisis, Italy's neoliberal response to a neoliberal and authoritarian EU came yet again in Summer, between 12 and 15 July. It included measures to promote development and reorganise the state, especially the public administration (Jones 2012: 90), but the markets deemed it not enough. Was it "too little and too late" (Jones 2012: 84)?

After further tensions on the bond markets, on 5 August 2011 a secret letter signed by the ECB's President, Trichet and its President-elect (in fact Mario Draghi, still Governor of the BoI), reached Berlusconi's government (Sacchi 2014: 6). The letter's contents would be revealed by the *Corriere della Sera* only in late September (Corriere della Sera 2011). Parts of it (Corriere della Sera 2011) strike for both the clear neoliberal inspiration and the openly authoritarian tone; in many ways, it is an imposition on a democratic, if economically strained, political system (Scicluna and Auer 2019; Matthijs 2017):

> The Governing Council [of the ECB] considers that pressing action by the Italian authorities is essential to restore the confidence of investors. ... [...] .... The Governing Council considers that Italy needs to urgently underpin the standing of its sovereign signature and its commitment to fiscal sustainability and structural reforms. ... [...] .... A comprehensive, far-reaching and credible reform strategy. ... [...] .... is needed. ... [...].... We consider essential for the Italian authorities to frontload the measures adopted in the July 2011 package by at least one year. ...
>
> [...] .... the government should consider significantly reducing the cost of public employees, by strengthening turnover rules and, if necessary, by reducing wages.

The letter quickly became one of the epitomes of the EU's 'coercive turn' (Scicluna and Auer 2019) towards a politicised yet unelected organisation, capable of forcing neoliberal policies and constraining democratic governments; a kind of 'technocracy by force', eroding democratic procedures especially in its less powerful members (Matthijs 2017) and clearly and directly attacking salaries and the public sector.

A significant part of the ECB's requests was accepted, including the abolition of provinces and the insertion of a norm on the obligation to balance the public budget in the Constitution. Yet recurrent tensions within the coalition, limited economic growth, financial speculation and rating agencies' downgrades led to further crisis and in September 2011 Italian bond yields overtook their Spanish correspondents (Jones 2012; Scicluna and Auer 2019).

Rushed reforms were not enough. On 7 August 2011, two days after the secret Trichet/Draghi letter, Professor Mario Monti, a well-known economist from Milan's Bocconi University (and with a Yale PhD) and former European Commissioner for the Internal Markets, Services, Customs, Taxation and later Competition (1995–2004), wrote a famous and somehow prophetic editorial for the *Corriere della Sera* (Monti 2011). In the piece Monti, who had often been tipped as a possible technocratic minister (or even Prime Minister), wrote about the risk of Italy being subject to a foreign '*podestà*', referring to a medieval tradition by which troubled *Comuni* ('free cities') were sometimes imposed foreign and external authorities to resolve their problems. According to Monti, Italy had lost a lot of time and its economy, especially in terms of economic growth, was ailing. Hence, the government was now subject to a *governo tecnico sopranazionale* ('supranational technocratic government', my translation), with a *mercatista* (that is, 'pro-market', my translation) orientation, and with several sites – Brussels, Frankfurt, Berlin, London, New York. 'Europe' and 'the markets' would better lead Italy and its elected government towards a return to growth, economic and political dignity, and full participation in European and international institutions. A rapid content analysis of Monti's short article for the *Corriere* immediately highlights the positive connotations he attributed to Europe and the markets, in the guise of tutors providing guidance to Italy's economic and ultimately political choices.

But what has been left of democracy in this chain of events? Does or did Italy really need a tutor? For all the flaws of Berlusconi's conservative, stagnant and self-serving governments, let alone his scandals and judicial issues, Italy still had strong elective institutions. The markets and Europe did not, except the rather feeble European Parliament. Monti's piece shed a strong light on the authoritarian face of technocracy, its incarnation in EU institutions, and its capacity to impose decisions even to the Eurozone's third biggest – if declining – economy. In 2011 Italy's unemployment rate was around 8.4% (The World Bank 2025d). In few years, the therapies imposed by the *podestà forestiero* would lead it to almost 13%.

5 Back to Technocrats – and to Populism (2011–18)

Ironically (or not?), it was the same Mario Monti who came to fully embody the *podestà forestiero*. After weeks of market speculations and the rise of the spread with the German bonds to 575 basic points, he was appointed lifetime Senator on 9 November and sworn in as Prime Minister on 16 November (Jones 2012), again thanks to a swift manoeuvre by the President of the Republic, Giorgio Napolitano, who 'ironically' had been a leading PCI intellectual, if a moderate one, during the Cold war. The extremely rapid turnaround suggests that some list of collaborators had been likely ready, at least in part, for some time. His government was entirely composed of unelected officers and had the task of enacting strong austerity measures in accordance with EU requests. In other words, Monti became the ideal typical agent of 'Integration through Crisis, ITC', the *modus operandi* of the European project (Scicluna and Auer 2019) that emerged after the financial crisis.

Monti's team was comprised of two top and mostly 'public' managers (Piero Gnudi, former IRI and ENEL President, and Corrado Passera, ex CEO of Poste Italiane and Intesa Sanpaolo), eight academics and eight *grand commis* with experience in Italian and EU institutions (Marangoni 2012: 136). It was by far the most technocratic government ever in European and Italian history (the parallel Greek experience with Papademos was in fact that of a technocrat presiding over a grand coalition of the main parties; Culpepper 2014; McDonnell and Valbruzzi 2014). It was also the executive with the strongest support ever from both chambers (Marangoni 2012: 138) and was widely perceived as an emergency government. As to its programme, a brief content analysis unveils the neoliberal inspiration: 18.52% of its pledges would refer to rationalising the public administration; 14.81% each referred to intervening in the labour market and encouraging growth (Marangoni 2012: 141). More than any previous technocratic government, Monti adopted a discourse of "promise and sacrifice" (Cozzolino 2020: 581), which tied current austerity to a promise of a prosperous future in Europe and the world. But for the time being, everything had to be about sacrifice and austerity.

Very early in his mandate, on 4 December, Monti adopted a decree law (*Salva Italia*, 'Save Italy') with fiscal measures worth about 30 billion Euros and aimed at achieving a balanced budget in 2013. It also included some tax breaks and pro-growth measures as well as a highly controversial pension reform (the Fornero law; on the decree law see Benvenuti 2016: 84). The retirement age was enhanced to 66 years and measures to make the job market more flexible were introduced. In an interview with a US magazine, the Economy Minister, Elsa Fornero, spoke about the necessity of sacrifices and denied that work was a 'right' (Giannone and Cozzolino 2023: 152). Neoliberalism was in full swing. Additionally, introducing in the Constitution the principle of a 'balanced budget' depressed an already sluggish economic growth. Monti's reforms remained mostly deflationary; pro-growth policies did not meet with strong EU support (after all, Italy was still a competitor, if enfeebled, to Germany and France), and liberalisations encountered entrenched hostility at home. Even more, Monti's government was an experiment in 'unmediated democracy', that is, a system in which political parties, social and interest groups (trade unions in particular) and lobbies (other than big business) were excluded from decision-making; concertation was not accepted and Monti had to backtrack on more ambitious economic change in order to avoid further tensions with unions, workers and small-size enterprises (Culpepper 2014). Without the mediation of some anchors in society, top-down reforms from unelected officers and sacrifices in the name of the EU are clearly not sustainable. Such practices can well be regarded as expressions of a strong authoritarian neoliberalism in a technocratic fashion.

Once the stability of the Eurozone and its Southern members was partly consolidated with draconian austerity plans and bailout packages, let alone Draghi's famous 'Whatever it takes' speech (26 July 2012; ECB 2012), the necessity of urgent austerity policies became less justifiable. Monti's popularity collapsed also in the wake of the episode of the *esodati*, that is, those workers who had retired before the increase in retirement age and found themselves without an income. The government later admitted that they might have been about 400,000 (Culpepper 2014: 1274). Trade unions, political parties, small- and medium-size companies and parts of the public sector rapidly withdrew their support to Monti. Berlusconi started aiming at early elections in 2013. In 2012 Italy's growth had been an embarrassing −3% (The World Bank 2023); youth unemployment had reached 35.9% (Datablog 2012); overall unemployment had jumped to 10.7% (The World Bank 2025d). The coveted dream of a European political union was morphing into an economic nightmare dictated by an inflexible technocracy.

In the meantime, Italy's political scenario was changing fast. A new political force, a movement usually understood as populist, the *Movimento Cinque Stelle* (M5S, 'Five Star Movement'), founded and led by a charismatic comedian, Beppe Grillo, was making inroads among hundreds of thousands of those disaffected by professional politics, parties, the 'caste' of allegedly colluding parties, media, and technocratic economic powers (Tronconi, ed., 2015; Mosca and Tronconi 2019). In a word, Grillo's movement was targeting the 'elite'. While (in a typically populist fashion) the strongest M5S's defining element was an anti-establishment position (Mosca and Tronconi 2019: 1266–70), on economic matters its direction was quite eclectic and hybrid. In the M5S's agenda, calls for more welfare, attacks on the EU and its 'bankers' and the advocacy of a universal basic income alternated with pledges of tax breaks and support for small-size companies. Whether these positions were mainly tactical or more deeply thought out, the attraction of the M5S grew in the aftermath of Monti's severe cuts and austerity politics. The February 2013 general elections proved among the most challenging, divisive and uncertain in Italy's political history.

The vote ended in an entangled stalemate; in the Chamber of Deputies, the centre-left obtained 29.55% of the votes; the centre-right, 29.18%, while a shocking 25.56% went to the M5S, which in fact became the biggest single party (Eligendo 2013). The preferred choice of President Napolitano, once again playing a crucial role and for the first time in Italian history handed a second mandate, was to facilitate the formation of a grand coalition between centre-left and centre-right to the exclusion of the M5S. Interestingly, Monti's newly formed party, 'Civic Choice' (*Scelta Civica*), and its allies did not go beyond 10.6% in the Chamber (Eligendo 2013). This seems to confirm the disappointment with a symbol of technocracy, elitism, austerity and unmediated democracy. Yet the newly appointed Prime Minister, Enrico Letta (PD), was himself at the border between politics and technocracy.

A relatively young but already experienced politician with government positions in the D'Alema and Amato cabinets, Letta was also a student of Andreatta's and an expert in international law, with excellent European credentials. In his team the key position of Minister of the Economy was still handed over to an independent economist, Fabrizio Saccomanni, Director-General of the BoI since 2006. With working experience also at the IMF, the EBRD (European Bank for Reconstruction and Development), and the EMI (European Monetary Institute, the ECB's predecessor), Saccomanni was in an ideal position to negotiate with the EU and implement its policies (Banca d'Italia 2019). Yet again, Italian politics had to be significantly influenced by European economic choices. Moreover, two other important ministries were assigned to independent experts: Justice to the Prefect, Annamaria Cancellieri and Labour to the statistician, Enrico Giovannini.

Letta's cabinet's choices were rather constrained by internal tensions (Berlusconi's intention to return to power independently), 'populist' external pressures (the M5S's rise) and the necessity to comply with the EU's stability rules. Some progressive reforms were attempted, but they were always characterised by small, incremental steps and within the EU neoliberal framework. Letta strongly committed himself to promoting youth labour (Chatham House 2013) and with this aim he adopted policies supported by the EU and its major countries. Youth unemployment was in fact still growing. Simplifications and tax cuts were also introduced as well as some rationalisation of the public sector. But all in all, no radical changes were made to promote growth and, if anything, Letta's policy erred on neoliberalism's side. Time and cabinet conflicts – together with a negative growth of –1.8% (The World Bank 2023) – played against the government's effectiveness and popularity. Furthermore, the PD itself seemed to prefer abandoning Letta's sober and technocratic style and embrace a more popular, approachable, or even populist approach, as expressed by Letta's successor, the youthful former Mayor of Florence and new PD Secretary, Matteo Renzi, who controversially replaced Letta as Prime Minister in February 2014.

Was Renzi's politics just a matter of style, or policy style? Not necessarily and not only, according to Piattoni (2016). In her view, Renzi may have tried to propose a 'communicative discourse' (Piattoni 2016: 12–15), that is, an attempt to sketch new institutional scenarios, to imagine a different country, one with a simpler political system (generally with a stronger executive), and to directly engage with voters in an effort to influence them. This was quite new, in a traditionally staid political system (although Berlusconi had in fact attempted a direct, unmediated style of communication) and in a rather technocratic centre-left, but would have it worked? And how have Renzi's policies and institutional choices translated in relation to neoliberalism and Italy's international political economy?

Despite Renzi's attempt to directly engage with voters in simpler ways, in a kind of centre-left 'populism' (Marcon 2014), the technocratic element was still maintained, especially in the Ministry of the Economy, entrusted to the long-time academic, IMF representative and OECD executive, Pier Carlo Padoan, a scholar of Economics (Cesaratto 2014) who in his youth had cultivated Marxist sympathies. Also, Renzi, who had grown in a centrist Christian democratic party, styled himself as a liberal reformist in the wake of Blair and Clinton, despite their questionable legacy (Anderson 2014), and was often called *Il rottamatore* ('The wrecker') because of his eagerness to lead rapid change and eliminate 'the old'. Driven by uncommon ambition, he envisaged reforming the Italian political system in a more presidentialist way and the country's economy in a liberal sense; additionally, he intended to implement his programme within the strict parameters set by the EU. Internationally supported by the likes of the ambitious, London-based, hedge fund founder, Davide Serra (Sanderson 2017), and by the consultant, Yoram Gutgeld (Panara 2013), the new premier gave precedence to changes in electoral laws and constitutional reforms, while simultaneously paving the way to more liberal economic policies. His Jobs Act (March 2014) made dismissals more likely while maintaining few and very basic employment protections. Precarious jobs became increasingly common. Limited tax cuts and modest demand boosts (e.g., an 80€ per month bonus for low-income workers), which would be adopted in the following months, can be read as (limited) means to relaunch the economy. On the whole, Renzi's political economy remained firmly tied to the EU. His reforms were mainly performative and did not bring substantial change. Was he thinking about bolder expansive measures over the longer term and perhaps in a presidential system?

Despite Renzi's rhetoric of peace and European unity, emphasis on merit, healthcare and education, figures tell a different story. After two years of premiership, the expenditure on healthcare and education had declined; the fiscal pressure had risen, from 43.4 to 44.1% (Airaudo and Marcon 2016: n.p.). Public debt further increased, while GDP growth moved from 0 (2014) to .8 (2015) to 1.3% (2016), literally too little to kick-start an economy in slow but steady relative decline (The World Bank 2023). While it is fair to say that, especially after 2015, the Prime Minister and his team concentrated their efforts on institutional change (which would flounder with the 4 December 2016 constitutional referendum; Zagrebelsky and Pallante 2016), there is no evidence that the PD-led government made any substantial effort to develop strongly expansive or 'Keynesian' policies.

Renzi's ambitious but insufficient plans ended with his resignation after the constitutional referendum's failure in late 2016. His successor, the moderate, soft-spoken and experienced former Foreign Secretary, Paolo Gentiloni, guided the country towards the 2018 elections, during a period marked by new challenges, especially those of migrations, growing Euroscepticism and populism. While in 2017 the economy grew by a 'surprising' 1.7% (The World Bank 2023), Gentiloni did not intervene on big economic issues, and the Ministry remained in the hands of Padoan.

Despite slight improvements, in part connected with the Quantitative Easing (QE) programme adopted by Draghi's ECB (Claeys, Leandro and Mandra 2015), Italy's basic socio-economic scenario at the end of 2017 was rather discomforting. Overall unemployment was still at 11.2% (12.4% for women); the share of youth not in employment, education or training (NEET) was 20%, by far the highest in Western Europe (The World Bank 2025b, c and d). Inequalities and resentment towards a 'caste' of 'Eurocrats', bankers, party politicians, intellectuals, journalists, and so on were also high. Italy approached the 2018 vote with strong winds in the sails of populism, antipolitics and nationalism.

6 Populism, Technocracy and Nationalism's Return (2018–)

As we have seen, technocracy and populism are sometimes opposed but often join forces (Bickerton and Invernizzi Accetti 2017 and 2018; Guasti and Buštíková 2020).

A supposedly strong leader, populist and nationalist, willing to communicate directly with the people, with limited parliamentary or party mediation, might want experts to approve and confirm her/his economic and political choices, or even serve her/his own power interests. Both the populist leader and the experts claim to know what is good for the people. Additionally, experts can enhance the leader's legitimacy both in domestic and international terms, in a complex coalition or in an international organisation. In the EU, conflict between national authorities and economic interests might arise because of the persistent tension between the economy, which is mainly governed at the EU level, and many other aspects of politics, which are partly in the hands of national and increasingly nationalist leaders. Yet conflict as such is not a necessity.

Potential for populist parties was already growing before the 4 March 2018 elections. The League, since 2013 led by the ambitious anti-immigration hardliner, Matteo Salvini, had cut ties with its regionalist and secessionist past and had become a national, nationalist, nativist, anti-immigration and anti-EU party (Albertazzi, Giovannini and Seddone 2018). Immigration and security throughout the country had clearly become the focus of the League's proposals (Albertazzi, Giovannini and Seddone 2018: 654–55). Additionally, Salvini conducted a strong social media campaign and appealed to businesses, including small enterprises, by proposing a 15% flat tax, even lower than that promised by the League's ally, *Forza Italia*. The Northern League changed its name to 'League for Salvini Premier (LSP)', dropping any reference to the North and attempting to appeal to Southern Italian voters as well. The M5S, for its part, campaigned mostly on socio-economic issues; with Grillo in the background, it was led by the young Luigi Di Maio, born in 1986, and promoted the *reddito di cittadinanza* ('citizenship income'), a kind of universal basic income for those in conditions of poverty; however, its positions on the EU and immigration remained rather ambiguous (Chiaramonte et al 2018). After several years in power, in contrast, the PD and *Forza Italia* looked rather discredited as they were often seen as symbols of the old establishment and its 'caste'.

The election's results rewarded populist parties far more than expected. With 32.7% in the Chamber and 32.2% of the Senate, the M5S emerged for the second consecutive time as the party with more votes nationally (Eligendo 2018a and b). It scored incredibly well in the country's South, among youngsters, students, the unemployed and other marginalised groups, but also in a range of other electorate fractions (Formigoni and Forni 2018). The League attracted more Northern Italians, working in factories, self-employed, shopkeepers or housekeepers. The PD lost ground in most groups, and maintained some support among managers, retired people, and those with higher education qualifications (Eligendo 2018a and b).

All in all, what emerged was a clear disillusionment with traditional parties (including *Forza Italia*, for the first time second to the League in the centre-right with a modest 14%) among large swathes of the electorate, and especially those who felt left behind, in the tax-burdened private sector (mainly in the North and in smaller companies), in the public sector, among the poor and the unemployed. More than problems with the EU, insecurity as such popped up as a key issue.

Forming a new government proved a complicated challenge, almost a disentaglable knot. At some point, the President of the Republic, Sergio Mattarella, even proposed another independent technocrat, the economist and former IMF Director, Carlo Cottarelli (IMF 2023), with the aim of adopting a new budget and preparing the country for new elections. Yet, after lengthy and protracted negotiations, the two key winners of the vote, the League and the M5S, were able to form a new executive with the ambitious name of *Governo del Cambiamento* ('Government of Change'). The agreement between the two parties, however, contained several contradictions between the League's neoliberal outlook and the M5S's more social orientation (Malagutti 2018; see Rossi 2023 for a study of the neoliberal element in the M5S as well).

Despite claiming to reject (or at least criticise) the EU and its rules, the new government stuck by them. Additionally, the technocratic element remained relevant. The new premier, Giuseppe Conte, was a little-known jurist without any political experience and with some proximity to the M5S (AGI 2018). He also appointed four independent experts; among them, and despite the choice of the controversial Eurosceptic economist, Paolo Savona, as Minister of European Affairs, there were staunch pro-EU sympathisers (Enzo Moavero Milanesi, Minister of Foreign Affairs, had been in the Monti cabinet!) and the usual technocrat in charge of the Economy, this time the conservative academic economist, Giovanni Tria. Moreover, and notwithstanding all claims of embodying direct democracy, a strong technocratic aspect had since the beginning characterised the M5S, which relies on a private online platform, Rousseau, which is mostly top-down led (Rossi 2023).

Neoliberalism survived the *Cambiamento* (Gasseau and Maccarrone 2023; Monaco 2023), and authoritarianism, in a nationalist fashion, clearly strengthened. Under Salvini's lead as Interior Minister, immigration was constructed as Italy's major issue and strong measures were enacted to stop NGO boats, abolish humanitarian protection and 'lock' the country in an ethno-nationalist way, not unlike Trump's USA (Dennison and Geddes 2022). Overall, in the first year of the M5S-League government, Salvini and the League won the limelight with strong anti-immigration rhetoric and aggressive policies, while the management of the economy was rather tentative, but did not diverge from a neoliberal path and did not help a country which in early 2019 was in recession again (Pianta 2019).

Salvini and the League clearly represented a nationalist, ethnicist, and anti-immigration viewpoint, which excludes refugees, asylum seekers, humanitarian protection and diversity more broadly. But at the same time, they promoted the interests and interpreted the feelings of a part of the bourgeoisie, in particular those small companies, shops and autonomous workers who felt increasingly peripheral in a globalising world of large corporations. Additionally, the League did not exclude the technocratic aspect, as is for example testified by the choice of an anti-Euro economist, Alberto Bagnai, as responsible for the League's Economy Department (Bagnai 2013).

The main social achievement of the M5S-League government, the M5S-sponsored *reddito di cittadinanza*, despite the normative value of a kind of universal basic income (Bronzini 2014), did not really shift Italy's political economy from a mainly neoliberal to a more socialist or socially oriented one.

Too many provisions of the new income's legislation pointed to conditionality and the income appeared more as a measure of workfare, that is, a temporary allowance while waiting for a job, than a piece of a larger and well-organised welfare state programme (Monticelli 2018). In a sense, the *reddito* was a one-off measure and ended up replacing welfarism, instead of representing a stepping stone towards it. Of course, it is important to acknowledge the difficulty of giving birth to a well-thought basic income in light of pressures and constraints from within the government (the openly neoliberal League) and the outside world (the EU with its constraints).

The coexistence between the League and the M5S became unsustainable also because of Italy's unexciting economic performance in 2019 (+1.6%; The World Bank 2023). The political crisis of Summer 2019, engineered by Salvini to cut ties with the M5S and give shape to a center-right coalition, ended up with the formation of another new and unprecedented government, with Conte at the helm of an unusual coalition between the PD and the M5S, in a sort of vague and imperceptible shift to the left of the latter.

The new government included a technocrat in a key position, Luciana Lamorgese, a prefect, as Minister of the Interior (ISPI 2020), and a historian and prominent PD politician, Roberto Gualtieri, who had been an MEP and a strong proponent of closer European integration (La Repubblica 2019), as Minister of the Economy.

Unfortunately, Conte and Gualtieri had little time to handle economic issues and the relations with the EU before the Covid-19 pandemic hit Italy, first among European countries, at the end of January 2020. Italy entered a strict lockdown on 10 March 2020 (BBC 2020), soon followed by most countries in Europe and the world. Amidst tragedy, the pandemic – immediately compared to a war – offered to citizens and governments the opportunity to rethink and revise economic and political models. The fear of an EU meltdown, especially to the detriment of its Southern members, was widespread. Conte's pro-European intervention on the Financial Times (Johnson, Ghiglione and Fleming 2020) on 19 March 2020 was soon followed by Draghi's proposals of private debt cancellations and the creation of EU bonds on the same newspaper (Draghi 2020). Despite opposition from some 'Northern' European countries (Austria, Finland, The Netherlands, only at times Germany), but with the support of France, Greece, Ireland, Italy, Portugal and Spain, on 27 May the EU Commission followed Draghi's advice and adopted a massive support package, focused on a green, equal, strong, digital and healthy reconstruction – Next Generation EU – 173 billion€ of which were destined to Italy (Next Generation EU 2020).

Was Next Generation EU, which in Italy became known as the PNRR (*Piano Nazionale di Ripresa e Resilienza*, 'National Plan of Recovery and Resilience'), a truly new beginning? Was it a new model for the post-pandemic age? A renunciation to entrenched austerity policies? Even the death sentence of neoliberalism itself, at least in the EU? No, not really.

The massive firepower of Next Generation EU (about 800bn €), the adoption of other significant measures to co-ordinate both economic and healthcare policies in the EU, the progressive nature of plans on issues such as gender discrimination, the environment and climate crisis, the circular economy, the European vaccination campaign and the ECB's Quantitative Easing, may seem to suggest a change in direction (Talani and de Bellis 2023). The EU would have moved towards a more solidaristic approach, away from the neoliberalism of the recent past, even if this would be a far cry from the end of orthodoxy and neoliberalism itself (Talani and de Bellis 2023: 164). Along similar lines, Schmidt (2022: 19) writes about a "great leap forward" but questions future evolutions. Will the EU return to the usual 'crisis management' mode or continue with coordinated economic policies along the lines of Next Generation EU, SURE (Support to mitigate Unemployment Risks in an Emergency), or the bond-buying programme, Pandemic Emergency Purchasing Programme (PEPP)? These are risks, which, in Schmidt's (2022) view, could be overcome with a move towards a more democratic and decentralised union. But how likely is it to happen? And in what ways would it represent a real change of paradigm?

Other authors are in fact more sceptical (see also Giannone and Cozzolino 2023). Dosi and Roventini (2022: 270) write about a "timid" change made by the EU. Being optimistic is hard, especially with regard to Italy and innovation policies, which have long been neglected in the EU as a whole and even more in Italy. Similarly, Pianta (2021) points to the necessity of some long-term change in Europe and Italy. Will the 'Washington-Berlin Consensus' (Fitoussi and Saraceno 2013) on austerity become history? In many aspects, Next Generation EU and the PNRR have entrenched and consolidated technocratic leadership in European countries (Giannone and Cozzolino 2023, Chapter 6) by inoculating a non-democratic international management of the EU economy into Italy and fellow EU members. This could be a promising development in the event of a truly democratic evolution of the European Union, but how likely is this to be the case? Not much, in light of the presence of many populist nationalist governments and the anti-European shift in the continent's public opinion since at least the 2007–08 financial crisis and its aftermath.

All in all, the Conte II government did not show the strength or the will to enact bold and transformative reforms. Once the PNRR was adopted on 12 January 2021 (PNRR 2021), questions arose about the cabinet's effectiveness and limits. Would Conte be able to reap the benefits of EU funds? The Prime Minister's loss of support from Renzi's new centrist party, *Italia Viva* (IV), led to a government crisis which rapidly ushered in the appointment as Prime Minister of the much-desired European central banker, Mario Draghi.

Also because of the pandemic and the economic emergency, the formation of the new government was surprisingly fast: it took only 18 days (Marangoni and Kreppel 2022: 134). Once again, Italy's politics was in the hands of a technocrat. However, Draghi's executive styled itself as a kind of 'national unity' government, in which all parties participated, except for the far-right *Fratelli d'Italia* (FdI, 'Brothers of Italy') and some forces on the left. In his inauguration speech, Draghi talked about the persistent conditions of emergency but he also somehow normalised the technocratic option, referring to his as a simple 'government of Italian citizens' (Giannone and Cozzolino 2023: 100). Together with party politicians, the government also included 8 independent experts; among them, Vittorio Colao, former Vodafone's CEO, took charge of Technological Innovation and Digital Transition; Daniele Franco, Director-General of the BoI, obtained the Ministry of the Economy; the physicist, Roberto Cingolani, was handed the Ministry of Ecological Transition (Governo 2022).

A former PhD from the MIT and a Goldman Sachs alumnus, Governor of the Bank of Italy between 2006 and 2011 and President of the ECB in the 2011–19 era, often recognised as the 'saviour' of the Euro with his QUANTITATIVE EASING programme, at the start Draghi enjoyed vast political support (including from the Eurosceptic League) and high popularity. Curiously, only another technocrat, Mario Monti, had enjoyed higher popularity at the beginning of the mandate (Garzia and Karremans 2021: 109). However, Monti's popularity declined fast, mostly because of the austerity measures he took. By contrast, Draghi had to kick-off a process of recovery (almost a rebirth of the republic) and allocate the loans and grants distributed by the EU. As Garzia and Karremans put it (2021: 11), "In contrast with the Monti government, which had to *take* resources, the Draghi government will have responsibility for *giving* resources to domestic socio-economic groups." This in part explains the widespread support among political parties, too. Draghi enjoyed international reputation as well. Janet Yellen, the US Secretary of Treasury, had worked together with Draghi in stabilising the Great recession during her mandate as Chair of the Federal Reserve, and shared with him a part of her educational trajectory at the MIT (Bergmann and Clark 2021). Draghi became a strong link between the two banks of the Atlantic. Additionally, he enjoyed a strong reputation in Europe at a moment when Merkel was leaving Germany's Federal Chancellorship and Macron was fighting a difficult battle to retain power and popularity in France (Marangoni and Kreppel 2021: 140). Was Italy becoming a crucial, or even the 'key', EU country in global affairs?

Draghi's style of government was also rather different from his predecessors. His leadership has always been decisive, result-driven and task-oriented, and such was his approach to Italy's premiership as well (Capano and Sandri 2022). Would this kind of managerial style pay off, in a country used to constant and lengthy mediations and negotiations among parties?

As a matter of fact, Draghi rapidly adopted and implemented a massive vaccination plan, led by an army general, Francesco Paolo Figliuolo (Capano and Sandri 2022: 123–24). At the same time, he revised and reapproved the PNRR by April 2021. Its new version revealed a more powerful hand from the Prime Minister, but the changes were minimal, apart from some slightly stronger emphasis on digitalisation, research, innovation and infrastructure (Di Quirico 2023: 117).

In the ensuing months Draghi continued adopting rapid decisions, reassuring European and international partners, and enjoying a generally broad support. Yet his centralised decision-making further alienated parliament; in the first year of government, 81% of the legislative initiatives were decree laws (Capano and Sandri 2022: 127), with the effect of driving a wedge between on the one hand parliament and parties, and on the other an increasingly authoritarian (and technocratic) government. The 2022 Budget Law, for instance, was not even discussed in the Chamber of Deputies. This *modus operandi* jeopardised the relations between the government and political parties, which became increasingly eager to return to the *status quo* ante.

Additionally, a lot of questions were left unanswered. What was the nature and impact of Draghi's reforms? What about their significance to Italian and European political economy and their characteristics? Dosi's and Roventini's words are sharp (2022: 270–71):

> For sure, Italy is still trapped in the adagio from the novel The Leopard: "everything must change to remain the same". And what must not change is the neoliberal policy framework mitigated by some cosmetic corrections, witnessed both by the Italian NGEU plan and the Draghi economic policies more generally.

Certainly, Draghi did not have enough time to reform Italy's political economy in some depth; however, something more was expected of a scholar who had worked with socially oriented economists such as Federico Caffè, Franco

Modigliani and Robert Solow (Chamedes 2021). The much-debated Eurobonds or a kind of permanent Next Generation EU plan, which would have made the EU less neoliberal and more popular among citizens, did not become reality. An EU industrial policy did not emerge and, specifically in Italy's case, bureaucratic simplification (which would clearly boost economic growth) did not go far; let alone the push for more innovation and technological research (Pianta 2021). Some commentators have criticised the managerial and neoliberal connotations of Draghi's close collaborators (Castellina 2021) and the overall 'supply-side' inspiration of his cabinet's economic policy (Artoni 2021).

The year 2022 was also influenced by the effects of the Ukraine war and the necessity to readdress Italy's foreign policy, with which Draghi engaged in depth, both in Europe and the Mediterranean, and with the aim of finding alternative gas suppliers to Russia. The Eastern European conflict contributed to harming an economy which was on the way to recovery. Italy's GDP growth in 2022 remained high – 3.7% (The World Bank 2023), but inflation, also driven by the war and energy prices, reached 8.7% (Simone and Pianta 2023), with negative effects in terms of poverty and inequality.

The rather abrupt end of the Draghi government (July 2022), mainly because of tensions with and within the M5S and between the executive and the centre-right (Giuffrida 2022a), led to the almost inevitable choice of a snap election on 25 September. Re-enter populism. Concerns about the Ukraine war, fast-rising inflation, post-pandemic tensions and broader disillusionment after about three decades of subtle and creeping neoliberalism, led to widespread disaffection and some sympathy for the only relatively major party which had constantly remained on the opposition, FdI. As a matter of fact, the 2022 elections were won by FdI with 25.98% of the votes for the Chamber and 26% in the Senate, far more than the sum of its centre-right allies (the League and *Forza Italia*), which did not even reach double digits (Eligendo 2022a and b). As was predictable, the turnout was a modest 63.91%, the lowest in Italy's Republican history. Giorgia Meloni, FdI's 45 years old leader, would become the first woman premier in the country's history.

FdI shares with its predecessor, AN (which in 2009 had merged with *Forza Italia*), a post-fascist legacy. Both AN and FdI are heirs to the MSI (*Movimento Sociale Italiano*, 'Italian Social Movement', 1945–95), a neofascist party. Just five of the nine FdI ministers in the new government (Meloni is not one of them) have never been in the MSI (Gagliardi 2022). Meloni herself had been a member of the *Fronte della Gioventù* ('Youth Front'), the MSI's youth wing. FdI's attitudes towards fascism have often been debated and seen as at least ambiguous (Gemma 2022; Giuffrida 2022b). Meloni claims she is no fascist because of anagraphic reasons, but at the same time she often quoted Giorgio Almirante (Sondel-Cedarmas 2022), the long-time MSI Secretary (1969–87), who in his younger years had written extensively in some of fascism's racist and anti-semitic journals (Eatwell 2003). Whatever the opinion on Meloni's ideology, there appear to be continuities between neo-fascist parties and FdI, especially in terms of organisation and ideology (Puleo and Piccolino 2022). This is true for aspects such as authoritarianism, illiberalism, and nativism (Vampa 2023). As is highlighted by Puleo and Piccolino (2022: 370), exclusionary nativism seems to deeply permeate FdI's ideology. Authoritarianism, especially in the form of harsh measures against migrants (for example, naval blockades), has also become a core component of FdI's rhetoric, together with populist tones and Euroscepticism (Puleo and Piccolino 2022: 374), going above and beyond AN's softer discourse. While stressing the softening of FdI's anti-European narrative in recent years, Baldini, Tronconi and Angelucci (2022) refer to the party's understanding of the family in traditional terms and its rejection of homosexual adoptions, while also shedding light on its emphasis on Christianity and the 'fatherland', together with attacks on migrations. FdI's and Meloni's views on gender, womanhood and LGBTQIA+ rights are also the object of heated debates (Torrisi 2022).

Whether FdI's electoral win is seen as a break or a 'new normal' (Giovannini, Valbruzzi and Vampa 2022), the sphere of political economy choices, which played a huge role in the defeat of traditional parties, seems to highlight continuity more than change. Neoliberalism, also in the context of a confederal 'Europe of Nations' which FdI seems to prefer, is in other words here to stay.

Despite insistence on the protection and promotion of the 'Made in Italy', FdI's programme was mainly neoliberal (FdI 2022). Emphasis on 'merit', private-public partnerships and a flat tax proposal were all on the agenda (Baldini, Tronconi and Angelucci 2022: 394), as well as the reduction or outright elimination of the citizenship income. Family benefits and limits to migration compounded a programme that can be defined as nationalist and neoliberal and serving the interests of the national fraction of Italian business. The new government, largely considered the most right-wing in Italy's Republican history (Pasquino and Valbruzzi 2022), includes 5 independents, among whom the hawkish prefect Matteo Piantedosi, Minister of the Interior, is probably the most prominent. Good relations with the EU are maintained by the Foreign Affairs Minister, Antonio Tajani (FI), a former President of the European Parliament, and by the Minister of the Economy, Giancarlo Giorgetti from the League, who is known for his moderate pro-EU positions. FdI also witnessed the arrival into its ranks of several politicians from *Forza Italia* and with a past in Berlusconi's governments, such as Raffaele Fitto, Lucio Malan and the former Economy Secretary, Giulio Tremonti, who is traditionally close to the League. Meloni's early moves also showed a clear and predictable sense of direction: strong alignment with the USA, NATO, Israel and the EU, especially on the Ukraine war and in Middle Eastern conflicts; measures to restrict immigration and enforce public order; the replacement of the citizenship income with less onerous subsidies. It is difficult to figure out significant differences with the neoliberal gist of previous governments. The authoritarian element is hard to deny, and so is the neoliberal one. Despite rampant inflation, the energy crisis and the Eurozone stagnation (in 2023, no measures have been taken to support incomes, while GDP growth has been a modest .9%; Ciccarelli 2023 and The World Bank 2023), the revision of the PNRR, enacted in July 2023, seems to favour private companies over state intervention in areas such as urban projects, the green economy and Southern Italy's recovery (Viesti 2023).

After all, Meloni's approach resonates with the ambitions and interests of the right of the USA Republican Party (Harb 2022), which regained the White House with Trump's large victory in November 2024; Meloni had attended and spoken at the CPAC (Conservative Political Action Conference) event in 2022 in the US and become one of Trump's key allies in Europe (Kazmin 2024). Additionally, she is familiar with national conservative circles, as is demonstrated by her participation and speech at the early 2020 Rome Conference (National Conservatism 2020). National conservatism promotes the ethics and some of the values Meloni supports – in terms of human life, family, religion, nationalism, nativism – and discards globalism, gender issues, multiculturalism, supranational unity while at the same time endorsing freedom of enterprise and the market. The windfall tax on banks' profits, which Meloni adopted in August 2023 and shocked the markets for some days (Sciorilli Borrelli 2023), can be interpreted as a populist measure. After all, banks are extremely unpopular throughout the West and a well-known populist leader who has recently attacked them is the Englishman, Nigel Farage (Savage and Isaac 2023). Who – Meloni or Farage – has taken the leaf out of the other's playbook?

To summarise, Meloni's politics is a case of authoritarian neoliberalism by which the illiberal and nativist tendencies of the government merge with the authoritarian thrust of EU rules and the pro-capital policies they support. Berlusconi's demise on 12 June 2023 (Forgnone 2023) may have created further instability, but the way out of the authoritarian neoliberal impasse for Italy looks highly cumbersome. By contrast, in many ways authoritarian neoliberalism seems to have become the country's new normal, whether it is enforced by pro-market EU regulations or by the more sinister forces of far-right political parties, which eventually comply with European technocrats' rules. Trump's return to the White House in 2025 may combine with the rise of right-wing forces in a vast range of countries, including in France and Germany, Argentina and South Korea, and with the shift to the right of traditionally more moderate fractions of capital such as those of the high tech and the Silicon Valley. Italy's future, also in consideration of Meloni's success in the 2024 EU elections (Parlamento Europeo 2024), does look neoliberal and authoritarian indeed.

CHAPTER 5

Britain between Neoliberalism and Nationalism

The toxic combination of neoliberalism and nationalism is often deemed typical of dependent economies (Scheiring 2022), for example in Central and Eastern Europe since the Cold war's end. These economies are particularly dependent on foreign investment, capital and technologies; they exchange these factors of production with a rather cheap and qualified workforce as well as with a relatively stable business environment. Yet an economy can be dependent in several ways; typically, it can rely on few commodities (such as agricultural products, minerals or energy resources) and export markets or, as is the case of some European and many developing countries, on the hegemony of transnational capital, especially in the financial industry (Musthaq 2021).

However, establishing a clear correlation between dependency and nationalist neoliberalism is problematic. Recently, some large economies which are traditionally seen as developed and diversified, have also manifested clear and strong signs of nationalist neoliberalism; this may be explained by the high degree of *inter*-dependence which globalisation has brought about since the 1970s. In a sense, core capitalistic countries such as Britain, several European states and the USA (Cozzolino 2018), which are clear cases of nationalist neoliberalism, have become increasingly specialised in few sectors (the financial industry or services in Britain) and dependent on the global economy in many other industries, within the framework of a worldwide division of labour. Certainly, Britain has been read as one of authoritarian (and nationalist) neoliberalism's forerunners, at least since Thatcher's premiership (1979–92), and is seen as one of neoliberalism's most iconic countries. Especially in recent years and under Conservative governments, the links between British authoritarianism, nationalism, and neoliberalism have become more visible and explicit, despite Britain's welfarist tradition in the decades after World War Two. This chapter begins with a short reconstruction of neoliberalism's roots in Britain, in the pre-Thatcherian era of the so-called post-war consensus – itself a debatable concept – and continues with a summary of the first significant emergence of nationalist neoliberalism under Thatcher and the subsequent Conservative governments. It proceeds by highlighting the ambiguities of New Labour and by focusing more strongly on the significant nationalist mutation which emerged during Cameron's premiership and ended up in Brexit, Johnson's nationalism, Farage's nationalism and the rise of national conservatism.

Historically a cradle of classical liberal thinking and its early diffusion, since the mid-nineteenth century Britain has seen the emergence of more 'social' liberal theories (J.S. Mill or J.A. Hobson were in this sense prominent authors), while subsequent governments embraced aspects of welfarism, if often just paternalistic, compassionate, limited to whites and men, and within the overarching framework of colonial and imperial domination. Yet after World War One British economic theory and practice started changing. The London School of Economics (LSE) became the most influential intellectual hub of a return to a rather classical liberalism, with a stronger emphasis on the market economy (Tribe 2015). Scholars such as Edwin Cannan (1861–1935) and Lionel Robbins (1898–1984) contributed to a shift towards a more traditional and less social form of liberalism, and it was Robbins who in 1931 called from Vienna a young academic, Friedrich von Hayek, to deliver classes at the LSE (Hayek 2012). In London Hayek had a number of important students and collaborators; some of them such as Ronald Coase or William J. Baumol would continue along neoliberal lines. Yet Hayek also found fiery opponents, led by John Maynard Keynes, who would set the guidelines of the welfare state and social democracy in the 1930s despite, after all, sharing with Hayek some key liberal ideas, notably the importance of individual freedom (Gamble 1996).

The immediate aftermath of World War Two in fact pitted Tories against Labour, Churchill versus Attlee, Hayek versus Keynes (the latter, however, was a member of the Liberal Party; Skidelsky 2003). Hayek's successful publication of *The Road to Serfdom* (1944) – in a nutshell, a strong argument about the pernicious impact of central planning on individual liberty – might have had some, if limited, influence on Churchill's policy choices (Shearmur 2006) but did not prevent Labour from winning the first post-war elections in July 1945 with a landslide of 393 seats vis-à-vis 197 for the Conservatives. In the six years of the Attlee governments (1945–51), the Labour Party held the premiership with the support of a strong majority and steered the economy in a deeply social direction. Companies in the industries of commodities, mining, transport, and the Bank of England were nationalised; a massive programme of public housing was started; in 1948 the National Health Service (NHS) was famously founded. Those were the golden years of the welfare state (Morgan 1984), which – it is important to remember – was also built by exploiting and extracting resources from a still large, if declining, colonial empire (Bhambra 2022). India and the other South Asian colonies would only gain independence in 1947, while African and other colonies, including in the Caribbean, had to wait even longer.

The unfortunate election defeat of 1951, when Labour lost despite obtaining almost 14 million votes (Nicholas 1952), opened a new era of Conservative leadership. But would the new governments, once again led by an ageing Churchill, espouse Hayek's ideas and solutions?

1 Consensus or Not Consensus?

It has long and famously been argued that after World War Two's national effort and until the 'Thatcher revolution' Britain witnessed an age of 'post-war consensus', based on mixed economy, Keynesianism and the welfare state (Addison 1975). After all, such socially oriented consensus came to characterise continental European societies as well (in France, it was the era of the *trente glorieuses*, from 1945 to 1975) and to some extent even the more market-oriented USA, after the New Deal and during the 'liberal era'. In the three decades after World War Two Keynes, not Hayek, became the intellectual source of inspiration of economic policies throughout the West, while even Germany's rigorous ordoliberalism was moderated by the 'social market economy'. That said, historians have questioned the real extent of the 'consensus' as well as its foundations in Britain and overseas. Was 'Butskellism', the fusion of ideas and policies between the Labour and the Conservative Chancellors of the Exchequer, Hugh Gaitskell (Chancellor, 1950–51) and Rab Butler (Chancellor, 1951–55) respectively, a reality or rather a slogan? How significant were the divisions between the two main parties and within them (Pimlott 1989)? Was the consensus just a myth? Some authors (Blackburn 2018) claim that, while there were important ideological differences, there was a kind of 'epistemological' consensus: in other words, the two leading parties and their intellectuals shared a pragmatic and empirical worldview and were determined to scrutinise and follow historical evolutions instead of imposing overarching ideas. Furthermore, we cannot forget that the construction of the British welfare state drew on the exploitation of its past and remaining colonies; while Britain was building welfare at home, huge debts towards India were cancelled and colonies such as Malaya were still exploited for many more years (Bhambra 2022: 12–3). Butskellism, in other words, was mostly for white British citizens.

Neoliberalism, in the meantime, was making some early inroads in the world of ideas, though not yet in that of policies. Within the marginalised Liberal Party, intellectuals such as Elliott Dodds (1889–1977) re-proposed liberal ideas of fairer distribution of private property and called for a 'welfare society', capable of limiting the interference of the 'welfare state' (Watson, ed., 1957; Jackson 2016). In 1955 a group of liberal and conservative thinkers such as the businessman, Antony Fisher (1915–88); the economist, Ralph Harris (1924–2006), and Arthur Seldon (1916–2005), another economist, founded in London the first neoliberal think-tank, the Institute of Economic Affairs (IEA), which would rapidly become pivotal in spreading the ideas of Hayek, Friedman, Stigler, Buchanan and other prominent US neoliberal economists. Additionally, the IEA would pave the way to the rise of Thatcherism in the 1970s (Jackson 2016; Jackson and Saunders, eds., 2012).

The premierships of Harold Macmillan (1957–63) marked the heyday of the co-existence between conservative, liberal, and welfarist ideas in post-World War Two British government (Hennessy 2007). The country was also experiencing strong economic performances and the Conservative elite looked firmly in control. It is difficult to claim that the Treasury resignations of 1958, including those of the Secretary, Peter Thorneycroft, and of Enoch Powell, represented a shift to a more business-oriented, 'neoliberal', policy (Green 2002).

And yet, the second half of the 1960s swept the Western world and most of the globe with a wave of new issues, new demands (of higher salaries, racial equality, gender equality, a cleaner environment, peace in Vietnam, a less authoritarian society, more and better socialism, more freedom), and relative economic stagnation. Britain was not immune and the new Labour government, led by Harold Wilson (1964–70), pragmatically combined pro-labour measures with pound devaluation and the necessity to resort to IMF support in 1968 (Clift and Tomlinson 2008). Yet Britain's growth remained sluggish, and its economic perspectives did not improve with the return to government of the Conservatives and the premiership of Edward Heath (1970–74), despite the accession to the EEC (European Economic Community) in 1973. Joining the European Common Market was seen favourably by the Conservatives, who had envisaged the possibility of expanding economic opportunities in a fast-growing group of countries and would be confirmed by 67.2% of British voters in a 1975 referendum (Nelsson 2015). New forces and ideas were meanwhile emerging. Within the Conservative Party, the politician who most embodied a turn towards pro-market policies (and a supporter of EEC integration) was Heath's Secretary of State for Health and Social Services, Keith Joseph (1918–94).

Joseph has often been considered the founder of Thatcherism. He has been regarded as an ideologue, an intellectual entrepreneur and an organiser of think tanks (in particular, the Centre for Policy Studies (CPS), founded in 1974 together with Thatcher); his crucial importance has been acknowledged by Thatcher herself (Thatcher 1995). The CPS, although formally independent, was immediately perceived as linked to its Conservative founders, Joseph and Thatcher, and, especially in the late 1970s, contributed to shaping a debate on the importance of neoliberal and monetarist policies. As to Joseph, there have been lengthy discussions on his own political inclinations. Was he at heart a liberal or a conservative (Denham and Garnett 2002)? Frankly such discussions miss the key point. Joseph was a (neo)liberal in so far as his economic ideas (in fact not particularly innovative and largely based on classical neoliberal thinkers) stressed the limits of state intervention, the efficiency of the market and the necessity to cut public expenditures to promote private entrepreneurship. In most ways this is the typical neoliberal playbook (Joseph 2014). At the same time, however, Joseph's experience tells us much more. He was both a (neo)liberal and a conservative, to say the least.

Born in Westminster to a wealthy family, a businessman, a young minister in Macmillan's government, Joseph embodied class privilege as well as a spirit of competition that is central to neoliberalism as well as to more traditional forms of conservatism. His approach to competitiveness was though selective and elitist, in a very questionable way. In his view, not everyone can be competitive. The less privileged, the poor, the subaltern, cannot afford this privilege. In Joseph's words in a 1974 speech (n.p.),

> The balance of our population, our human stock is threatened ... [...] ... a high and rising proportion of children are being born to mothers least fitted to bring children into the world and bring them up ... [...] ... Many of these girls are unmarried, many are deserted or divorced or soon will be. Some are of low intelligence, most of low educational attainment ... [...] ... They are producing problem children ... [...] ... A high proportion of these births are a tragedy for the mother, the child and for us.

In simple and tragic words, Joseph appeared to be calling for eugenics and birth control to dispose of those deemed unfit for the competition. Attacked and criticised, he quit the race to lead the party, but his competitive spirit remained a part of the neoliberal discourse.

Joseph's neoliberal attack on the poor was in fact matched by Enoch Powell's assault on immigrants, in a toxic blend of neoliberalism, nationalism and racism. Powell's life and speeches have prompted Shilliam (2021: 239) to consider him, the most infamous British racist politician, "Britain's first neoliberal politician". Powell was in favour of free markets and free entrepreneurship, but his was not the view of an economist or an ideologue; nor was he particularly keen on adopting specific social or economic policies. Powell's *habitus* was neoliberal – and nationalist and racist. In his view, English history was one of freedom, markets, and 'orderly independence' (Shilliam 2021: 243–44). Neoliberalism was in a sense quintessentially tied to English history. That was not applicable to migrants – they had a different history, a different culture. Some of them were exporting communalism. Hence, Powell's infamous no to migrants, unfit to adapt to the English system (Shilliam 2021). This way Powell rejected immigration as well as European integration and empire or any form of Commonwealth; in all cases 'pure' English values would have been compromised. Of course, many neoliberals were and are neither racist nor nationalist, but Powell's narrative captures one key aspect of neoliberalism, which in specific places and circumstances has blended and blends with populism, nationalism and even racism. That was the case of Thatcherism, at least in some of its manifestations, and regardless of Thatcher's own personal convictions. That is the case of contemporary neoliberal populism, as expressed by Farage's political creations.

As a matter of fact, while Thatcher became the Leader of the Opposition (1975) and Labour was still in government (under Prime Ministers Wilson and later Callaghan, 1976–79), some neoliberal measures were introduced. Labour's overall direction remained socially oriented, with a range of new policies on public housing, child poverty, health and safety at the workplace, gender equality, and so on. At the same time, especially under Callaghan, the Labour Party had to adapt to the changing conditions of the world economy and became more neoliberal even regardless of the oil crises, the 1976 pound crisis and the subsequent resort to IMF funds. Some austerity policies were introduced as well as massive cuts in social expenditures (Humphrys and Cahill 2014: 680–81). If only to some extent, Labour started adapting to an incipient globalisation and neoliberal competition. This was a part of a general movement which also included the Labour Parties in Australia and New Zealand, and the Democrats in the USA during the Carter presidency (Humphrys and Cahill 2014). It was also the end of any consensus, if it had ever existed, between left and right on welfarism and Keynesian policies. Thatcherism was truly beginning.

2 Thatcherism in Power with Thatcher and Major (1979–97)

The 1978–79 'Winter of discontent' was not only pivotal in handing over British democracy to Thatcher; it witnessed the first massive wave of strikes (of truck drivers, waste collectors, nurses, railway workers, and more) against austerity and was carefully constructed by the Conservatives as the ultimate defeat of Keynesian welfarism (Hay 2009 and 2010).

Thatcher won the 1979 elections with 339 seats – 70 more than Callaghan's beleaguered Labour (BBC 1997a). She would remain Prime Minister for eleven years and leave a crucial and lasting legacy in British and world politics. The first woman premier in British history, Thatcher was hardly committed to feminist values and remained divisive also among women (Purvis 2013). A lot has been written on her politics and legacy, but to our purposes its most important aspects are the combination of neoliberalism and nationalism (the latter bordering with racism in the case of Enoch Powell's experience; Tribune 2021), the praise of competition among citizens and countries, and the moment of 'authoritarian populism' which was illustrated by Hall (1979). In broad terms, Thatcher proposed as the key solution of social and political issues a 'strong state', if 'small', limited, working *for* the market or – better said – for big business, capital. This is especially clear in Gamble's early interpretation (1979, reformulated in 1988) about 'the free economy and the strong state'. In line with Hayek's view, such strong state values negative, formal liberty (Berlin 1969) more than democracy; it is a state which frontally attacks public administrations and trade unions and *rolls* them *back* before *rolling out* a new and neoliberal political body. It is also nationalist, populist, racist and authoritarian (Hall 1979); it expresses Powellism despite Enoch Powell's earlier political demise. It claims to represent the people in opposition to the Labour-led 'state', but is far more elitist and exclusionary (Hall 1979). Stuart Hall's views, while being pioneering and powerful, have sometimes been criticised for not including a comprehensive analysis of the forces, the 'historical bloc', that supported Thatcherism (Jessop 2015; Jessop et al 1988) and for not having explored the ways such forces would become entrenched in British institutions. As a matter of fact, it was a multifaceted, complex bloc.

Thatcher relied on the endorsement of the City and large financial institutions more than that of declining industrial capital. Financialisation was a key aspect of her politics (Davis and Walsh 2017), which aimed at breaking the strength and unity of the working class and its trade union representatives. She was also largely supported by the media and made use of the emerging 'creative' sector; Saatchi & Saatchi famously helped her campaign. Yet she made decisive inroads in the middle classes and even took some working class support away from Labour (Butler and Kavanagh 1980). In other words, her historical power bloc was large and distributed across classes and her ability to attract and shape the middle classes would have later been emulated by New Labour (Moran 2005). Additionally, Thatcher was able to rely on parts of the white working class which chose to defend its relative privileges vis-à-vis their immigrant, often black, peers (Shilliam 2018).

That said, her first years in government were incredibly challenging and ridden with risks. The Conservatives were rather divided between staunch Thatcher loyalists and more traditional Tories, linked to tradition and a paternalistic, compassionate welfare (Young 1989). The Exchequer was in the hands of Thatcher's supporter, Geoffrey Howe (1926–2015), while Keith Joseph held the Industry portfolio. In 1981 other loyalists were appointed to secretarial positions; among them, Nigel Lawson (1932–2023) took Energy and Norman Tebbit (1931–) was handed Employment. Yet Thatcher's battle was uphill. 'Rolling back' (Peck and Tickell 2002) the state and public employment brought about skyrocketing unemployment rates and hard-hitting recession. In 1980 the GDP declined by 2%, followed by –.8% in 1981 (The World Bank 2024b). Strikes, factory closures and race riots multiplied, especially in 1981 and as a reaction to a return of a mounting racist discourse (Trilling 2013). Despite some decisive and controversial neoliberal moves (for example, tax cuts and the 1979 Right to Buy Act, which allowed categories of tenants to cheaply buy their flats), Thatcher faced severe initial difficulties in implementing her programme (Jessop 2015: 19). A stronger opposition might have taken advantage: by contrast, under the more leftist leadership of Michael Foot, Labour lost several MPs, who were attracted by the rise of the Social Democratic Party and its new alliance with the Liberals (the Liberal Democrats). At the same time, Thatcher managed to recover, also thanks to the nationalist rally engendered by the military victory in the Falklands War (April–June 1982) and to the fragmentation of opposition parties which did not find a way to come together and oppose a cohesive platform to Conservative neoliberalism (Jessop 2015; Fry 2008).

Thanks to some economic recovery and high degrees of patriotism and nationalism bolstered by the Falklands War, Thatcher approached with some confidence the 1983 vote. She was re-elected with a landslide majority of 144 seats (BBC 1997b) and could then speed up the adoption of her neoliberal project. Unemployment remained well above 3 million, but tax cuts, privatisations (for instance, of British Telecom) and the fight against unions (in 1984–85 the government engaged with massive miners' strikes) continued and in fact gained momentum. With a convinced neoliberal, Nigel Lawson, at the Exchequer, Howe dealing with Foreign Affairs and Brittan as Home Secretary, Thatcher could also rely on a stronger and potentially more loyal government. Economic growth reached 4.1% in 1985, 3.2% in 1986, 5.4% in 1987 and 5.7% in 1988 (The World Bank 2024a). Traditional factories were gradually replaced by brand-new shopping malls, while more and more multinational companies started producing in Britain, for example in the automotive industry, with the arrival of Peugeot and Nissan. Even more significantly, 27 October 1986 was the day of the 'financial Big Bang', that is, the opening of a computerised London Stock Exchange (LSE) to foreign companies. London was to later undergo more and intense doses of financialisation (Treanor 2006). And yet, despite all these changes, unemployment figures remained largely above 3 million at least until 1987, while income inequality kept growing. Neoliberalism truly created a country of 'two nations' (Jessop et al 1988), which would often be held together by nationalist ideas and symbols, especially in opposition to migrants and European integration and in the 1980s' second half.

Encroachment on local authorities, the financial and housing market crisis in late 1987, and especially the widely resented 'poll tax' led to a decline in Thatcher's fortunes. In June 1987 the 'iron lady' was anyway able to win the national vote for the third time, despite a loss of 21 seats and Labour's adoption of a more liberal and centrist platform under Neil Kinnock (BBC 1997c). Yet inflation's return, strikes in public healthcare, a firmly nationalist position in handling European integration, whose process was cruising towards the Maastricht Treaty and the single European currency, and the protests following the adoption of the controversial poll tax, led to tensions within the party and Thatcher's eventual resignation in November 1990 (Jessop 2015: 21). Yet she had remained at 10 Downing Street for about 11 years, combining neoliberalism with hostility towards both immigration and the European project, according to a logic which had been earlier illustrated by Powell. Thatcher's core values have usually rotated around a triad – free enterprise, nationalism, and an efficient state – and its sometimes-challenging contradictions.

But Thatcherism was far from dead. Thatcher had contributed to founding the Eurosceptic Bruges Group, another think-tank, in 1989, after a famous anti-European speech in the Flemish city (Jones 2016). John Major's subsequent premiership (1990–97) has often been considered a failure (Hickson and Williams, eds., 2017), while in fact it was a key moment of transition when Thatcherism had to face some of its own contradictions and paved the way to the more reassuring and moderately pro-European synthesis of the 'New Labour' era. While Major might have been the embodiment of a "Thatcherism with a grey face" (Jessop 2015: 21), his government continued along fully neoliberal lines and adopted highly controversial measures such as the privatisations of the coal and railway industries. 16 September 1992 is the date of the infamous 'Black Wednesday' (Inman 2012), when Britain was ousted from the European Exchange Rate Mechanism (ERM); it marked a massive humiliation for Major's cabinet, even if the economy subsequently recovered (with a peak growth of 3.8% in 1994; The World Bank 2024a), and the government even contemplated the possibility of using the EU as an 'external constraint' on inflation and devaluations. Some of the policies pursued by the Chancellor of the Exchequer, Kenneth Clarke (1993–97), would be continued by New Labour and the same can be said of many aspects of Thatcher's general politics. Major's conservatism, for its part, took some distance from Thatcher's nationalism and opened avenues for a more technocratic, pro-EU posture, in line with what was becoming the dominant narrative of the 1990s.

The 'New Labour's' avalanche was coming. In part following in the footsteps of Kinnock, a youthful and dynamic lawyer, Tony Blair (who had become Labour's leader in 1994), had completely refashioned the Labour Party. Strongly supported by the media and keen on spinning and public image, Blair, Peter Mandelson, an ambitious spin doctor, and a journalist, Alastair Campbell, refurbished the party's brand and directed their electoral attention towards the centre, the middle classes, that is, employees, administrators, managers, and an increasingly emerging 'creative class' which, especially in London and the South of England, had replaced the old working class and was leading Britain into the global age; or at least it was constructed as such by New Labour. As early as 1994, Blair had rejected the party's commitment to nationalisations (the clause IV of the Labour Party Rule Book) and reoriented its economic policies in a strongly pro-market direction, with workfarism in the place of welfarism and the 'Third way' ideology more as a slogan than a coherent set of policies. These ideas were also advanced by the Shadow Chancellor, Gordon Brown (1951–), who apparently left room to Blair as party leader. The Labour Manifesto ('New Labour because Britain deserves better'; Labour Party Manifesto 1997) was a clearly neoliberal document. It proposed a vision of a rejuvenated, dynamic, competitive society. Amongst its key points, there were a more corporative (rather than confrontational) approach to trade unionism, a full acceptance of the global economy, emphasis on competitiveness and efficiency in education and healthcare, attention to the environment, focus on low inflation as well as lower taxation, emphasis on rules and regulations, and a renewed interest in the EU, with the proposal of a referendum on the participation in the European Monetary Union (EMU) and the single EU currency. There was a shift from Thatcher's muscular nationalism, but some continuity with Major's more internationalist approach. The 1990s were the heyday of global neoliberalism and for some time it looked as if Blair, Clinton, Germany's social democratic *Neue Mitte* (a kind of New Labour 'the German way'), the EU, Yeltsin's Russia, the WTO (World Trade Organisation, a new global trade organisation), and even a nominally communist but increasingly neoliberal China were all embodiments of a brave, new, and neoliberally planetary compact.

3 From Blair's Neoliberals to Nationalist Neoliberals

Nationalism, however, had not disappeared. In parallel with the ascendancy of Blair's 'New Labour', a Eurosceptic and nationalist party was gaining ground as well. In 1994 the Anglo-French millionaire, James Goldsmith, founded a new and anti-EU force, the Referendum Party, with the specific aim of calling a referendum on the nature of the EU and Britain's role in it (Heath et al 1998). The referendum's proposed question was: "Do you want the United Kingdom to be part of a Federal Europe or do you want the United Kingdom to return to an association of sovereign nations that are part of a common trading market?" (Heath et al 1998: 25). Goldsmith's resources helped mobilise voters especially in Southern and Eastern England. While in other respects they did not share common political positions, the party's voters had mostly and distinctively Eurosceptic traits. In the 1997 elections the Referendum Party ended up garnering more than 800,000 votes and ranked fourth among British political forces, behind the two main parties and the Liberal Democrats. Goldsmith would pass away soon (in July 1997) but other anti-EU and nationalist forces were emerging; among them there was the UKIP (UK Independence Party).

Founded in 1993 by a Eurosceptic academic, Alan Sked, the UKIP gained some traction only after 1997 and the demise of the Referendum Party (Ford and Goodwin 2014). After gaining 3 seats in the European Parliament vote in 1999, the UKIP made a breakthrough in the 2004 EU elections (which coincided with the EU enlargement to most of Central and Eastern Europe), when it obtained more than 16% of the votes (Lynch, Whitaker and Loomes 2012: 736). A decisive change, however, would occur only in later years. To perform better, the party needed a populist and charismatic leader, and it found one in Nigel Farage (1964–), a former City broker with some alleged sympathy for Enoch Powell (Mason and agencies 2014; Mason 2014a; Tournier-Sol 2019). While the initial core of UKIP voters was mainly composed of 'left behind' white working class and elderly men (Goodwin 2014), Farage was able to broaden the party agenda from a mostly anti-EU to an anti-immigration and anti-elite, right-wing nationalist and populist platform (Ford and Goodwin 2014; Goodwin 2014). At the same time, he proposed a clearly neoliberal project, promoting tax cuts and flat taxes (Davies 2016). By carving out a space on the right, between the Conservatives and the moribund, fascist British National Party (BNP), Farage led the UKIP to a shocking result in the 2009 European Parliament elections, when it obtained 16.5% of the vote and 13 seats, more than Labour and less than only the Conservative Party (BBC 2009c). The UKIP was thus positioning itself on the right as a possible alternative to the Tories. Yet the time span between 2004 and 2009 had been characterised by the furious unfolding of the subprime financial crisis and the initial stages of the 'Great recession'. Before returning to the 2009 vote, it is therefore crucial to reflect on what had happened to Blair's New Labour.

After his triumph in the 1997 general elections (with the largest majority in British political history until then: 418 Labour MPs vs 165 for the Conservatives; BBC 1997d), Blair marched quickly towards promoting economic reforms.

Granting independence to the Bank of England (Quaglia 2005: 557), a move reminiscent of Italy's choice in 1981 (see Chapter 4.2), was a step into a technocratic direction and was followed by measures to support devolution to Scotland and Wales. The Labour leader maintained a degree of welfare, though in a more targeted way and in a workfarist sense. In continuity with the Major government and in parallel with the emergence of the technocratic EU of the Maastricht criteria, Blair and the Chancellor, Gordon Brown, adopted a 'politics of depoliticisation' (Burnham 1999 and 2001). Since the main issues were still, in some order, "maintaining foreign confidence in sterling; preventing inflationary wage settlements; and capping public expenditure" (Burnham 2001: 129–30), it became increasingly convenient, especially for the Labour Party, which had often been criticised for its management of the economy, to transfer part of the responsibility to agencies, public/private bodies, 'New Public Managers', rules, regulations and ultimately technocracy. In many ways, Blairism represents the technocratic moment of British politics *par excellence*; it constructed a 'politics of numbers' which Labour would often not hesitate to manipulate (Clift 2023).

Blair and his long-lasting Chancellor of the Exchequer, Gordon Brown (in government between 1997 and 2007), who had a more traditionally social democratic point of view, proceeded along the Thatcherite way (Jessop 2015: 22), rejected 'old' Keynesianism and the traditional welfare state, while at the same time returning to a 'one Nation' approach and adopting selected social policy measures. Expenditures on education and healthcare rose and some anti-poverty policies were introduced. Yet the government's overall direction remained decidedly neoliberal (Jessop 2007).

Blair also launched the idea of a 'knowledge economy', that is, a society of creative workers-entrepreneurs, who in a context of competition would have strengthened the British economy (O'Donovan 2021) and would have reinforced the new middle classes on which New Labour depended for its own success. However, as is highlighted by O'Donovan (2021: 188–90), the adoption of knowledge-driven development models would ultimately lead to growth but also to higher inequality. Additionally, labour market reforms were made in a spirit of tough workfarism (Jessop 2003: 10–8). As Blair had announced in his 1997 Leader's victimising speech (n.p.):

> it is compassion with a hard edge. A strong society cannot be built on soft choices. ... [...].... The new welfare state must encourage work, not dependency. ... [...].... We want single mothers with school age children at least to visit a job centre, not just stay at home waiting for the benefit cheque every week until the children are sixteen.

Together with the knowledge economy and workfarism, Blair and Brown revitalised the usual catalogue of neoliberal reforms, from liberalisations to deregulation, from privatisations to commodification of what remained of the public sector, from internationalisation (or globalisation) to the reduction of direct taxes (Jessop 2003). In many ways, it becomes clear why Thatcher considered Labour's transformation under Blair "her greatest achievement" (McSmith, Chu and Gardner 2013: n.p.).

New Labour's economic achievements in its first term were enough to grant another landslide win in the 2001 national vote. Blair's party obtained 413 seats, while the Conservatives stood at 166. However, the turnout was only a worrying 59.4%, the lowest figure since 1918 (BBC 2001). New Labour's legitimacy was in some decline. Taxes meant to fund education and healthcare rose in 2002, and the second Blair ministry was mostly marked by much-debated foreign policy choices. Nationalism was still an important driver of Britain's foreign policy and was framed by Blair in terms of messianism, exceptionalism, even 'liberal' imperialism, as per the expression of his diplomatic adviser, Robert Cooper (Foley 2023). The interventions in Afghanistan and especially Iraq were a part of this 'mission', but they would prove costly in terms of loss of lives, energy, and international credibility, notably in the Middle East and Europe. Britain seemed to return to the imperialist rhetoric of the early 20th century. Despite an overall pro-EU orientation, Blair had to slow down on fast-accelerating European integration and mainly focus on the enlargement to Central and Eastern Europe, Cyprus and Malta, which was itself in line with a neoliberal interest in investment in new markets and producers. GDP growth peaked at 3.1% in 2003 (The World Bank 2024a) and then started slowing down. The EU enlargement, however, shed light on the emerging issue which immediately gained prominence in the 2004 EU Parliament vote: immigration from European countries, on which Britain chose not to impose restrictions (Ford and Goodwin 2017: 22). In the 2005 general elections, Labour still relied on the legacy of several years of significant economic achievements, and obtained 355 seats, 48 less than in 2001. The Conservatives, led by the tough former Home Secretary, Michael Howard, who waged a campaign centred on limiting immigration and severity on crime, earned some 32 seats more than in 2001 but ended up with just 198. The UKIP did not win seats but, with more than 600,000 votes, rose for the first time to the position of fourth most voted party in a national election (Bartle and King, eds., 2005).

Blair's final term was cut down to two years, which were mostly focused on domestic affairs and issues of terrorism, especially after the London attacks on 7 July 2005, themselves a sign of an increasingly shaking neoliberal globalisation. As was predictable, Blair left room to his Chancellor Brown, widely perceived as being less neoliberal and more welfarist. Brown became Labour leader on 24 June 2007 and Prime Minister three days later (BBC 2007a). The new government, in which the Exchequer portfolio was assigned to Alistair Darling, would though soon undergo the most severe test, that of the 'Great recession'.

4 From the Great Recession to the Tories' Return and Brexit

The financial meltdown's and the Great recession's main impact would be on political actors, and especially New Labour, rather than on neoliberalism as such. In contrast, neoliberalism would not die (Crouch 2011); it did survive and became much more nationalist and even racialised. The crisis of traditional institutions dragged with it ideas and political parties and would lead to a level of nationalist neoliberalism far higher than that of Thatcher's era.

Once the US subprime crisis started spreading internationally in August 2007, the most vulnerable British bank, Northern Rock, faced liquidity problems and asked for the Bank of England's intervention on 12 September 2007 (BBC 2007b). After extending the loan several times, the Bank of England nationalised Northern Rock in February 2008 (Staff and agencies 2008). In a nutshell, British authorities responded by bailing out the country's banking system. The fear engendered by the bank's default and the economic contraction in 2008's second term hit Labour hard, in both opinion polls and local elections. While Lehman Brothers was collapsing in the USA (September 2008), Brown's reaction was though prompt. Royal Bank of Scotland (RBS) was nationalised and Britain adopted a £50 billion plan to recapitalise the banking sector, which would set some example for other countries, too (Wearden 2008; Krugman 2008). Yet the economy entered recession for the first time since 1991 (BBC 2009b) and the unemployment rate rose steeply. Historic companies such as the retailer, Woolworths, closed down, while others suffered heavy losses, including for instance Marks and Spencer. Further losses were announced by RBS in February 2009 (BBC 2009a) and, in the middle of an uncontrollable recession, the 2009 budget included tax rates of 50% for incomes above £150,000. Labour would pay dearly for its attempt to save neoliberalism by making it more 'progressive', and despite hosting the April 2009 London G20 summit, in which Brown appeared to lead in terms of proposals for a global financial recovery. In the 2009 EU elections, Labour would end only in the third place, with just 15% of the votes and 13 seats (BBC 2009c). The recession was hitting very hard. The nationalist, anti-EU UKIP had become a force to be reckoned with and the Conservatives, led by the youthful David

Cameron, had returned to leading the opinion polls. In fact, despite a slight economic recovery, which may have helped Brown, and the lack of a controlling parliamentary majority, the Conservatives won the 2010 elections with 36.1% of the votes (7.1% more than Labour) and 306 seats (BBC 2010b). Parliament remained hung and the Tories had to forge an alliance with the more progressive and usually pro-European Liberal Democrats. However, the change was not one of ideas, policies and practices; it was rather a rotation of political personnel under the persistent banner of neoliberalism. Nor was nationalism losing steam. The UKIP, despite Pearson's rather erratic leadership, obtained more than 900,000 votes and remained the fourth most voted party in the general elections. The far-right, fascist, British National Party (BNP), garnered 564,000 votes (BBC 2010b). Additionally, Euroscepticism was an important part of Cameron's agenda and enjoyed significant support in the ranks of the Conservative Party. The red line was defined as a further deepening of EU powers, which would have been accepted only after the consent of the British people in a referendum (Conservative Party Manifesto 2010). Moreover, the Tories intended to return to the UK some powers on specific matters and further emphasise the flexible and mainly economic dimension of the EU. Immigration from within and without the EU would have to be more controlled and, when necessary, limited.

In most respects, despite (generic) promises and the coalition with the Liberal Democrats, Cameron's politics was highly neoliberal (Vail 2015). Cuts to the public sector, to taxes, welfare, and debt were superficially compensated by some emphasis on the NHS and especially on a 'big society', an ambiguous, slippery term that referred to charities, volunteerism, and decentralisation, which were mostly seen as ways to help citizens catch up with austerity policies in the public sector (Conservative Party Manifesto 2010; Scott 2011). Another area where Cameron committed conservatism to some change was that of the environment (Carter 2009). It is difficult though to envisage in his politics something genuinely new; it was rather an attempt to adapt conservatism to a more media-savvy, populist, PR-driven form of politics; an aspect on which Cameron to some extent borrowed from Blair's Labour.

Facing a budget deficit of £156 billion, the new Chancellor of the Exchequer, George Osborne, immediately adopted provisions for austerity policies; with the aim of balancing the budget by 2015, he proposed 77% spending cuts (Wamsley 2023) and established technocratic bodies such as the fiscal watchdog, the Office for Budget Responsibility (OBR; Clift 2022, 2023 and 2024), which had a mandate to make forecasts and check public accounts. The welfare reform of late 2010 (BBC 2010a) and the contextual rise of university tuition fees heralded an era characterised by a stronger rhetoric of work ethics and individualism; after all, the Conservatives were truly back. Unrest and riots quite suddenly became more common. The abrupt explosion of urban riots in several English cities in August 2011 led scholars and commentators to think that welfare cuts, deprivation, social exclusion and marginalisation had led to the outbursts of violence (Chakraborty 2011). The government's and Cameron's rhetoric were by contrast quick in neoliberally pointing to individual or gang criminality and responsibility and in returning to the shallow narrative of the 'big society' as a solution (Cameron 2011b). And yet the 'big society' discourse, the further shift from welfare to workfare, the stress on individual work ethics were not functioning; nor were austerity policies. Unemployment reached almost 2.7 million in March 2012 (BBC 2012) and the EU became increasingly identified as a likely scapegoat. The veto cast by Cameron on a new EU treaty in December 2011, in the middle of the Eurozone crisis, was a concession to Conservative Eurosceptics as well as a sign of a stronger nationalism on European affairs. Britain was witnessing the Eurozone's meltdown with strong concern and fear of getting too much involved in the troubles. More Conservative MPs and politicians started promoting the idea (which had historical precedents, especially when Britain joined the European Communities in 1975; Glencross 2015) of a referendum on Britain's membership in the EU (BBC 2011). At the same time, Cameron also addressed the issue of terrorism by denouncing the failure of multiculturalism and how it had passively allowed the emergence of Islamist fundamentalism, and by advocating a new, more active, 'muscular', liberalism (Cameron 2011a), to be achieved also through a stronger emphasis on shared national values in education. The attack on multiculturalism took place roughly at the same time in several European countries, also as a way to scapegoat migrants, and in the context of a broad turn to the right (Bhambra 2017b), which in 2011 was in government in all the larger EU countries (Germany, Britain, France, Italy, Spain). In the meantime, in 2011 the new Education Secretary, a neoliberal with neoconservative leanings, Michael Gove, came up with the proposal of an education reform, which would move in the direction of a less global and more England-focused teaching of history (Bhambra 2017b). Britain was going back to an identification as England and especially a white, little England; this was an underlying stream of thought which, after all, had never truly disappeared and resurfaced at a moment of economic difficulties.

The year 2012 was one of some economic recovery (+1.5%; The World Bank 2024b), but also of tremendous turbulences in the Eurozone, especially in Ireland, Greece and the latter's Southern neighbours. Fear of further migration (mostly from Eastern and Southern Europe) and of the possibility of some consolidation in the Eurozone bloc, which started undergoing significant change and some institutional deepening, urged Cameron to take a clear stance on the EU, which he did in January 2013 with the famous 'Bloomberg speech'. In it he affirmed the character of Britain as an 'island-nation' and its instrumental relationship with the European Communities which, after having been successful in bringing peace and stability to the continent after World War Two, were now struggling to promote prosperity. The way out of the impasse, in Cameron's view, was that of a revision of the EU institutions in the direction of a single market, abandoning any further political ambition, followed by a referendum on the UK's membership in it (Cameron 2013). Apart from the fact that the United Kingdom stretches over two islands, it had been an empire as well (Bhambra 2017b) and it was now again posturing in an imperial, dominating way, including towards the EU and the other EU member states.

At the same time, support for the UKIP and Euroscepticism were rising rapidly. In 2012 Theresa May, the ambitious Home Secretary, declared her intention to "create ... [...] ... a really hostile environment for illegal migration" (Griffiths and Yeo 2021: 522). While such an anti-immigration discourse and policy had precedents even under Labour governments (Griffiths and Yeo 2021: 525), with May the discourse became more pervasive and aggressive. 'Go Home' vans started touring some areas of London while draconian deportation measures, enhanced police checks, controls in schools and universities, removal of access to financial and healthcare services, not to mention the racialisation of several controls (Bhambra 2017b), contributed to an atmosphere of growing panic and hatred (Broomfield 2017; Goodfellow 2020).

In these circumstances, the UKIP obtained its best result ever at the 2013 local elections (Watt 2013) where its anti-EU, nationalist and anti-immigration rhetoric became ever more tangible (Harris 2013). Cameron's more moderate Euroscepticism found itself increasingly squeezed between on the one hand the UKIP's hard anti-EU attitudes and growing discontent within the Tories' conservative right and on the other hand the party's more centrist factions (Vail 2015), within the context a stalling British economy (Heppell 2014: 159–60). The choice of nationalism and a referendum on EU membership by 2017, despite its risks, seemed in 2013 the most rational course, at least from the Conservative government's point of view. 2014 and 2015 would be years of decisive elections as well as of Scotland's independence referendum.

The UKIP and Farage were the true and only winners of the 2014 European Parliament vote. For the first time since the early 20th century a party other than Labour or the Tories won a British election, be it national or European. The UKIP obtained almost 4.4 million votes and 24 MEPs, ahead of both Ed Miliband's Labour and Cameron's Tories (BBC 2014a). Migration, especially from Central and Eastern Europe, and relations with the EU were the key and only big issues of the UKIP campaign (Wintour 2014). Farage's party exploited the atmosphere of 'hostile environment' created by the government and by the right-wing media attacks to migration to promote further 'Othering' of both Eastern Europeans and Muslims (Shaw 2022). A new rhetoric of Powellism was getting hold of important parts of the country; narratives of 'little England' and 'global Britain', both rooted in an idea of England/Britain as a hard-working, market-oriented, white and threatened country, were gaining visibility (Melhuish 2024).

At this stage, Cameron felt compelled to act fast. Pressure from the EU combined with that of Scotland, whose threat to leave the United Kingdom was to some degree motivated by economic issues. While only 44.7% of Scottish voters opted for independence in the referendum on 18 September 2014 (BBC 2014b), some of Scotland's more deprived areas (Scottish Government 2013) voted for separation from London.

Preparing the 2015 general elections proved to Cameron a challenging task. In late 2014 he would again make clear that Britain was committed to controlling immigration, reforming the EU, and putting the reforms' final outcome to UK citizens in a referendum (Cameron 2014). Additionally, as far as economic policy was concerned, Cameron insisted on attacking Labour's mismanagement and chaos as opposed to a Conservative-led "Great Revival" (Conservative Party Manifesto 2015: 7). This claim was not substantiated by data. In the years 2010–15, economic growth had been a non-exciting 2.05%, still less than the figure of 2.07% of the 1997–2009 Labour governments' period, which had included the nadir of the Great recession (IMF 2023b). While there had been stronger recovery since 2014, data on deficit and public debt were not comforting at all. The latter had even risen to 82.1% in May 2011 (ONS 2023). Lower taxation on companies and upper classes had also contributed to the deficit and to debt's enlargement (Fuchs 2016). Moreover, a vast number of the newly created jobs were precarious and part-time (Fuchs 2016: 173). Cameronism's neoliberal appeal to 'hard workers' and meritocracy unveiled its somewhat hidden populist nature (Fuchs 2016: 174), while its constant emphasis on oppressive EU regulations and rules expressed the sentiment of a growing anti-EU faction within and without the Conservative Party (Fuchs 2016: 175–76).

The 2015 Conservative Party Manifesto insisted on recent economic achievements (which in fact were modest and far from consolidated), law and order policies, a referendum on the EU and limits on migration. Despite predictions of another hung parliament and Ed Miliband's Labour's early lead in exit polls, Cameron's Conservatives obtained a convincing victory, with a total of 330 seats against 232 for Labour (BBC 2015a). With 12.6% of the votes (although only one seat won) the UKIP was a surprising third, while the severely punished Liberal Democrats ended in the fourth place, with less than 8% of the votes (BBC 2015a). Interestingly, the Tories fared far better among men, over 65 years old, whites, and upper and middle classes, with percentages of 38, 47, 39, and 45 respectively. The UKIP did quite well among the same groups, in addition to a surprising 19% in the C2 class (that of skilled manual workers; Ipsos 2015). A key influencing role, much more than that of the ascending social media, was likely played by the traditional national press: *The Sun, The Telegraph, The Daily Mail, The Times* were all on the Conservative side (Jackson and Thorsen, eds., 2015).

After rapidly forming a new government largely based on the previous one (but without the Liberal Democrats and with more room for manoeuvre), Cameron adopted a new budget, which included a National Living Wage (UK Government 2015), and started focusing his attention onto the forthcoming EU referendum.

So much has been written on Brexit (the referendum actually took place on 23 June 2016 and Leave won with 51.9% of the total votes; BBC 2016) and its root causes. Certainly, long-term and traditionally British issues such as entrenched Euroscepticism and the defence of UK sovereignty played some important role (Curtice 2017; Taylor 2017). A weak European identification, which has been evident throughout most of Britain's recent history, together with a nostalgia of the imperial legacy and of its Commonwealth links, has doubtless been important. Also, a significant part of British public opinion has traditionally and vocally lamented the loss of sovereignty inherent, among others, in the principle of the primacy of EU law or in that of a common EU citizenship; not to mention resentment towards the increased power of the unelected Brussels bureaucracies. Breaking down the data on pro-Leave variables, levels of education and age played a highly significant role. Higher education and younger age in fact pushed in the Remain direction (Goodwin and Heath 2016b; Zhang 2018). 75% of those aged 18–24 voted to stay in the EU, while the most pro-Brexit age band was that between 65 and 74 years old (66%; Ipsos 2016). 68% of voters with a degree or higher were also Remainers. This applies to 80% of students as well, while 70% of those without qualifications opted for Leave (Ipsos 2016).

A lot has in fact been written on the role of the "Left Behind" (Goodwin and Heath 2016b: 7; Ford and Goodwin 2014), that is, those British (more often English) voters who are usually older, male, white and socially conservative and who traditionally supported Labour in less affluent areas such as parts of the Midlands and the North; they would have felt marginalised by the advance of neoliberal globalisation and competition, especially in large cities such as London and in the South East; they would have feared migration and potential competition from 'foreign' workers (Ford 2016). In other words, these groups would have felt abandoned, 'left behind', and marginalised by the global, European, and British elites, both economic and political, both left and traditional right. In many cases, and particularly in rural areas with little history of ethnic diversity, these groups would have also felt highly strained by the rise of immigration, which may have played an important role especially where demographic change had been incredibly rapid such as in some parts of the East of England or the Midlands (Goodwin and Milazzo 2017).

While all the interpretations above can draw attention to the ruthlessness imposed by neoliberalism on some social groups and the feeling of alienation caused by it as well as to the perceived convergence of interests between some EU and British neoliberal elites, these aspects are only a part of the story, and a limited one. Another, and more important part, has been the rise of a narrower form of English nationalism, exemplified by the likes of Farage, Gove and especially Boris Johnson, as a catalyser of a new stage of Conservative statecraft, aimed at gaining the support of the declining middle and working classes (Gamble 2021b). Brexit expresses a new middle-class nationalism. Additionally, dominant narratives have neglected the importance of the racial factor: there is strong evidence that the white middle classes, including in rich Southern and Eastern England, supported Brexit in the millions (Dorling 2016), while the (largely working class) non-white minorities significantly sided with Remain (Bhambra 2017a): only 36% of the BAME groups would have chosen Leave (Goodwin and Heath 2016a). Brexit, in other words, was a distinctively white and middle-class phenomenon (Bhambra 2017a: 215), linked to a legacy of racism and imperialism which dates to at least the 19th century, re-emerged after World War Two with the Windrush scandal (Virdee 2013) and resurfaced in the ugly context of the narrative of the so-called 'uncontrolled migration' running through Europe and the West, including the USA (Bhambra 2017a). Migrants, be they white Europeans or Arabs, Asians, Africans, or others, have been interpreted as a threat to a fundamentally essentialist and racialised view of British culture (Melhuish 2024). The political and ideological discourse of Brexit was of course developing in parallel with changes in the economic structures. Something new was also lurking on the horizon of global capitalism; something that was more similar to a combination of neoliberalism with illiberal forms and ideologies, or a 'neo-illiberalism', according to Hendrikse (2021). Otherwise, as is maintained in this work, we can use the term 'authoritarian/nationalist neoliberalism'. New forms and fractions of capitalism were emerging and some of them expressed their support to Brexit.

Overall, big businesses tended to support Remain but, without strong trade union opposition and within a broadly pro-business political framework, they remained quite silent and quiet (Feldmann and Morgan 2021a). By contrast, small and medium-size companies often pursued different interests and at times supported Brexit. 14% of a survey sample of small and medium-size companies claimed that the EU was making their employment decisions easier, while 31% claimed the opposite (Inman 2016). Too many regulations and constraints would be impairing the growth of smaller UK companies in the EU framework; let alone the potential competition from other EU countries such as Germany and its neighbours (The Netherlands, Belgium, Austria, Denmark, France itself, etc). Yet also bigger groups' representatives felt that Brexit might have offered new opportunities; in particular, delinking Britain from the EU could have opened new markets and may have provided the chance of signing more favourable trade agreements without the need to rely on the single EU trade policy (Partington 2018). Additionally, some businesses such as Wetherspoons (but also some large retailers), the pub chain founded and owned by the outspokenly pro-Brexit businessman, Tim Martin, had little economic interest in the EU market and promoted Brexit. Other companies looked at the opportunities to open new global markets by withdrawing from the EU's centralised trade framework and returning to rely on an independent UK trade policy, with the potential to act faster in key world regions such as the Americas or South and East Asia. The inventor and billionaire entrepreneur, James Dyson, vocally supported Brexit and invited to look to Asia, well beyond Europe (Ruddick 2016). Likewise, another billionaire (Forbes 2024c), the founder of the chemical giant, INEOS, Jim Ratcliffe, complained about the intrusiveness and extra powers gained by the EU over time (INEOS 2016). In other words, a significant fraction of the British bourgeoisie powerfully supported Brexit with the persuasion that a more autonomous Britain would have better played its cards on the world markets and would have been liberated from the shackles of EU rules, regulations and competition policies. A part of British capital, to sum up, looked away from Europe and towards the rest of the world, but with Britain at the core.

Brexit was thus much more than a 'left behind' issue. To a significant extent, it was fostered by the white British middle classes and by sections of the British business which expressed an 'economic', utilitarian form of nationalism. But it was also another episode of an imperial history of 'othering' migrants, be they other white Europeans or non-whites from many world regions. The much controversial and often vilified Director of the Vote Leave Campaign, Dominic Cummings, a promoter of industry and technology, wrote in 2017 (n.p.):

> Leave won because 1) three big forces [the immigration crisis, the 2008 financial crisis and the euro crisis] created conditions in which the contest was competitive, AND 2) Vote Leave exploited the situation imperfectly

> but effectively, AND 3) Cameron/Osborne made big mistakes. If just one of these had been different, it is very likely IN would have won.

On the one hand, Cummings's campaign was an assemblage of populist elements and recurrent, brutal attacks on opponents, often directed at the establishment of both main parties and beyond. On the other hand, it unveiled a form of 'technocratic nationalism' (a concept often associated with Modi's India and smart cities; Datta 2015) according to which Britain would aim at becoming a scientific and technological superpower, leaving behind the European Union and its regulatory burdens, and returning to its glorious past as an autonomous tech powerhouse (Bagehot 2016). In this sense, companies such as Dyson and INEOS somehow subscribed to an agenda of technocratic nationalism. Vote Leave found some difficulties because of the co-existence with Farage-supported Leave.EU, a parallel campaign which was more populist and targeting broader discontent, against white as well as non-white migrants but also multinational corporations (Jennings and Lodge 2018: 80). At the same time, and sadly in agreement with Cummings, it is also correct to say that the incumbent government did little to attempt to remain in the EU. Nor did Corbyn's Labour embrace the European cause, which it could have done with the goal of deeply reforming the EU institutions in a socialist sense. Cameron's campaign was feeble and unconvincing; the case for Remain was presented in a tepid way, more focused on Brexit's risks than on EU membership's benefits; Cameron himself, often perceived as a quintessential representative of the 'establishment', did little to stop the Leave tide (Curtice 2017). As to Labour, Corbyn stuck to his personal, highly Eurosceptic viewpoint, and made limited efforts to defend the EU, even if in its current neoliberal form (Shaw 2022: 96–8). If we put together racist leanings, imperial nostalgias, the interests of some business fractions and the clear weaknesses of the Remain campaign, the referendum's nationalist outcome becomes clearer. Neither Cameron nor Corbyn proved ardent pro-European leaders. What about then the timid support to Remain of the business world? For all the mistakes of the various agents, the Brexit referendum's outcome reflects deep-seated Euroscepticism, a challenging international context, and a fast-growing anti-immigration sentiment. With the benefit of hindsight, a different result may even appear unlikely.

5 From Brexit to Post-Brexit

The choice of a 'one-nation' (Hickson, Page and Williams 2020) Remainer, Theresa May, as the Leader of the Conservative Party and new Prime Minister (on 13 July 2016), seemed to signal the party's intention to avoid the unleashing of divisive forces and a disorderly Brexit. The new government in fact included vocal Brexiters such as Boris Johnson (Foreign Secretary), David Davis (Secretary for exiting the EU), and Priti Patel (International Development), all to the right of Cameron's outgoing cabinet (Stewart 2016) but at the same time was led by a woman who had been Home Secretary under Cameron (Agerholm 2016), when her attitude had been harsh, unforgiving and fundamentally against immigration. Hostility towards immigration, in a sense, was the main common thread between May and the Brexiters. After triggering Article 50 of the EU Treaty to start the Brexit negotiations (March 2017), May confidently went to popular vote with the aim of strengthening the support to her way of handling Brexit negotiations. And yet the move failed. In the June 2017 elections the Conservatives were able to gain only 317 seats and lost an overall majority, a fact which forced them to form a coalition with the 10 MPs of the hawkish Northern Irish Democratic Unionist Party (DUP). By contrast, Corbyn-led Labour, which ran on a democratic socialist programme and a 'soft Brexit' mandate, surprisingly obtained 262 seats and 40% of the votes (Dorey 2017). Almost 13 million Britons appeared to reject long-time neoliberal politics (UK Parliament 2017). Arguably, with a stronger pro-EU position, Corbyn might have even won the elections.

Managing at the same time Brexit negotiations, Conservative Party infighting, EU technicalities, a series of challenges old and new (terrorist attacks, climate crisis, relations with Putin's Russia, Trump's USA and a more aggressive China, technological evolutions such as the emergence of Artificial Intelligence, AI) proved a tremendous task for May and her fractious, constantly changing cabinet. Despite several U-turns in key policy areas, on immigration May remained inflexible; her ministry was marred by the emerging of the 'Windrush scandal', that is, the revelations of the harsh policies (including detention and deportation, and especially during the Cameron and May ministries) directed at those UK residents (mostly of Caribbean origins) who had come to Britain in the aftermath of World War Two (Gentleman 2021). The revelations shed light on inhumane decisions affecting tens of thousands of senior Commonwealth citizens who had lived in Britain for more than fifty years and had never been required documents or proofs of residence, mostly because at the time of their arrival their countries were still a part of the British empire (Gentleman 2018). While the Home Secretary, Amber Rudd, resigned on 29 April 2018, May vowed to continue the 'hostile environment' policy (Merrick 2018).

Boris Johnson's more charismatic, if essentially opportunistic, availability to lead the country (especially after his resignation from the Foreign, Commonwealth and Development Office, FCDO, in July 2018), Farage's simultaneous 'withdrawal' after Brexit's achievement, and the emergence of new right-wing forces in the Conservative Party set limits to May's leadership possibilities. After the umpteenth attempt to package a Brexit deal, May resigned from the party leadership and the position of Prime Minister in June and July 2019 respectively, leaving the job to the quintessential Brexiter, Johnson. Energised by Johnson's promise to 'get Brexit done', British voters would emphatically vote Tory in the 12 December 2019 general election (BBC 2019a). Johnson obtained 365 seats, while Corbyn's Labour sank to 203. In terms of votes, the Conservatives went close to a 44%. The Brexit Party, which succeeded the UKIP, managed to garner slightly more than 640,000 preferences, a disappointing result after the triumph at the 2019 EU elections (with more than 5 million votes; BBC 2019b). A new government, mostly composed of Leavers and in a climate of growing racism, xenophobia and Islamophobia (let alone antisemitism in the Labour ranks), was getting ready to finalise the Brexit deal (Shaw 2022: 121–24).

Come the end of January 2020, Britain left the European Union. Johnson seemed to succeed where May had failed, but a new and tremendous storm was in fact already hitting the United Kingdom and the world: Covid-19, the pandemic. The pandemic would of course attract the world's and Britain's attention throughout 2020 and most of 2021. Yet even setting aside Brexit, on which a last-minute deal with the EU was reached by 24 December 2020 (Boffey and O'Carroll 2020), several other key political events took place during the pandemic time, and not just in relation with Johnson's erratic and consequential Covid-19 mismanagement, which was also caused by the neoliberal healthcare cuts of the previous decades. Global events such as Black Lives Matter protests, the rise in Channel immigration and the election of a Democrat, Joe Biden, to the White House in Autumn 2020, intersected with appalling sanitary emergency, economic slump and a series of scandals (including Johnson's lockdown parties and Cummings's infamous trip to Durham during lockdown; BBC 2020b) on which there is still little clarity. At the same time, Tory nationalism and far-right conservatism moved further to the right.

A new generation of Conservative politicians emerged around well-known (and controversial; Monbiot 2018) think-tanks such as the historical Institute of Economic Affairs (IEA). As early as 2012, Priti Patel, a zealous Thatcherite hardliner (Mason 2014b), Kwasi Kwarteng, a successful historian and businessman, Dominic Raab, a pro-Brexit lawyer, Liz Truss, a former Liberal Democrat, and Chris Skidmore, a Eurosceptic historian, had joined forces and jotted down a kind of manifesto for a new Conservatism in a new Britain, in the book *Britannia Unchained* (2012). The work (overall, extremely superficial) combined strong emphasis on Thatcher-style neoliberalism and competition with a renewed nationalist thrust. The authors lamented Britain's loss of competitiveness and work ethics vis-à-vis countries such as those in East Asia, the USA, Canada, and others. All the authors were members of the Free Enterprise Group, a kind of spin-off of the IEA, and some had roots in former colonies of the British empire.

In her position as Home Secretary, Patel would become well-known for aggressive and restrictive immigration policies. The Nationality and Borders Bill (which would become an Act in 2022) of 2021 introduced major obstacles to the acceptance of asylum seekers and refugees and even "criminalized assistance to them even for humanitarian reasons" (Shaw 2022: 130–1). After proposing a points-based immigration system (HM Government 2022), Patel would sign the Rwanda Asylum Plan on 14 April 2022, with the purpose of deporting asylum seekers to Rwanda. The plan would immediately become controversial because of its alleged violations of both international and domestic law (Syal 2022a; Daly 2022). Aside from Patel's anti-immigration positions and other controversies, it is interesting to notice how Johnson's Home Secretary, as a manager in corporate communication and relations, represented an emerging fraction of the middle class, which located itself outside of the traditional Oxbridge stronghold. Similarly, although educated at Oxford and Cambridge, Raab, a lawyer, often expressed critical positions on immigration and feminism and had been a part of the Brexit campaign, also in the name of strongly neoliberal ideas. A financial analyst and a Cambridge PhD in History, Kwarteng has then both expressed neoliberal views and a more 'nuanced', or 'revisionist', history of British imperialism (Kwarteng 2011). For her part, Liz Truss had started her political career in the Liberal Democratic Party, had worked on issues of childcare and education, had qualified as an accountant and held other positions in the government, for example as Foreign Minister under Johnson (UK Government 2022). A new bourgeoisie was in the making, one with both nationalist and neoliberal sympathies, and some degree of highly questionable imperial nostalgia, to say the least.

6 The Rise of National Conservatism?

Which new political forces and ideas have emerged since Brexit? Is a new and more nationalist generation of Conservative politicians, who rose during the Johnson premiership, on the verge of taking over power, at least within the party? How are they positioning themselves in relation to Farage's return to mainstream politics? The answers to these and similar questions are in fact highly complex, although it is important to remember that the whole British political climate, not just one party, has become more nationalist. This has also been confirmed by the latest (4 July 2024) general elections, in which Reform UK, Farage's new creature, obtained more than 4 million votes (BBC News 2024). But how has politics in more recent years translated into the relations between nationalism and neoliberalism?

The pandemic, characterised by Johnson's erratic and highly criticised decisions, a flurry of scandals, including those related to Cummings and to the Prime Minister's behaviours, and the overall perception of growing and unprecedented corruption (Sanders 2023), proved to be Johnson's ultimate undoing. Despite a range of possible interpretations and Johnson's often pragmatic and opportunistic attitudes, his premiership, which centered on Brexit (Hayton 2021), can clearly be read as nationalist. In particular, Johnson refocused the Conservatives' attention onto regaining ground on the right wing and mainstreaming the "far-right rhetoric of nativism, anti-immigration and Islamophobia" (Worth 2022: 823) as well as by espousing a more narrowly English form of nationalism (Gamble 2021b) as a key dimension of his own statecraft. While his premiership did not last long enough to start off significant constitutional changes and to fend off power struggles within the party, Johnson's legacy would remain. His shift towards a more nationalist and anti-immigration statecraft would be the starting point of a reshaping of the Conservative Party in a more inward-looking and isolationist direction. As is illustrated by Melhuish (2024), there is no necessary tension between 'little England' and 'global Britain'. Both have roots in the imperial and colonial legacy and the former is in a sense a condition of the latter. Stronger nationalism and unity at home set the scenario for expansion overseas, at least in an economic sense.

After Johnson's spectacular loss of party confidence in July 2022, when an almost endless series of mass resignations took place in a few hours, a new cabinet would begin its work on 6 September 2022, under the leadership of the Thatcherite (and Johnson loyalist), Liz Truss, the former Foreign Secretary. Among her key collaborators there were her co-writer Kwarteng at the Exchequer, Lt. Col. James Cleverly as Foreign Secretary, and the already controversial Attorney General, Suella Braverman, as Home Secretary (Crerar, Elgot and Lawson 2022).

Truss would be mostly remembered for the 'mini-budget', which was seen as an expression of her 'Trussonomics'. It was adopted in the context of a rising 'cost of energy crisis', in part triggered by Russia's invasion of Ukraine, and a massive wave of strikes throughout 2022. Inflation was reaching 10%. In a nutshell, the mini-budget (or 'Growth Plan'; The Growth Plan 2022) included significant tax cuts with the aim of relaunching growth to at least 2.5%/year and using increasing borrowing as a replacement for taxation. Among the most controversial measures there were massive tax cuts for the highest earners and the scrapping of several duties and of corporation taxes from 25% to 19%. It was a kind of typically populist neoliberal plan, but it came at an economically wrong moment and had been poorly prepared. Truss and Kwarteng had refused to have the endorsement of the OBR, the body in charge of forecasts and a kind of fiscal watchdog, and had not considered the importance to neoliberalism of strong rules and regulations, especially since the Great recession. While the reaction of some businesses was positive, that of the markets was shocked and shocking. The pound's exchange rate collapsed vis-à-vis the dollar, the Bank of England intervened to calm capital markets (Thomas and Nanji 2022), and even international authorities such as the IMF (Sherman and Espiner 2022) and US President Biden (the latter, of course, in a highly diplomatic manner) stepped in to criticise or question the plan.

The 'mini-budget' was in fact a 'budget for the wealthy' (Russell 2022), which would have further exacerbated socio-economic inequalities, and destabilised the national economy in the context of already rampant inflation and skyrocketing fuel prices. In many ways it was pure Trussonomics and represented neoliberalism's 'master narrative' (to use Lacan's terminology; Maher 2023) of freedom and growth, combined with a nationalist spirit; not by chance it was praised by Farage (The New European 2023) as an expression of a quintessentially British form of economics. It was also a response to the more rule-based, disciplinarian, technocratic neoliberalism of the OBR, the IMF and international bodies. Truss's government's collapse due to the mini-budget in fact led to the emergence of neoliberalism's second narrative, that is, following Lacan and Maher (2023), the 'university narrative' of stability, austerity and, in a broad sense, technocracy. Its leader was Truss's former rival for the premiership, Rishi Sunak (1980–), the first Asian British in the role and one of the country's history's youngest Prime Ministers. A Stanford MBA, with work experience in Goldman Sachs and major hedge funds, Sunak immediately recalled to mind the profile of the 'technocrat' (The Economist 2023) and was handed the top job also to calm down the markets. At the same time, he was a technocrat with a clearly political profile, which has usually been understood as nationalist and socially conservative (New Statesman 2023).

Such combination of tough, uncompromising neoliberalism and nationalist conservative positions seemed to characterise most of Sunak's new cabinet. While prominent nationalist Conservatives such as Cleverly, Braverman and Gove maintained their roles, the experienced, Jeremy Hunt, who had replaced Kwarteng after the mini-budget's collapse, was confirmed Chancellor of the Exchequer, and 42-year-old Kemi Badenoch, already in charge of International Trade, was handed over the role of Minister for Women and Equality.

The first acts of Sunak's government reflected its nationalist neoliberal orientation. The Autumn 2022 Statement, which was delivered by Hunt in the context of the highest inflation since 1977 (11.1%; Elliott 2022) and rising interest rates, was comprised of both deflationary and mildly expansive measures. While announcing some tax increases, Hunt committed to moderate rises in spending on healthcare and education and a rise in the national minimum wage, according to a typical populist playbook (BBC 2022a). At the same time, Sunak reneged on climate change commitments by opening the first new coal mine in three decades (BBC 2022b) and introduced further restrictions on asylum seeking in the country (BBC 2022c).

The most nationalist side of Sunak's government would again be expressed by a Home Secretary, this time, Suella Braverman. A pro-Brexit barrister and a former Attorney General (2021–22), Braverman came to the fore because of her strong right-wing positions, especially on issues of migration and regarding asylum seekers, and for her revival of the 'Rwanda plan'. Also, she defined herself as 'proud of the British empire' (Syal 2022b). Such positions soon translated into law in the Illegal Migration Act 2023 (Harrison, Casciani and Sheils McNamee 2023). The latter, and the fact that some of its provisions are at odds with those of the ECHR (European Convention on Human Rights), has raised the question whether some form of national conservatism is taking shape and gaining power in Britain.

In the Anglo-American tradition, national conservatism has roots in thinkers such as Burke and Hamilton, Webster and Lincoln, but it gained traction especially in the Cold war generation of Buckley, Hayek, Strauss, Robertson and others (Hazony 2022). In the contemporary context, national conservatism has manifested itself in Orbán's Hungary (Szaló 2021) and in a significant range of countries (noticeably, in Central and Eastern Europe – Poland, Slovakia, Romania, Bulgaria, but also in Austria, Belgium, France, Italy, Spain and Sweden) where it incarnates the more traditionalist and reactionary forces within the Global Right (Varga and Buzogány 2022). National conservatism has also some roots in Britain (in part, in the tradition of Enoch Powell) where at the same time it has arrived via the US CPAC (Conservative Political Action Conference) and other conservative networks, in addition to a number of media outlets, from tabloids to GB News (founded in 2021), think-tanks like Policy Exchange (Fekete 2023: 93) and politicians such as Braverman. The latter, according to Fekete (2023: 92),

> was warmly received at the Conservative annual Conference for decrying a 'hurricane of mass immigration', calling the Human Rights Act the 'Criminal Rights Act', and declaring that she stood with 'the hard-working common-sense majority against the few … the privileged woke minority, with their luxury beliefs', which included saying that a man can be a woman.

Braverman's far-right attacks against the alleged loss of traditional values, the rise in immigration and the leftist elites would find some echo in the USA and Europe, and Braverman herself would intervene at the National Conservatism (NatCon) Conference, held in London on 15–17 May 2023. The conference, whose first edition dates back to 2019, saw the participation of influential radical right Americans, including Kevin Roberts, the President of The Heritage Foundation (which is providing intellectual support to Trump's presidency), as well as some well-known British politicians such as the Secretary of State for Levelling Up, Housing and Communities, Michael Gove, and the much-debated ultra-conservative MP, Jacob Rees-Mogg (Dearden 2023; National Conservatism 2023), who traditionally locates himself at the crossroads between nationalism and neoliberalism.

The significance of the diffusion of national conservative ideas and practices in Britain cannot be underestimated. Themes such as low birth rates have become more popular throughout the West, as is testified by the Tory MP, Miriam Cates, who intervened at the NatCon Conference (Walker 2023; Fekete 2023: 98) and by Goodwin's recent statements on immigration (Fekete 2023: 98). Such topics are usually typical of ultra-nationalism and the radical right, including in Hungary or Meloni's Italy, and are a part of the repertoire of the populist narrative.

At the same time, British national conservatism looks like a work-in-progress, with an uncertain future. Many participants to NatCon 2023 were in fact just moved by curiosity or simply economic liberals (Walker 2023). Is UK national conservatism mainly an instrumental political tool? Is Braverman attempting to use national conservatism for political and electoral purposes? Is she attempting to capture conservative voters from the right? As a matter of fact (Walker 2023: n.p.),

> it remains to be seen whether the UK is receptive to this as the US, not least because the primary American audience for such views – evangelical Christians – are both much less numerous and different in outlook here.

Braverman's nationalist version of conservatism may succeed or not, but a further torsion to the right of British Conservative (and not only) politics is already taking place and is here to stay. NatCon 2023 was also attended by diplomats (David Frost), intelligence heads (Richard Dearlove), anti-immigration writers (David Goodhart; Freedland 2017), anti-immigration academics (Eric Kaufmann), scholars in theology (James Orr), and historians (David Starkey). This further testifies to the transformation of the Conservative Party (Bale 2023), but also to the right-wing shifting pendulum of British politics as a whole.

The persistence of British national conservatism is testified by the return of Braverman, Farage, Cates, and others at the 2024 conference, this time at the heart of much-vilified EU, in Brussels. Interestingly, the event hosted well-known far-right speakers such as Viktor Orbán and the French presidential candidate, Éric Zemmour. Additionally, it might have gained more resonance because of the decision of a Brussels's local mayor, Emir Kir, to shut it after one day of works (Abrahamsen and Williams 2024). Shutting down NatCon, as offensive as the conference may be, can backfire and play into nationalists' hands. They would in fact feel legitimised to criticise the elitism of the 'leftists', 'Marxists', 'globalists', or whoever their target is.

But what are the core principles of national conservatism, which, as a global movement, is supported by the Edmund Burke Foundation (Burke Foundation 2024)?

A look at their core discourse unveils some ambiguities, but also clear basic traits. 'The nation' is mentioned repeatedly, and in rather belligerent terms. Point 1 among the core principles refers to the will to "endorse a policy of rearmament" (Burke Foundation 2024: n.p.); point 3 supports the necessity for national governments to "intervene energetically to restore order" (Burke Foundation 2024: n.p.). What about religions other than Christianity and Judaism? What about families other than "the traditional family, built around a lifelong bond between a man and a woman" at point 8 (Burke Foundation 2024: n.p.)? Or the proposal of a moratorium on immigration or anyway "much more restrictive policies" (point 9)? Is the call for racial equality a nice periphrasis to perpetuate white privilege (point 10; Burke Foundation 2024: n.p.)?

While the core NatCon social and cultural narratives suggest a nationalist, far-right agenda, the economic dimension is clearly neoliberal, with a strong emphasis on freedom and the market economy (point 6 in the core principles). More than any other influential and current group or institution, the National Conservative umbrella seems to hold together nationalism and neoliberalism, in addition to calls for traditional families, traditional faith, and a basic rejection of immigration and supranational organisations.

But how entrenched is National Conservatism in British public and political life? Despite its rise in politics, the media, the academia, public institutions, it is far removed from achieving any kind of vaguely hegemonic position. Yet some of its ideas have spread, also because in the latest years the whole of British political life has turned to the right.

Sunak's rather feeble premiership – always conditioned by Conservatives' internecine strife – has mostly focused on the nationalist aim of curbing immigration. After months of recurrent public sector strikes, pay rises were approved, also after enhancing visa and healthcare fees for non-British citizens (Allegretti 2023; Iacobucci 2023). Furthermore, the cornerstone of Sunak's premiership became the infamous Rwanda Bill, after the rejection of the Illegal Migration Act 2023 by the UK Supreme Court (The Supreme Court 2023). Notwithstanding abstentions, rebellions, and opposition from the right of the Conservative Party, three difficult readings in the Commons and further dissensions in the House of Lords, The Safety of Rwanda Bill became Act on 25 April 2024. It has been defined "a pointless exercise in performative cruelty" (McKee 2024: n.p.). It is highly likely that it may never be implemented, also because of the Conservative defeat in the July 2024 vote. Yet the cruelty of its message, the disrespect of international and domestic law, and the persuasions of those who wanted even more insensitive regulations, will have a legacy. British nationalism is a reality to be reckoned with. It has manifested itself in other dimensions of Sunak government's politics. On environmental issues, after early promises, Sunak postponed the petrol car ban by five years (Holton and James 2023); he also cancelled the High-Speed railway 2 (HS2), between Birmingham and Manchester, which may have lowered the impact of road traffic and contributed to the North's levelling up (Zeffman and Whannel 2023). On many other issues, including those related to gender, social and LGBTQIA+ rights, Sunak has proved to be a most conservative Prime Minister (Elgot 2023). In simple words, too many times he has been a follower rather than a leader; and he has often followed the most vociferous, radical and nationalist voices of the Conservative right. The existence and persistence of these voices as well as their connections with international forces bear witness to the enduring power of Britain's nationalist neoliberalism.

What has been the impact of the 4 July 2024 elections on nationalist neoliberalism and conservatism? To start with, the election had an unsurprisingly very low turnout – 60% (–7.6% in comparison with 2019) – which suggests overall dissatisfaction with politics (BBC News 2024). These data invite reflection on the significance of Labour's apparent triumph. After all, Starmer's party obtained 411 seats (290 more than the Conservatives), but less than ten million votes, that is, less than the 10.3 million Labour had won under Corbyn's socialist and internationalist (though tepidly pro-European) leadership in 2019. Starmer's Labour has increasingly moved to centrist positions with a pragmatic and cautious attitude and has embraced a form of 'thin labourism' (Manwaring, Duncan and Lees 2024). Despite Starmer's early socialist background and some interesting initial campaign promises (for example, the renationalisation of railways and other public utilities; Brown and Stewart 2022), challenging neoliberalism will be difficult. If anything, a move towards a more progressive neoliberalism (Saad-Filho 2020) may perhaps take place. Others have noticed Starmer's legalistic attitude (Johnson, Thomas and Basham 2024), which reflects a broader tendency to juridify neoliberalism in a technocratic way. As to nationalism, after some early talk about 'patriotism', there is little clarity. Starmer vowed to scrap the Rwanda plan (Francis and Seddon 2024) and declared it "dead and buried" as soon as he was elected (Francis 2024), but doubts remain on which immigration policies the Labour government would choose. Rachel Reeves, the new Chancellor (and the first woman in this role in British history), has work experience in the Bank of England and a past with pro-business positions, if moderate and somewhat progressive. Her proposal of a national wealth fund (Makortoff and Kollewe 2024) has yet to be fully evaluated. On the whole, the majority of the Starmer cabinet members have ties to the 'New Labour' experience and share little with Corbynism's democratic socialist orientation. Gauging their positions on nationalism remains difficult and dependent also on the attitudes of the opposition and the public opinion. As to the opposition, with 23.7% of the votes and 121 seats the Conservatives have to face the worst result ever in their entire electoral history. A part of their right wing has been eaten out by Reform UK, Farage's last creature, which managed to win 14.3% of the votes and 5 seats, including one for Farage, who had never entered Westminster before (BBC News 2024). Led by Farage and by a businessman, Richard Tice, Reform UK is organised like a company. It combines neoliberalism with nationalism in a clear and rather consistent way. Support to small companies would be matched by possible taxes on banks; scrapping High Speed railways and net zero targets would combine with the promise of an extra £17 billions a year for the NHS, also by engaging with the private sector. At the same time, the UK would leave the European Convention on Human Rights (ECHR) and put a freeze on all non-essential immigration (Sandford 2024). Such programme, which has been expressed as a 'contract with voters', risks creating divisions within the Conservative Party and giving Reform UK a leading position among right-wing voters. It is possible Reform UK's nationalist and neoliberal stances will have a growing impact on the choices of Labour and especially the Tories. That said, the 2024 election also showed some rejection of both nationalism and neoliberalism (the Green Party obtained a record 4 seats and 6.7% of the votes) and of nationalism only (the internationalist Liberal Democrats won 72 seats, 61 more than in 2019). Of course, the evolution of Britain's nationalist neoliberalism keeps depending on the influence of the world political economy and particularly of the country's main political and economic partners, the USA and the EU.

As of Spring 2025, the most significant domestic moment in the life of Starmer's executive has been the 30 October 2024 budget (Autumn Budget 2024), Reeves's first. Tax rises combine with expenditures of £22.6 billion for public healthcare, £20 billion for Research and Development, and some further expenses for schools, education, the environment and housing. Reactions have been mixed but the overall impression is that it is not a strong blueprint for growth (Pratley 2024). In general, it aligns with the kind of mild progressive neoliberalism embraced by New Labour and Starmer. Yet the nationalist element has not disappeared, also because of two key events.

In the first place, on 2 November Kemi Badenoch became the Leader of the Conservative Party. She is the first black person ever to become the leader of a major party in Britain. Usually associated with the party's right, Badenoch has in fact criticised 'critical race theory' and in general opposes gender theories, in addition to expressing a nationalist position on immigration and foreign policy (Geiger 2024). In the second place, few days after Badenoch's election, Donald Trump won the US presidential vote for the second time and with some ease. Co-existence and cooperation between the Trump administration and Labour Britain will not be easy. The USA has asked Britain to spend more on defense and will likely ask it to further tighten up immigration policies (Urban 2024). Additionally, there are already tensions about Musk's sympathies for Reform UK, with or without Farage.

Whatever the White House's choices, opinion polls in Britain seem to suggest declining support to Starmer and more shifts to the right. Badenoch's Tories would remain at a disappointing 22% (vis-à-vis Labour's 24%), while Reform UK would obtain an incredible 24% (Poll of Polls 2025). It is likely Labour's rise in taxes and perception of softer tones on immigration, if only apparent – have opened the gates to a clearly neoliberal, nationalist and anti-immigration force. Whatever will happen in the coming years, it is clear that British nationalist neoliberalism is a force to be reckoned with.

CHAPTER 6

Russia and Authoritarian Neoliberalism

As we have seen, in several countries neoliberalism has been imposed from above, often in a technocratic manner and with the cooperation of at least a fraction of the national bourgeoisie. In other countries neoliberalism has ultimately paved the way to discontent and facilitated the emergence of nationalist forces, which have been supported by nationally oriented businesses and have adopted increasingly authoritarian and nationalist policies while remaining within a formally democratic framework. Yet other countries have moved from authoritarianism to authoritarianism, with a brief and usually fragile democratic interlude. Precisely during that interlude, however, the unleashing of neoliberal policies led to a rapid return to authoritarianism and to the consolidation of the most traditional, idealtypical case of combination between authoritarianism and neoliberalism.

Russia belongs to this third group. The 'shock therapy' and the structural reforms of the early 1990s in the former USSR and the European Soviet bloc triggered a chain of reactions which over time led to Putin's regime in Russia and to broadly similar ones in neighbouring and comparable states (on Kazakhstan and Uzbekistan see Gallo 2021; on the former Soviet space see Lane 2013). The seeds of neoliberalism were already brewing in Russian politics in the mid- and late 1980s, the days of Gorbachev's *perestroika*. Russian neoliberalism has not been fully imposed from outside and above; it has also domestic origins, in Russia and the rest of the Soviet Union. Certainly, Gorbachev had little or nothing to do with neoliberalism (Rutland 2013: 337) and his momentous reformist attempt, at least in its early stages, aimed at *reshaping* communism and state planning, not *replacing* them. Yet it is important to remember that *perestroika* was in part a response to a neoliberal offensive which had launched on a global scale under Reagan in the early 1980s (and in part, even earlier, in Carter's presidency's final stages). Additionally, *perestroika* would unleash pro-market forces which in a few years would contribute to the end of the USSR and the birth of an entirely new state, the Russian Federation, together with other 14 post-communist republics. In the periphery of the Soviet system neoliberal ideas were in fact already circulating (Rupprecht 2020). Since 1986 a group of Russian economists and scholars had started meeting outside what was then Leningrad, in a place called Snake Hill (*Zmeinaya Gorka*). Among these early Russian neoliberals, we can recall the Muscovite, Larisa Piyasheva, who was a convinced Hayekian economist; the pro-authoritarianism historian, Andranik

Migarjan; the pro-Pinochet economist, Vitaly Nayshul (Rupprecht 2020: 8). Yet neoliberal ideas remained distant and detached from political practice, at least until the breakup of the USSR. Gorbachev had introduced elements of a market economy, but within the temporarily resilient framework of Soviet economic planning.

In the economic, social, nationalist and international convulsions which followed the late 1980s' changes, the once-shining star of Gorbachev declined in parallel with the rise of a charismatic reformer, if at times erratic, unpredictable and populist: Boris Yeltsin. Neither an expert nor particularly competent on economic matters, Yeltsin became President of Russia in the 1991 elections, when he defeated Communist opponents, spoke, if vaguely, about democracy, and called for more autonomy for the Russian Republic (Steele 1991). He would seize his chance by defying a military coup (largely orchestrated by the traditional security apparatuses) against Gorbachev on 18 August 1991, after which he raised to the position of leading figure in what remained of the USSR. He later quite suddenly agreed on the dissolution of the union with his counterparts in Belarus and Ukraine, in the much-debated Belavezha Accords of 8 December 1991 (Shushkevich 2013). On 25 December the Soviet flag waved for the last time over the Kremlin. It was now Russia's and Yeltsin's hour.

1 The Age of Shocking Reforms

Yeltsin set up a strongly pro-market and rather pro-Western cabinet. His Foreign Minister, Andrei Kozyrev, was in favour of good relations with the USA and Europe and approved of liberalism and the market economy (Kozyrev 1991; Kubicek 1999). Yegor Gaidar (1956–2009), who was appointed to oversee the Economy and Finance portfolio, was a famous liberal economist with some good reputation in the West (Columbia University 2007). Anatoly Chubais, responsible for privatisations, was a well-known scholar and had already started privatising programmes in Leningrad in 1990 (Commanding Heights 2012). In other words, there was a significant neoliberal component which had origins in Russia. In the meantime, the IMF, Western governments (especially the US Treasury) and their leading economic advisors (Jeffrey Sachs from Harvard University was the most famous of them) were attending to the double transition, from authoritarianism to democracy as well as from a planned to a market economy. Come 2 January 1992, Yeltsin and Gaidar adopted a vast range of neoliberal measures, which they included in the so-called 'shock therapy'. In other words, the thinking was: the earlier the reforms, the better. More reforms, and all together, the better. And shock it was.

In few hours and days, and amidst incredible uncertainty, in a huge country which had long been almost totally unfamiliar with a market economy, many policies were abruptly adopted: the liberalisation of prices, foreign trade, foreign exchange; a rise in interest rates; the announcement of massive privatisation plans, and other wide-ranging pro-market measures (Murrell 1993: 131–7). The key idea was that the depth and simultaneity of several economic reforms adopted at the same time would have maximised their positive effects and would have lent credibility to a country willing to undertake a rigorous transformation towards a market economy. Additionally, the 'shock' would have made a return to any form of socialism or communism basically impossible. Yet the effects were so challenging – and shocking indeed – that in 1993 there already was widespread criticism (Murrell 1993), not to mention rampant poverty; in 1992 alone, the GDP collapsed by 14.5% (The World Bank 2025a), while prices were skyrocketing, basic services started shrinking and politics entered a phase of turbulences both at a macro and a micro level. Neoliberalism's initial impact on Russia was tremendous. After all, the incompatibility between shock therapy and democracy has been widely recognised (Marangos 2004).

Towards the end of 1992 inflation was reaching 1,600% (Rutland 2013: 346). The effects of the shock, which had been contained in other countries (for instance, Poland), were terrible. Its justification lay in the perceived necessity to convey credibility and will to change to markets and investors, who may have been cautious considering Russia's poor history as a market economy, its communist legacy, and actual issues – the newly-born state had inherited an enormous public and external debt from the USSR. The reformers had also to engage with domestic infighting. The old communist *nomenklatura* was in part still in its place; many of its members took advantage and benefitted from early privatisations. Gaidar's battle was a daunting one, against both some of the old forces and large swathes of the Russian population, which was impoverished and felt ruined by the market transition, which brought about the demise of many welfare provisions. Furthermore, it was a battle against fractions of the communist regime which in few years would create an oligarchy instead of an idealised market economy; they would set up a series of oligopolies in the place of competition. The transition, as Chubais would cynically put it, was only 5% economics and 95% politics (Rutland 2013: 342). The difficulties of the reforms' early stages, in the 1990s' first half, have later spurred reflections by key protagonists such as Gaidar himself (1999), who recalled his loneliness and marginalisation, and the best-known US academic advisor to the Russian government, Jeffrey Sachs (2012).

Sachs (2012) defended his work in Russia and laid the blame for the problems onto a range of different actors: the IMF, the USA and the Russian authorities.

In the first place, the IMF and the World Bank never intervened with any economic assistance, which, in Sachs's view (2012: 6) should have been in the range of $15bn per year for many years and should have consisted of both grants and concessional loans. This would have been a kind of 'Marshall Plan' for Russia and the former Soviet bloc. Why did the Washington Consensus institutions refuse support? Why was the USA reluctant to aid, under both Bush Sr and Clinton? After all, Russia could have become a key market and a privileged resource provider. The USA's (and the EU's, especially Germany's) attitude remains open to interpretation. Was the West interested in dealing with a weakened Russia in the role of a cheap exporter of raw materials, fossil fuels and commodities? Was the West intent on demolishing Soviet Russia's industrial legacy? Was the USA, itself facing economic problems under Bush Sr, unable and unwilling to help? As to Sachs, he also criticised the inefficiencies, corruption and infighting within the Russian state. In particular, he attacked the legislature's resistance to change, its constant opposition to Gaidar, the errors of the Central Bank Governor, Viktor Gerashchenko, and Yeltsin's lack of interest in economic matters throughout 1993 (was he more interested in enhancing the country's international status or busy fighting his own internal enemies?). Cronyism was rife and influenced privatisations, in which Sachs had almost no involvement, and corruption was particularly widespread in politically 'hot', strategic industries such as that of fossil fuels. After all, this should be no surprise; it has happened worldwide.

While a massive plan of economic support may have contributed to the establishment of a more sustainable and efficient form of Russian capitalism, Sachs's support to the 'shock therapy' testifies to his difficulties in dealing with Russia's historical specificities and to the importance of fine-tuning any type of economic or financial intervention. Previous experiences of neoliberalisation, such as that of Poland (where Sachs had also played an advisory role) or the Czech Republic, had taken place in very different contexts; also, their 'success' is far from controversial; suffice to say that in the most symbolic case of a successful market transition – Poland – the unemployment rate was still a staggering 17.7% in 2005 (The World Bank 2025e). If perhaps more limited than in other countries, Gaidar's neoliberal reforms immediately paved the way to a return of authoritarianism, as was expressed by the reaction of a part of the old, ex-communist elites and the rapidly emerging nationalist ones. This was possible also because, at the same time, Russia was plunging into desperate socio-economic conditions. As of 1993, inflation was still around 900% (The World Bank 2024b). Nor was politics of any help.

Yeltsin immediately lost the support of his Vice President, the nationalist and war veteran, Alexander Rutskoy. Meanwhile, Chubais started a programme of massive voucher privatisations, which, after some initial success (Boycko, Shleifer and Vishny 1993), continued with very mixed results in a country which was still unfamiliar with private ownership. Strong opposition to privatisations and liberalisations was coming from the legislative bodies, that is, the Congress of People's Deputies of Russia and its expression, the Supreme Soviet of Russia, whose members were mainly from the old party hierarchy and whose leader, Ruslan Khasbulatov, a Chechen and a former ally of Yeltsin's, was a strong opponent of neoliberal reforms (Khasbulatov 1993). A temporary compromise was reached in December 1992, when Gaidar was replaced by the experienced and pragmatic former Minister of the Gas Industry and founder of Gazprom, Viktor Chernomyrdin, a kind of astute technocrat in the middle of heated political confrontations (Erlanger 1992).

1993 would immediately become a year of violent authoritarianism. The clash between legislative and executive became increasingly harsher, with Congress and the Supreme Soviet rejecting any constitutional proposal from the President and the President taking on increasingly stronger powers; Yeltsin avoided impeachment and was emboldened by the positive result of a referendum on confidence in him (on 25 April, 59.9% of the electorate expressed confidence; Clem and Craumer 1993), while parts of the federation (Tatarstan and above all Chechnya) started attempting to escape Moscow's control. When Yeltsin, acting against the Constitution, dissolved Congress on 21 September 1993, the legislature responded by nominating Rutskoy Acting President. In 1992 Rutskoy had already denounced Yeltsin's policies as 'economic genocide' (Ferdinand 1992). The executive-legislative standoff ended with street fighting and an armed conflict around the Ostankino Television Tower and Congress (in Moscow), which was eventually won by Yeltsin and the pro-Western forces thanks to the decisive support of the army (Brudny 1995). Yet, in what became a real battlefield, at least more than a hundred people were left dead (Goncharenko 2018). Russia's infant democracy was already ailing, wrecked by the economic and political effects of neoliberal reforms and by the stalemate between authoritarian supporters of both the 'old' and the 'new' in the country.

Nevertheless, on 12 December 1993 Russian citizens went to the elections for the first time in the post-communist era. On the same occasion, they were also asked to vote for a new constitutional draft proposed by Yeltsin. The results were mixed but confirmed Russia's new authoritarian and nationalist tendencies. On the one hand, authoritarian forces did well in the Congress vote. The far-right Liberal Democratic Party of Russia (*Liberalno-demokraticheskaya Partiya Rossii*, LDPR) even came first, with 22.9% of the votes. Its ultranationalist leader, Vladimir Zhirinovsky, was calling for Russia's expansion, racist and fascist policies and was an early example of ultra-nationalist populism (Kipp 1994; Lentini 1995). Simultaneously, the new Communist Party, led by Gennady Zyuganov, obtained 12.4% of the votes (slightly less than Gaidar's Choice of Russia, *Vybor Rossii*, which ended up with a disappointing 15.5%) and ran on a platform which combined communism with nationalism (Lester 1997). On the other hand, a new Constitution, which had been drafted by a special assembly and provided for a strong presidency, was adopted by referendum with a majority of 58.43% of the voters (Sakwa 2020a). While it contained some elements of liberalism and democracy, it would be subsequently used to expand presidential powers in an authoritarian sense (President of Russia 2010).

Russia's underlying social and economic problems, however, were very far from being resolved. While inflation was slowly subsiding, in 1994 Russia's GDP declined by 12.6%, followed by −4.1% in 1995 and −3.8% in 1996 (The World Bank 2025a). Chernomyrdin's cautious and technocratic government continued with moderate reforms adopted by some of his few liberal ministers. Yevgeny Yasin, Minister of the Economy between 1994 and 1997, was an independent liberal economist. Oleg Davydov, Minister of Foreign Economic Relations (1994–7), started negotiations with the WTO. Yet the emerging political figure of the years 1993–6 was the Communist leader, Gennady Zyuganov. In the middle of seemingly endless impoverishment, military engagement in Chechnya (since December 1994) and economic meltdown at home, the sinister promise of a 'nationalist' socialism, with emphasis on traditional Russian and Soviet values, social cohesion and collectivist inspiration, started having some purchase (Vujacic 1996) and contributed to the decline in popularity of Zhirinovsky's ultra nationalist right to the benefit of Zyuganov's Communists.

Aside from economic indicators, Russia was also showing signs of societal and demographic collapse. In 1994 and 1995, life expectancy went down (The World Bank 2022); Russia's demographic and economic decline since *perestroika* had been bigger than that of Germany in the early 1930s (Nolan 1995).

Reforms still had support, but a limited one. With Yeltsin's backing, Chernomyrdin and a group of technocrats and businesspeople founded a new centrist party, Our Home – Russia (*Nash Dom – Rossiya*, NDR). Another moderate and reformist group, Yabloko, took shape around the economist, Grigory Yavlinsky, and proposed a more socially oriented form of liberalism, in addition to insisting on the fight against corruption (White, Wyman and Oates 1997: 770). Yet nationalism, patriotism and communist nostalgia were the electors' strongest sentiments. They largely contributed to the outcome of the 1995 legislative vote, when the Communists ended up as the most voted party, with 22.7% of the preferences and 150 seats. Zyuganov's party had about one million members and was highly structured; its popularity was highest among senior Russians, in rural areas, among workers and pensioners. Zhirinovsky's LDPR, which was a distant second with 11.4% of the votes, enjoyed stronger support in the military. Yabloko (7%) attracted younger and highly educated voters. The NDR obtained only 55 seats and ended up third in terms of votes. All in all, the 1995 elections, despite minor controversies about their fairness, expressed a clear outcome; they confirmed Yeltsin's and Chernomyrdin's severe problems, even if no party gained enough support to claim a hegemonic position (White, Wyman and Oates 1997: 786).

In many ways, in a president-dominated system, the 1995 *Duma* vote was a prologue to the Summer 1996 (with the first of two rounds on 16 June) Kremlin elections, the first since the USSR's end. The field of candidates looked extremely 'crowded' and competitive. Together with Yeltsin, Zhirinovsky and the largely favourite Zyuganov, in fact even a rather unpopular Gorbachev, the liberal, Yavlinsky, and a popular (and populist) general, Alexander Lebed, who advocated for the end of the Chechen war and against corruption, made a presidential bid.

Because of the early 1990s' socio-economic decline, Yeltsin's popularity was in shatters. His campaign was a tremendously uphill battle and the President himself was not sure whether to run or not (McFaul 1997). And yet, with characteristic political intuition and resolve, on 15 February he decided to attempt (Hockstader 1996). His reformist campaign demonstrated a good degree of political astuteness. Originally inclined to run on a nationalist platform, Yeltsin chose to transform the campaign into a struggle between him and Zyuganov's communism, which he framed as a clash between the future and the past. Together with anti-communism he mobilised the economic firepower of the early oligarchs, who decided to use their financial might to support him, both legally and semilegally (Sakwa 2020a: 192–93). Chubais became the leader of Yeltsin's official campaign, and the oligarchs of the *semibankirschina* (the 'seven bankers'), led by the media moghul, Boris Berezovsky, rallied around the president. Among the seven (in reality, they were more) pro-Yeltsin businessmen of the *semibankirschina* there were a young and rampant trader, Mikhail Khodorkovsky; bankers such as Fridman, Potanin, Smolensky and Vinogradov; two media tycoons, Berezovsky and Gusinsky; a young collaborator of Berezovsky, Roman Abramovich; a technocrat and banker, Petr Aven. These new 'oligarchs' lent capital to the government in exchange for shares in some companies (Sakwa 2020: 191–92) in case of government default – an operation which gave them effective leverage over the state ('loans for shares'). In addition to financial and media support, Yeltsin engaged in relentless campaigning around the country (Brudny 1997: 262–63) and enjoyed the benefits of a massive IMF loan of some $10 billion (Sakwa 2020a: 193). Together with the backup of British and especially USA advisers, Yeltsin could also reap the benefits of a ceasefire with Chechen rebels on 27 May 1996. In June, polls started being favourable to him for the first time. This happened also because Zyuganov had begun moving backwards. His strategy of endorsing nationalism and eroding Zhirinovsky's support, especially by promising a nationalist foreign policy, was initially successful but would eventually backfire. The slogan "Russia, Motherland, the Nation" (Brudny 1997: 267) was not really appealing to younger generations. Zyuganov surprisingly lost the first round of the poll with 32.5% of the votes, a slight defeat to Yeltsin's 35.8. Yet the Communist candidate had tremendously lost steam. Yeltsin's election campaign managed to secure the endorsement of Lebed, who had garnered a significant 14.5% in the first round. With Zhirinovsky downsized to 5.7%, the way to the Kremlin was again paved for Yeltsin. In the second round the incumbent secured 53.82% of the votes versus Zyuganov's 40.31 (Sakwa 2020a: 217).

The new cabinet reflected the increased influence of oligarchs and businesses. It was a clearly neoliberal government, if somewhat more moderate than the earlier Yeltsin-Gaidar cabinets. While the enigmatic and ambitious Chernomyrdin was reappointed Prime Minister, the banker, Vladimir Potanin, became one of the First Deputy Prime Ministers. Yeltsin balanced Potanin's appointment with that of the more traditionalist, Yevgeny Primakov, as Minister of Foreign Affairs. Primakov, a respected scholar of international affairs (with expertise on the Middle East and especially Arab politics) and a diplomat, had been a KGB agent and later the Director of the SVR, the *Sluzhba Vneshney Razvedki*, that is, the Foreign Intelligence Service (1991–96). He incarnated a more pro-Soviet and statist mindset. Despite changes in personnel, however, economic conditions hardly improved. A distressed Yeltsin started suffering from severe health issues; in March 1997 he and Chernomyrdin tried to inject new reformist energy into the government by again resorting to technocrats such as Anatoly Chubais and the highly regarded independent scholar and corruption-fighter, Boris Nemtsov, as Deputy PMs (Sakwa 2020a: 241).

In 1997, for the first time since independence, the Russian economy was recording growth, if limited (+1.4%; The World Bank 2025a). Yeltsin felt it was time to speed up with reforms and strike a blow to Chernomyrdin's ambivalent aspirations. On 23 March 1998, while the East Asian financial crisis was already affecting Russian exports, Yeltsin appointed Sergey Kiriyenko, a 35-year-old economist and technocrat, Acting Prime Minister. About a month later, Kiriyenko formed a government of economists, jurists and other experts. Among them, a prominent place was occupied by Kiriyenko's mentor, Nemtsov, along with several other liberal economists, such as Viktor Krishtenko and

Oksana Dmitriyeva. The new government quickly found itself in the middle of a deep crisis and squeezed between many obstacles. Banks and the oligarchs were resisting taxation; international investors started losing trust; defending the rouble proved a challenging task; Kiriyenko was forced to let the state partly default on 17 August 1998 and was dismissed six days later (Sakwa 2020a: 243). Russia was at a turning point. Its first and lasting liaison with neoliberalism and the global economy had not worked (Robinson 1999). While the economy was again losing heavily (−5.3% in 1998; The World Bank 2025a), and Yeltsin was severely ill, new (even if 'old' and backward-looking) forces were gaining prominence. The former intelligence head, Yevgeny Primakov, a *silovik*, a 'man of force', that is, a representative of the security services, would soon be appointed Prime Minister.

2 Primakov's *Intermezzo*

Primakov had diplomatic and intellectual capital and vast experience in the intelligence field. As an international affairs scholar and practitioner, he was well-known for a fundamentally anti-USA posture, which was expressed in the so-called 'Primakov doctrine' (Weitz 2017). The doctrine advocated for a Russian sphere of influence in the Middle East and Central Asia, and some political proximity to states such as Iran, India and especially China. But what were the effects of such doctrine on Russia's economic policies and economics? Was Russia retrenching and rejecting Western neoliberalism? In a sense, it was. Primakov knew what Russia was against, but not exactly what it could stand for. As a pragmatic diplomatist, he could even support some reforms; yet as a leader of a non-reformist cabinet, he clearly stood against them. In Primakov's cabinet there were two Communists, among whom Yuri Maslyukov was the First Deputy Chairman of the Government for Economy and Finance; there was also and one representative of the LDPR. The reformists had disappeared, apart from the moderate banker, Boris Fyodorov.

Primakov refocused on stronger state intervention (Kotz 1999). The age of what he would later call 'pseudoliberals' (Primakov 2013) was over. In his view, there were no conditions or possibilities for neoliberalism in Russia. Supported by rising oil and gas prices and by rouble devaluation, Primakov presided over a first period of significant economic growth – about 6.4% throughout 1999 (The World Bank 2025a). This combined with a turning point in foreign policy, symbolised by the 'Primakov loop' on 24 March 1999, when the Prime Minister ordered his flight to the USA to turn back, as a reaction to the beginning of NATO's bombing of former Yugoslavia (BBC 2015b). Primakov's move expressed a double shift, in foreign and economic policies. It was time to reject the superficial allure of Western-sponsored politics and economics.

Yet Primakov's popularity and prestige may have not pleased Yeltsin, who was also looking for a successor. Even more importantly, Primakov had reopened to the Communists and had closed to reformers. On 13 May 1999, Yeltsin decided to replace Primakov with Sergei Stepashin, another former intelligence agent and Interior Minister under Primakov. Stepashin's cabinet was mostly composed of independents while there were no Communist Party members at all. Yet the new PM's lack of experience and charisma led to another change of mind of a beleaguered Yeltsin, who on 9 August dismissed Stepashin, handed the role of PM to a little-known Vladimir Putin and proposed the latter's candidature also for the role of President (Rosenberg 2019).

A former KGB officer with extensive experience in Dresden (1975–91), Putin had also worked in the more liberal Government of St Petersburg (1990–96) and later moved to Moscow to become the director of the KGB's successor, the FSB (*Federal'naya Sluzhba Bezopasnosti*), in 1998. Despite somewhat limited political credentials and lack of experience at the highest level, his 'law-and-order' approach to politics, his brutally effective handling of the Second Chechen War (1999–2009) and his relative distance from the oligarchs' power games, made Putin rapidly popular among ordinary Russians and interesting to Yeltsin. At a time of extreme uncertainty and lasting, massive economic problems, Putin started to be seen as a solid choice for Russia's future (Sakwa 2020a: 247). Probably, as of 1999, few imagined the political, economic, international and cultural consequences of Putin's appointment. But how exactly has the new leader – ever since in power as Prime Minister or President – combined authoritarianism with neoliberalism throughout his long political career?

3 Putin and Neoliberalism: an Ambiguous Relationship

In a sense, Putin's choice as a leader represented a shift from the era of shock therapies, deregulations, and privatisations. The shift towards a more statist understanding of politics had already started with Yeltsin's appointment of Primakov in 1998 and had continued with that of the more malleable, Sergei Stepashin, in 1999. But what about Putin? What were his plans? And how did he and his various teams relate to the ideas and practices of neoliberalism in Russia's problematic socio-economic context? Additionally, what were Putin's views on democracy and authoritarianism?

To start with, once in power Putin had to think about a vision, an ideology, and a party organisation as well. In September 1999 Yeltsin and Putin supported the foundation of a new party: *Yedinstvo* (Unity). It competed in the December Duma elections with the favour of the media and against robust opponents such as the Communists, Zhirinovsky's bloc, Yabloko and especially the newly-born OVR (*Otečestvo – Vsya Rossiya*; Fatherland – All Russia), led by Primakov and the popular mayor of Moscow, Yuri Luzhkov. Unity obtained a surprisingly high 23.8% of the votes, just below the downsized Communists (24.8%), while OVR stopped at a modest 13.6% (McFaul 1999). Yeltsin decided it was time to take advantage of the momentum; 1999 had also been the first year of strong economic growth since the USSR's end. On 31 December 1999, he resigned from the presidency and Putin became Acting President. Due to his links with some oligarchs (notably, Berezovsky) and their control over the media, Yeltsin probably thought it was the best time to pave the way for the Kremlin race to the loyal, apparently unassuming, Vladimir Putin, and provide him with the opportunity to shape his own image in a positive way. In exchange, Putin immediately offered guarantees to Russia's first President and his family that there would be no prosecutions related to potential charges of corruption (Traynor 2000a).

As a KGB officer, Putin was seen as a possible supporter of a return to a strong, better organised, more interventionist state; and of course, to a less liberal and less democratic one (Nesvetailova 2005: 249). In the run-up to the 2000 presidential elections, Putin upheld a generic stance on specific policies and played on his well-crafted image as a strong, effective leader who was putting a brutal end to the Chechen conflict, proposing a 'law-and-order' approach to Russia's problems and restoring the pride of a former superpower whose GDP had become smaller than Switzerland's or Taiwan's (WITS 2024). How Putin initially deciphered neoliberalism remains though more difficult to guess. In principle, he was in favour of a market economy, but with more state intervention in it; and he envisaged a state capable of restoring economic conditions more aligned with Russia's political history and traditions. This latent ambiguity is well-expressed by Putin's words in late 1999 (Karasik 2000: 181):

> Russia will not soon become, if it ever becomes, a second copy of, say, the U.S. or England, where liberal values have deep historical traditions. ... [...].... A strong state is for Russians not an anomaly. ... [...].... but on the contrary is the source and guarantor of order, the initiator and main driving force of all change.

'Discipline' and 'patriotism' were other key words used by Putin; after a decade of chaos and foreign economic interventions such words resonated with many Russians. But how would Putin resolve the inherent tension between order and change, between stability and progress? Here we are left rather clueless.

The young leader's success was prepared by many factors. Both Luzhkov and Primakov, after the December electoral disappointment, renounced their candidacy to the Kremlin. Zyuganov partly opened to neoliberalism and argued in favour of a 'regulated market' (BBC 2000). Yavlinsky was a victim of moments of hate campaign which targeted Jews and homosexuals and their presumed links with liberal politicians like him (Traynor 2000b). These were already examples of authoritarian neoliberalism and its toxicity. They somehow worked and, together with the benefits of media support, can explain Putin's landslide win, despite his relative lack of experience and rather limited political exposure at the highest levels. He won in the first round with 52.9% of the votes; Zyuganov was a distant second (29.2%) and Yavlinsky a very distant third (5.8%; Sakwa 2020a: 217–18). The new cabinet immediately reflected Putin's imprint. It was full of liberal economists who had collaborated with him during his time at the Government of St Petersburg (1990–96). The rather lacklustre new Prime Minister, who would soon become a victim of Putin's centralising drive, was Mikhail Kasyanov, a technocrat who had experience as a Minister of Finance and a negotiator of Russia's international debt. Most prominent were scholars and practitioners such as: Alexei Kudrin, Minister of Finance and financial economist with a background in St Petersburg; Herman Gref, another St Petersburger, a financial technocrat and new Minister of Economic Development and Trade; Putin's adviser, the well-known liberal economist, Andrey Illarionov; last but not least, the moderate diplomat, Igor Ivanov, as Minister of Foreign Affairs (Sakwa 2020a). While the cabinet members' names seemed to express a clear neoliberal outlook, as we will see, Putin would always pursue a pragmatic and flexible policy.

How much of Putin's early economic policy was neoliberal and how much of it was a 'hollow paradigm' (Khmelnitskaya 2021), that is, an attempt to engage with, and mobilise, policy experts, specialists, technocrats, and the broader civil society without any 'real' effects and without sharing any 'real' power? In other words, how far were Putin's neoliberal plans mostly performative and devoid of substance?

As a matter of fact, Putin early embarked on a strong course of neoliberal reforms. He decided to embrace the world's dominant political paradigm and to aim at attracting Western attention – and Western investments. In most aspects, Russia's economic and foreign policies were and are often intertwined. According to Matveev (2019: 36),

> Thus the connection between neoliberalism and authoritarian tendencies characterized not just the period of 'shock therapy', but the period of Putin's early reforms as well.

The reforms were rather significant. As early as August 2000 Putin introduced a 13% flat tax on personal incomes (Ivanova, Keen and Clemm 2005), which would be followed by other cuts and simplifications in tax rates in the subsequent years. Fiscal revenues, which had been declining because of persistent evasion, rose significantly, even if the effects of the flat tax on the Russian economy have remained largely controversial (Ivanova, Keen and Clemm 2005; Gorodnichenko, Martínez-Vázquez and Sabirianova Peter 2008). Private pension funds were introduced as well as a new Labour Code (2001) which made it easier to dismiss workers (Matveev 2019: 35). Economic growth responded tremendously well: after a 10% peak in 2000, it stabilised at 5.1 and 4.7% in the two following years (The World Bank 2025a).

Another important reform, which was adopted towards the end of Putin's first presidential mandate (January 2004), was the introduction of a stabilisation fund (Hanson and Teague 2013: 13), which aimed at cushioning the country's public finances in case of a decline in oil prices. Putin and Kudrin were well-aware that the economic achievements of the early 2000s were also linked to the high prices of oil, gas and other commodities. Yet, while Kudrin and other technocrats managed to transform parts of the state in a more neoliberal way (Huskey 2010), in order to reaffirm the strength of the public sector and provide opportunities to the growing lobby of *siloviki*, Putin had to face the oligarchs and the manner they had captured state power under Yeltsin. After all, even in the early stages of Kasyanov's government, corruption was extremely high (Sakwa 2020a: 247). Putin intended to gain control over the media, and investigations on media barons such as Gusinsky and Berezovsky began soon (Tompson 2005: 182). Berezovsky had paved the way for Putin's succession to Yeltsin, but this fact did not help him at all (Duncan 2007: 3). His tensions with Putin started at least in 2000, when Berezovsky's ORT TV began criticising the President, and continued in 2001, when his media empire was taken over by the Russian state and Berezovsky was forced to settle in London as an exile (Elder 2013a). Meanwhile, on 28 July 2000 Putin had met the 21 most important oligarchs, excluding Gusinsky and Berezovsky. It seems that he had proposed (in fact, imposed) a kind of deal: Putin would have not prosecuted them if they had stayed away from opposing him and limited their activities to business (Duncan 2007: 10; Guriev and Rachinsky 2005). Was Putin intent on creating a 'state market' on the ashes of a 'market state' (Sakwa 2020a: 116)? Certainly, he wanted to give shape to a more stable, predictable political system, with the state, not the market (or private plutocrats) in the driving seat; and the state should have been a rather authoritarian one, with little room for the 'niceties' of democratic debate and peaceful exchanges of views. After all, in his view Yeltsin's flawed democratic experiment had led to the emergence of powerful and greedy economic oligopolies. Putin's political moves immediately reflected the collaboration, but also the tensions between authoritarianism and neoliberalism. How far could an open market economy combine with Western geopolitical pressures and the reaction they engendered among the *siloviki* and a re-emerging Russian securitocracy?

A decisive passage in the transition to strong authoritarianism was the story of the rapidly emerging oligarch, Mikhail Khodorkovsky. Starting in the age of *perestroika*, the young chemical engineer set up various businesses, in import-export, finance, banking, oil; later he won Yeltsin's support. When he started entering the oil industry, however, after dubious privatisation processes, some problems emerged. Under Putin's presidency, oil and gas became of strategic state importance, and the President had made it clear the state would have controlled them, directly or indirectly. In 2003, Khodorkovsky started modernising his new oil company, Yukos, and initiated talks of a merger with another oligarch, Roman Abramovich, who owned the oil company, Sibneft (Sakwa 2014). Additionally, Khodorkovsky was expanding its activities outside Russia and supposedly had conversations with large US majors like ExxonMobil and ChevronTexaco. In the same 2003 he became Russia's richest person and one of the world's wealthiest (BBC News 2013). If we add to his business expansion the fact that he and some of his collaborators were funding liberal opposition parties and even the Communists, we can understand why Khodorkovsky drew Putin's attention and wrath (Gessen 2012; Sakwa 2014).

In October 2003 the magnate was arrested, with a list of allegations ranging from tax evasion and fraud to other and dubious ones. There is little doubt that the trial was politically motivated; it led to a sentence of nine years to be spent in a penal colony. Among many possible explanations, what is more important in giving account of Putin's behaviour? After all, Khodorkovsky was contributing to the Russian economy's rapid growth of the early 2000s. His punishment may be due to many causes. Khodorkovsky had made no mystery of his economic and political ambitions and was creating a mighty pole of economic and political power. Moreover, and perhaps crucially, opening the gates of the energy industry to major US corporations was against Putin's core political views, especially at a time when the Russian economy was still internationally fragile. Yet the way the 'Khodorkovsky affair' was handled suggests there was something more. Putin chiefly wanted to hit a blow to the oligarchs and teach them a lesson (Tompson 2005). The ghosts of chaos and instability which had haunted the Yeltsin era had to be eliminated once and for all. Russia was not against the market, but it should have been one controlled by the state, and the executive in particular; a Putin-style neoliberalism, informed by nationalism, also in the economic domain, and authoritarianism.

The authoritarian turn was also an effect of other events. Putin's early collaboration with the West, as had been the case in the Afghanistan war and in the global war on terror, was about to end. Russia was against the Iraq war (2003), which after all divided the EU (and the world) as well and was partly the outcome of powerful unilateral and unipolar forces in the USA such as those of the neoconservatives and the military-industrial lobbies. In part as a reaction to worsening relations with the West, Putin started increasingly relying on his own men (usually they were men), both the St Petersburg's liberals and the *siloviki*, that is, more specifically, "the representatives or former representatives of the security services" (Duncan 2007: 10), with whom Putin had spent a large part of his career and whose *habitus* he basically shared. Russian politics was becoming more authoritarian, rigid, and conservative. Putin's success at the 2003 Duma vote can in part be explained by Chechnya's stabilisation as well as by fast economic growth (7.3% in 2003; The World Bank 2025a), but also by pro-Putin media campaigns as well as by problems in the elections themselves and their regularity (OSCE 2003). In several aspects the 2003 vote was bordering that of a fully authoritarian regime (refworld 2024).

A new party, 'United Russia' (*Yedinaya Rossiya*, YR), which was the result of a merger between Putin-supporting Unity and the OVR, garnered a massive 37.6% of the votes and 222 seats, leaving the stagnant Communists (12.6%) and the LDPR (11.5%) way behind. All other parties, except the nationalist *Rodina* ('Motherland'; 9%), did not even reach the representation threshold of 5% (Sakwa 2020a: 326). Putin was now in control of the legislature. He could dismiss Kasyanov, a victim of Putin's early centralisation of power, and prepare the presidential elections by appointing premier the less-known Mikhail Fradkov, an economist rumoured to enjoy sympathies among the *siloviki* (Sakwa 2020a: 248). Ivanov was replaced as Foreign Minister by the experienced diplomat, Sergei Lavrov, while Gref and Kudrin maintained their positions. Five new Ministers were from United Russia; everyone else was independent, once again highlighting the importance of technocratic knowledge and expertise in Putin's cabinets.

The 2004 elections marked the beginning of a more authoritarian phase. Putin, who had dominated the state media in the election run-up, won with more than 71% of the votes. The only liberal opponent, Irina Khakamada, did not go beyond a disappointing 3.8%; the lacklustre Communist, Nikolay Kharitonov, ended up with a modest 13.7%. All in all, the elections' democratic nature was clearly flawed (OSCE 2004). Western pressure was having somehow opposite effects.

Western (especially US) pressure was in fact becoming a key factor in shaping Russia's political economy. In November 2003, Georgia witnessed the first of the so-called 'coloured revolutions', the Rose Revolution, in which cuts in IMF/USA aid and Western support to pro-democracy groups brought to an end the semi-authoritarian Shevardnadze regime. One year later, Ukraine's Orange Revolution empowered the reformist, Viktor Yuschchenko, who replaced the more pro-Russian candidate, Viktor Yanukovych. Early in 2005, Soviet-educated Askar Akayev, President of Kyrgyzstan, fled the country to leave room to Kurmanbek Bakiyev. Although these uprisings had strong domestic causes and support, their endorsement in the USA and the EU strained relations between on the one hand Washington and Bruxelles and on the other Moscow (Ó Beacháin and Polese, eds., 2010). Furthermore, NATO had continued expanding eastwards. The Czech Republic, Hungary and Poland joined it in 1999; Bulgaria, Estonia, Latvia, Lithuania, Romania, Slovakia and Slovenia followed suit in 2004. There were also early talks about Georgia, Ukraine and countries in the Balkans. Russia felt excluded and threatened by these developments and Putin expressed his clear concerns in a famous speech at the Munich Security Conference in 2007 (President of Russia 2007). Why would NATO keep expanding? To defend and protect a part of Europe from whom? Certainly, NATO's enlargement did not go down well in the Kremlin, particularly among former KGB officers who had fresh experience of the Cold war.

Putin took note and thought it was also time to concentrate domestic efforts on what he held most important to the Russian economy, that is, fossil fuels and their state control. Oil prices in the early 2000s were high and contributed to Russia's economic rise; yet the country needed stronger growth to propel its economic and political ambitions; in 2004 its GDP was still just the world's 16th biggest, that is, lower than far smaller countries such as The Netherlands' or South Korea's (IMF 2024).

Rosneft was already Russia's largest oil major. After acquiring the licence to develop oilfields in Sakhalin, the company purchased Yukos's main assets and became Russia's biggest oil corporation, largely under state control. Meanwhile, under the leadership of Putin loyalists such as Alexei Miller and Dmitry Medvedev, Gazprom became the leader of the gas industry and Russia's biggest company. Was Putin now – also as a reaction to Western political and economic encroachment – turning towards a developmental or *dirigiste* (sometimes also called 'statist') model (Matveev 2019)?

The answer is, yes and no. Certainly, the developmentalist moment became more visible, but developmentalism is not incompatible with neoliberalism. In fact, *dirigisme* saved neoliberalism; traditional developmentalist economies (for instance, in East Asia) fully opened to neoliberalism after a statist phase and combined the two ideologies and sets of practices. As to the creation of bigger state-controlled companies, especially in the energy industry, it was not necessarily a way to cronyism and clientelism, as is for example claimed by Hanson (2007; 2009). Throughout the 2000s in fact Russia remained one of the world's fastest-growing economies (The World Bank 2025a); Gazprom and Rosneft became efficient corporate giants by international standards; the aircraft producers merged into one large company, United Aircraft Corporation (UAC), of which the state is still the main shareholder. At the same time, however, Russia was still a fully neoliberal economy (Matveev 2019: 38). While in 2006 it adopted the National Priority Projects, which were meant to support the welfare state, healthcare, housing, agriculture and education (Matveev 2019: 39), the Finance Minister Kudrin prioritised caution, austerity and the repayment of foreign debt, aims which Russia met in 2006 also thanks to years of high commodity prices and deflationary policies. A degree of welfarism was anyway important to both obtain further popular support and to strengthen capitalism's long-term stability. All in all, the combination of authoritarianism and neoliberalism proved successful to Putin, but up to some point. With better services and higher salaries, a middle class was growing fast. Throughout 2007 Russia's major cities such as Saint Petersburg, Moscow, Nizhny Novgorod, Samara, Chelyabinsk, and others witnessed the start of significant protests, which were dispersed by public force (Lankina 2014). Among the protesters there was a variety of prominent personalities and representatives of important groups, from the neoliberal chess champion Gerry Kasparov to the nationalist, Eduard Limonov, former PM Kasyanov, Irina Khakamada, Andrey Illarionov, far-left forces, but what was missing was something holding all of them together, other than the rejection of Putin's emerging regime. The regime was instead delivering reasonably well in terms of the fundamentals of the economy and stability. These two aspects – a fast-growing, if increasingly unequal, economy and higher stability, including some feeling of restored pride in relations with the West – contributed decisively to the outcome of the 2 December 2007 Duma elections. On the eve of the 'Great recession', Russia's economy had grown by another massive 8.5% (The World Bank 2025a). YR became more and more associated with Putin and proposed a 'Putin's Plan', which was strongly connected to: 1) the idea of a great Russian civilisation; 2) the commitment to building a competitive economy, 3) new quality of life, and 4) a stronger civil society; 5) the establishment of a 'sovereign democracy', that is, a top-down managed regime, which in reality had little to do with sovereignty and even less with democracy (McAllister and White 2008; Sakwa 2016). A sovereign democracy would mainly mean one-party hegemony at home and a confrontational, if mostly defensive, posture with other 'Great Powers' abroad. Yet most Russians, after the collapse of the 1990s, were chiefly interested in good economic standards; Putin-led YR had proven capable of delivering them, at least in part, and was promoting further improvement in basic living conditions.

Despite the achievements mentioned above, YR took no chance and benefitted from an intense and at times unfair election campaign, dominating the media, harassing opponents, intervening directly in schools and universities to enforce compliance, and so on (McAllister and White 2008: 938–43). This time it obtained 64.3% of the votes and 315 seats, becoming a fully-fledged single dominant party. The Communists, the LDPR and Rodina garnered what remained and adopted programmes to some degree aligned with Putin's party. Yabloko and the liberal opposition disappeared (McAllister and White 2008).

Eight years after Putin's accession to the Kremlin, and despite lingering protests, Russia looked more stable and economically far stronger. Yet the price to be paid had been big. Putin had dispossessed some of the early oligarchs, although new ones were emerging and usually had strong loyalty connections with the Kremlin. Economic inequality was high and neoliberalism was co-existing with an increasingly authoritarian regime. The Gini Index had risen from 37.1 to 42.3 (The World Bank n.d.). As of 2007, Russia had 53 billionaires; according to Forbes, only the USA and Germany were home to more of them (Krastev 2007).

The year 2008, which was fraught with a worldwide financial and economic crisis, would bring some change, but in a 'transformist' sense. Some variables would change in order to keep the whole edifice intact.

4 Medvedev's Presidency: a Second *Intermezzo*

Putin was constitutionally prevented from running for a third consecutive term. Who would have replaced him? A *silovik*? A technocrat like Fradkov or the temporary Prime Minister, Viktor Zubkov, who was an expert on financial crime?

Soon after the 2007 Duma elections, Putin announced his choice of Dmitry Medvedev, who would then be confirmed by United Russia. Medvedev reciprocated by expressing his preference for Putin as Prime Minister. How would the tandem work? Which vision would they express? The tandem took centre stage in the middle of the 2007–08 worldwide economic storm. Which solutions did they propose?

A lawyer, a collaborator of Putin's in Saint Petersburg and a moderate politician, Medvedev was generally seen as a Putin loyalist, having managed his presidential campaign in 2000 and having acted as Chairman of Gazprom from 2000 and later as a First Deputy PM (2005–08). He was also seen as generally more liberal and certainly more neoliberal than his mentor. In a state divided into at least four broad (and often overlapping) factions (Sakwa 2011; 2020b: 31–3), Medvedev was seen as a representative of the 'legal liberals' (Sakwa 2020b: 32), that is, those intellectuals and practitioners who aim at achieving a kind of rule of law or, in the German tradition, *Rechtsstaat*, and at eliminating the Russian state's dualism between a liberal constitutional form and a non-democratic, opaque, administrative regime (Sakwa 2010). Legal liberals would be more focused on democracy and rights than, for instance, purely 'economic liberals' such as Kudrin (Sakwa 2020b: 32).

Why did Putin choose Medvedev at a key juncture, in late 2007, when the global financial crisis was worldwide looming large, and neoliberalism was falling into discredit? Possibly Medvedev, with his entourage of legal and economic collaborators, was seen as a solution to both potential economic problems and in relations with the West. Possibly choosing Medvedev was a way to balance between the liberals and the *siloviki*, who had grown in power under Putin. Whatever the reasons, Medvedev's campaign was quite lacklustre, also because he could easily reap the benefits of having been selected by a highly popular Putin, while the opponents were the usual (and by 2008 rather worn out) candidates, Zyuganov and Zhirinovsky. Without much fanfare, on 2 March 2008 Medvedev won with 70.3% of the votes, far more than Zyuganov's 17.7 and Zhirinovsky's 9.4. Even without fraud and irregularities (The Economist 2008), Putin's choice would have likely won anyway.

Since the inauguration speech (American Rhetoric 2008), Medvedev more strongly emphasised values of rights, liberties, economic freedom and innovation. Yet, while the Medvedev-Putin 'tandemocracy' (2008–12) maintained and even strengthened neoliberal characteristics, Russia did not evolve at all in a liberal-democratic direction. The new Putin cabinet, to begin with, was comprised of several *siloviki*. Sergei Ivanov, a career KGB officer, became Deputy PM, together with the much-talked businessman, Igor Sechin. Often seen as one of Russia's most powerful individuals (Walker 2017), Sechin had been the Chairman of Rosneft and stood at the conjunction between the energy industry and the FSB; in a sense he was protecting the security community's interests in the oil industry. Igor Shchyogolev, another FSB officer, was appointed in charge of Telecommunications. At the same time, liberals such as Kudrin remained in their job, Zubkov and Siluanov became First Deputy PMs and the economist, Elvira Nabiullina, a 2007 Yale World Fellow, obtained the Economic Development and Trade portfolio (Yale News 2007). Overall, the cabinet included members of a variety of factions.

Who was the tandem's leader, Putin or Medvedev? In some ways, both had their own spaces, also because Putin wanted to keep a balance between different groups. However, despite the promises and hopes of some liberalisations, the road to them immediately proved rockier than expected. The NATO Bucharest Declarations, which referred to Georgia's and Ukraine's eventual membership of NATO (April 2008), and Georgia's military attack on Russia-supported South Ossetia (August 2008), led to a five-day war between Russia and Georgia in August 2008 and to a sudden and deep deterioration in the West-Russia relations (Sakwa 2009: 592). Medvedev and Putin remained though poised to pursue economic reforms in the name of neoliberal modernisation and could benefit from Obama's election in the USA and his promises of a 'reset' in USA-Russia relations (Harding and Weaver 2009).

Medvedev's reforms touched several areas: energy efficiency and nuclear energy; medical technologies; IT and communication; space technologies; privatisations. Many reforms, however, remained dead letter, in part because of the 2009 recession, which led to a GDP collapse of 7.8% (The World Bank 2025a; the worst decline among G20 countries; Matveev 2019: 40) and in part because of domestic opposition, especially from Sechin and the *siloviki* (Matveev 2019: 41). The latter feared that privatisations would have led to the emergence of an independent power base for Medvedev. In general, power struggles more than different ideologies have been at the roots of many of Russia's current problems. As a matter of fact, Medvedev's much-touted programme of modernisation hardly materialised.

If we had to locate along a spectrum the positions on political economy of Russia's key political actors in the late 2000s, Medvedev and perhaps Kudrin would have been at the neoliberal end, with the new President often intervening to defend or promote forms of democracy and some change (Hahn 2010: 232–34). Putin would have maintained a more authoritarian yet pragmatic and flexible stance (Hahn 2010: 230–32), while the bulwark of the public sector and the *siloviki* (like Sechin) fully defended authoritarianism and broadly endorsed a market economy. Yet no leader truly embraced democracy and all favored a degree of neoliberalism and economic reforms, but not political ones. This attitude, and the ensuing 'disappointment' generated by Medvedev's presidency, was also a response to the global financial crisis, which in Russia was mostly interpreted as an unwelcome 'Western' import, and to the hardening of the position of the *siloviki*, who once again felt entitled to defend Russia from Western encroachment by resorting to a strong and controlling state.

Despite some improvements in Russia-US relations thanks to Obama's 'reset' (which led to dropping Bush Jr's missile defence plans for Eastern Europe and to adopting a New START Treaty in 2011; Pifer 2015) and despite some steps in Medvedev's reforms of elections and anti-corruption policies (Hahn 2010), authoritarianism was in Russia to stay. The financial crisis and the 'Great recession' provided it with the opportunity to redefine itself as the solution to market-engendered chaos, while both geopolitical and economic tensions (especially the search for new markets for oil and gas, beyond Western Europe) persuaded Russia to join the first group of the BRICs countries, which included also Brazil, China, and India and whose Heads met for the first time on 16 June 2009 in Ekaterinburg in the Ural district (BBC News 2009).

Unresolved tensions with the West and fast-growing relations with a booming China soon led to the perception that Russia was moving even closer to the emerging powers. In 2010 South Africa joined the BRICS, which, spearheaded by China (by then the world's second biggest economy) and despite their economic and political differences (Armijo 2007), started drafting a financial and economic order alternative to that of the IMF and the World Bank, the US Treasury and the Washington Consensus. At the same time, the economic and social repercussions of the global economic turbulences which were following the 'Great recession' began hitting hard regions such as Southern Europe, North Africa and the Middle East. The events of the Arab spring (2011) and the rapid toppling of authoritarian leaders in Tunisia, Egypt, Libya, Yemen and other countries had a strong impact on Russia as well. Especially the events in Libya, where the long-time authoritarian leader, Muammar Gaddafi, would end up brutally executed on 20 October 2011 (Sakwa 2020a: 248), played a significant role at a macro level in Russian politics. Medvedev, who was more aligned with US and Western policies, chose to abstain on the UN Security Council Resolution which was establishing a no-fly zone over Libya (Anishchuk 2011). Putin, by contrast, saw the Libya intervention as yet another instance of US/Western imperialism, notably in a country which had significant economic relations with Russia. Putin's 'zero-sum' geopolitical vision led to conflict with Medvedev and ultimately to the senior leader's choice to run again for the Kremlin's top position (Sakwa 2020a: 248). His confrontational, KGB-influenced worldview left little room for compromise and accommodation, particularly when the West was seen as expanding. This more traditional and realist geopolitical orientation would accompany Putin throughout all his subsequent terms as President. Medvedev, who did not reject authoritarianism but expressed a softer neoliberal position, had to step down and accept the subordinate role of Prime Minister.

With a GDP growth of 4.5 and 4.3% in 2010 and 2011 respectively (The World Bank 2025a), Russian leaders could still capitalise on significant economic achievements. Although Putin represented a more statist and authoritarian position than Medvedev, both promoted combinations of authoritarianism and neoliberalism. At the same time, however, Russia's economic development, especially in large cities, had contributed to the emergence of a more affluent, open-minded and cosmopolitan society. Putin's and Medvedev's promises were no longer attracting significant parts of the Russian population. United Russia's political platform for the 2011 elections emphasised welfare and the social dimension, but also the role of the police and armed forces. Such a combination of paternalism and preference for order and stability did not go down well with millions who were thinking otherwise and were now reclaiming civil and political freedoms. On Duma election day (4 December 2011) United Russia lost 77 seats and garnered 'only' 49.3% of the votes. The Communists stopped at 19.2% and the LDPR at 11.7%. 'A Just Russia' (*Spravedlivaya Rossiya*), previously linked to YR but later closer to social-democratic policies, obtained a surprising 13.2% (Sakwa 2019: 329).

These elections were widely criticised as fraudulent and rigged. Significant protests, which also reflected the perceived opportunity of taking advantage of YR's loss of momentum, started taking place, particularly in Moscow and other large cities (Colton and Hale 2013). While not new in Russia's post-Soviet history, they somewhat surprised Kremlin officers. According to one of them, "No one expected that tens of thousands of people would go out on the street" (Treisman 2013: 1). The digital media in this context played a significant role (Denisova 2017); however, no kind of 'Arab spring' or 'coloured revolution', materialised, partly because of the wide variety of interests and divergencies among the protesters and partly because a majority of Russians was anyway satisfied with the economic conditions that were prevalent in the Putin-Medvedev era (Colton and Hale 2013; Monaghan 2012a). Among the protesters there were though many of the leaders of a growing civil society, the 'creative class' (Treisman 2013) of white-collar professionals which in Western countries was often backing up neoliberalism in combination with democracy. The anti-corruption journalist, Alexey Navalny, was flanked by the social liberal, Boris Nemtsov; Kasyanov and Yavlinsky stood in Bolotnaya Square with writers and journalists (News Blog 2011). Other rallies were later attended by Zyuganov, Kasparov and even the former Finance Minister Kudrin, who had retired from government in 2011 after tensions related to public spending. Yet the protesters' agendas were once again very different; a dialogue between

Zyuganov's bloc of rural pensioners and the young liberal urbanites following Nemtsov or Navalny was highly unlikely, not to mention the positions of ultra-nationalists within and without Zhirinovsky's party. Even among the liberal groupings there were different leaders with different groupings of followers.

Despite the protests, Putin managed to master the 2012 presidential campaign. He even did it with some ease. The campaign was better organised and mobilised far more citizens than in the past (Monaghan 2012a: 13–5). Liberals lost to *siloviki*, but some balance was maintained; while Medvedev was overall side lined, some of his ideas were adopted: in particular, the proposal to return to direct popular elections of regional governors (Monaghan 2012a: 12). Other proposals were completely dismissed, for instance in relation to creating an international financial centre at Skolkovo. Repression of opponents (especially, Navalny) combined with identification of economic targets and promises of a boost in public spending (Treisman 2013). The lack of teeth of the competitors – spearheaded by the usual Zyuganov and Zhirinovsky – did the rest. Sergei Mironov, in 2004 a Putin supporter, ran on a platform combining nationalist and socialist elements (Al Jazeera Staff 2012). The independent businessman, Mikhail Prokhorov, campaigned on a pro-EU and pro-market platform. All in all, there was little to disrupt Putin's well-oiled *sistema* and mighty political machine, which made use of a blend of persuasion, co-optation, subtle threat and repression.

On 4 March 2012, Putin won back the presidency with a massive 63.6%. Zyuganov followed with 17.2% and a surprising Prokhorov was third with 8%. The other candidates were way distant (Sakwa 2020a: 221). The Medvedev *intermezzo* had ended, even if Putin's mentee remained Prime Minister. Russia's supreme arbiter, however, was again sitting on the country's most important chair.

5 Putin's System of Power and Neoliberalism

Once back at the heart of the Kremlin and with a strong electoral legitimacy, despite claims of fraud, massive protests and international criticism, Vladimir Putin did not kickstart any revolution. He did not even attempt to enact important reforms either. After all, he did not have any grand visions to adopt or implement, other than trying to restore some of Russia's past greatness. But in what sense and in what ways? With the support of which groups? And how do neoliberalism and authoritarianism fit into this picture?

Penetrating Putin's statecraft (or, simply put, politics) is no easy exercise. Sakwa (2020b: 77) strikes a chord when he writes about the "Putinite strategy of permanent compromise." In Putin's actions or ideas there is little evidence of visions or ideological convictions; there is evidence of rationality, pragmatism, calculation, at times uncertainty. Putin handles power like an alchemist, always calculating what is more beneficial to himself and often to an abstract idea of the country, which he understands in a conservative and geopolitically realist way. Always following Sakwa (2020b: 77), Putin is mostly a "faction manager" and not really an omnipotent, almighty, and visionary leader. He looks rather like the manual micromanager of an informal, convoluted, complicated, yet somehow working, *sistema* (Ledeneva 2012 and 2013).

What relationships are there between Putin's manual micromanagement and the adoption (or not) of neoliberal policies? This remains a complex issue, on which Sakwa expresses doubts (2020b: 79), while Ledeneva (2012), despite similar concerns, interprets his era (although mainly in the early stages) as one of 'consolidation of capitalism'. Sakwa illustrates Putin's pragmatic combination of "heavy-handed political management" (2020b: 79) and pro-market choices, including capital's penetration into education, healthcare and labour law; he concludes by aptly referring to the notion of "authoritarian neoliberalism" (2020b: 79; see also Morris 2021). Yet there is still something more; specifically, it is important to recall Putin's emphasis on technocracy (also mentioned by Sakwa 2020b: 79–80) and expertise, which is deployed to foster economic growth, in an almost titanic and somehow fruitless effort to catch up with the West and avoid being caught up by China and other East Asian countries, which in the 2010s gained technological advantages over Russia. Sympathy for technocracy is also expressed by the choices for the key roles in the first Medvedev government (2012–18) and would continue with the ministerial appointments of economists until present days (as of Spring 2025). Neoliberalism, nationalism, and authoritarianism end up combining their forces; Putin's micromanagement in decision-making and a degree of contingency dictate which of them in turn prevails, but each of them relies upon the others. The effects of Putin's *sistema* on everyday political economy are complex and multidimensional. The much-talked 'vertical of power' (Monaghan 2012b) descending from Putin down to local officers has always been slightly more than a mere ideological discourse. While the President and his bureaucracies have usually extracted from and 'milked' Russian citizens, the latter have learnt how to resist and have developed informal systems of 'infrapolitics' and 'nomadism', to use Deleuze's terminology (Morris 2019). In this sense, it is important to recall the everyday resistance and distance from power as well as from formal authority of tens of millions of Russians. Forms of resistance such as evading signatures or negotiating fines are ingrained in an always ambivalent co-existence with an extracting and exacting state (Morris 2019). That said, also in light of Putin's pragmatism and adaptability, it is important to have an overview of the political economy he contributed to shape in a chronological sense, bearing in mind the challenges Russia has faced since 2012.

The first Medvedev government (2012–18) reflected more continuity and rotation than change (Monaghan 2012a: 16–7). Igor Shuvalov, a top civil servant and an economist, not without his own flamboyant life (Butler 2022), remained the only First Deputy PM. The economist Arkady Dvorkovich, a Medvedev loyalist, maintained the portfolio of Deputy PM for Industry and Energy. Kudrin, who had criticised high military expenses (Matveev 2019: 41), was replaced by another economist, Anton Siluanov. An independent economist, Andrey Belousov, obtained the portfolio of Economic Development. In other words, despite the presence of new names and faces, and despite stronger *siloviki* control with Putin back at the helm, the neoliberal element and the economic experts remained, even if many of the latter by 2012 had a party affiliation, usually with United Russia. At the same time, a Putin loyalist, the nationalist and military expert, Dmitry Rogozin, became Deputy PM for Defence and Space. Oleg Govorun, a Putin aide on foreign affairs, obtained the Regional Development portfolio (Monaghan 2012a: 16–7). In other words, some degree of balance among the factions was maintained.

Putin's re-election in 2012 represents though a turning point in the relations with the West and authoritarian consolidation. Hardening relations with the USA and the EU in Syria were matched by the 'Foreign agent law', which put severe restrictions on NGOs working in Russia and set the stage for further democratic backsliding (Elder 2013b). The law would soon be followed by a clampdown on LGBTQIA+ rights in the name of 'traditional values' (Wilkinson 2014). Putin was now further distancing Russia from 'Western' liberal values.

In the meantime, Russia's economic structure was increasingly moving away from a traditional neoliberal and towards a more statist model. Throughout his career, Putin consistently demonstrated a pragmatic attitude and might have probably opted for 'more market' if that had brought about a strengthening of the Russian state. Yet, in a country which was feeling threatened by the West in key world regions (Syria, a bridge to the Mediterranean and the Middle East and host to Russian military bases, and increasingly Ukraine), strengthening the economy via a stronger role of the state seemed the most appropriate route. Hence, in 2012 privatisation programmes came to a standstill. Rosneft, the mainly state-owned oil giant, was still chaired by the powerful *silovik*, Igor Sechin, who in 2012–13 presided over the acquisition of TNK-BP and made it the world's biggest listed oil company (Neate 2013). Rostec, a military industry colossus, was rebranded in 2013. It was controlled by another *silovik*, CEO Sergey Chemezov, who had been a friend of Putin's since their common days in the intelligence in East Germany (Matveev 2019: 42). The brewing tensions between Russia and the West exploded in 2014, with the Ukraine crisis and the much-debated annexation of Crimea by referendum (16 March). Understanding why Russia became internationally more assertive is a difficult conundrum, which cannot be resolved by generic references to Putin's KGB mindset or the fear of Western encroachment. Authors such as Götz (2017) have highlighted various reasons why Russia became geopolitically more confrontational. Putin's leadership and mindset may have well contributed and so did Russia's attempts to divert attention from domestic issues as well as its growing ideological nationalism and concerns with Western geopolitical expansion. None of these elements, however, can alone explain Putin's rapid reaction to the events in Ukraine; rather, it is their combination. What followed the Crimea episode generated a fracture with NATO countries; sanctions were imposed on Russian companies and individuals, which, together with falling commodity prices, led to the country's subsequent economic decline (–0.7% in 2014 and –2% in 2015; The World Bank 2025a). Sanctions might have cost Russia $160 billion, according to Putin himself in a 2015 statement (Connolly 2016: 751). The timing of this moment of decline was particularly important since Putin intended to concentrate his third mandate on Russia's economic and technological development, and international investments would have been crucial to that goal.

By contrast, the years 2014–16 were characterised by profound stagnation. The Russian economic elites had little incentive in investing in industry and remained mainly reliant on commodities (Inozemtsev 2016). Russia's growing relations with the BRICS translated into a deeper partnership with China, which became 'strategic', and in which Beijing had the upper hand, at least since imposing its own terms on the building of the massive 'Power of Siberia' gas pipeline, whose construction started in 2015 (Gallo, Wu and Sergi 2020). China became a supplier of industrial goods and a recipient of commodities and energy sources, with a negative impact on Russia's industrial diversification. A collapse in FDI followed suit, together with the rouble's devaluation and general economic decline (Connolly 2016).

Yet to some extent the effect of sanctions was even to help Putin. As is often the case when sanctions are imposed on authoritarian states, isolation convinced the President to adopt an Import-Substitution Industrialisation (ISI) strategy and generated a kind of 'rally around the flag' effect (Connolly 2016). As a result, in the 2016 Duma vote United Russia once again prevailed with a strong majority of 54.2% (Sakwa 2020a: 330), while the opponents remained far behind: the Communists with 13.3% and the LDPR with 13.1%. As a Prime Minister, Medvedev consolidated neoliberal measures, though mostly in the sense of austerity and stability (Sakwa 2020a: 249). Putin strengthened authoritarianism, with further crackdowns on protests and control over the media, the judiciary and various forms of dissent. Stronger economic growth, 2.8% in 2018 (The World Bank 2025a) helped Putin once again win the Kremlin elections. In another case of highly questionable electoral procedures, he obtained almost 76.7% of the votes. An agricultural cooperative entrepreneur, Pavel Grudinin, ran for the Communists with a significant social programme, but reached only 11.8%. Zhirinovsky garnered 5.7% and the liberal journalist, Ksenia Sobchak, 1.7% (Sakwa 2020a: 221). As of 2018, Putin's system of power was consolidated. Economic recovery, China's support, the EU's weaknesses and the ambivalences of Trump's politics in the White House seemed all to play in favour of the Kremlin's long-time tenant.

6 Towards and beyond the War in Ukraine: What Future for an Increasingly Authoritarian Russia?

The new Medvedev cabinet (2018–20) included several economists, one of whom was Siluanov, who became the only First Deputy Prime Minister. There were also new *siloviki* such as the independent candidates, Dmitry Patrushev (son of Nikolai Patrushev and in charge of Agriculture) and Yevgeny Zinichev (responsible for Emergencies), who would die in office in 2021. Taking advantage of improving economic conditions, Medvedev announced an increase in the retirement age (Sakwa 2020a: 249) on the same day the FIFA Football World Cup started in Moscow (14 June 2018). Many Russians, however, were not distracted by the mega sport event and began a new wave of protests, under the leadership of both senior politicians and emerging ones like Navalny, and with a range of motives from anti-corruption to anti-systemic attitudes (Fomin and Nadskakula-Kamarczuk 2022). The proposed pension reform broke the compromise which had long supported an 'authoritarian welfare state' (Logvinenko 2020). Protests continued throughout 2018 and forced Putin to intervene and partly backtrack on the reform, if only to a limited extent. After all, the disappearance or monetisation of welfare (Morris 2019b) had long been a reality, to which millions of Russians had responded by both internalising neoliberal subjectivities and resorting to informal jobs or semi-legal activities.

2018 and 2019 were years of further restrictions to rights but also of moderate economic growth (2.2% in 2019; The World Bank 2025a). Putin started working on the country's (and his own) political future beyond Medvedev's executives. In January 2020 he proposed to the Duma a series of constitutional amendments, to be adopted after a referendum (Hutcheson and McAllister 2021). The amendments were a blueprint for a harder authoritarian regime and for Putin's life-long presidency. Among them there were: the removal of a consecutive two-term limit to presidential mandates; the declaration of the supremacy of Russian over international law; references to Christianity and traditional families, with the banning of same-sex marriages. These aspects would provide Putin with the opportunity to further consolidate his grip on Russian politics. Medvedev's government immediately resigned and was replaced by a new one (21 January 2020), which once again confirmed both Putin's ability to rely on several groups and factions and the growing influence (also in an economic sense) of the *siloviki*.

The newly appointed Prime Minister, Mikhail Mishustin, was by all means a technocrat (Syrovátka and Holzer 2024). As the Director of the FTS (Federal Tax Service) between 2010 and 2020, he had revolutionised tax collection, thanks to strong emphasis on digitalisation and AI. His appointment reflects Putin's long-time commitment to relaunch Russia's technological and economic performances. His new government included other 15 independent ministers, among whom another technocrat, the economist, Andrey Belousov, became prominent as First Deputy PM. At the same time, political heavyweights such as Shoigu, Siluanov and Lavrov maintained their key roles in Defence, Finance, and Foreign Affairs.

In the meantime, the role of the *siloviki* became increasingly important. Sergei Shoigu, one of them, had been Minister of Defence since 2012. As was mentioned earlier, a former FSB Director and a Leader of the Security Council, Nikolai Patrushev, could now also rely on his son as Minister of Agriculture. Sergei Ivanov Jr, son of the former Minister of Defence, was by 2018 working with Gazprom at the highest levels. In other words, since the final moments of Medvedev's presidency, Russia had seen the emergence of 'dynasties of *siloviki*' (Brancaleone 2021: 11–2); the *siloviki* themselves started increasingly looking for wealth with the aim of consolidating their positions and becoming 'silovarchs' (Treisman 2008; Markus 2017); some authors have even written about the rise of a 'new nobility' (Galeotti 2016: 3), in a process we can also call the 'neoliberalisation' of the *siloviki* themselves. As has been the case with many historical monarchies, however, there are significant divisions within the new 'nobility'. Hence, neither the *siloviki* nor the silovarchs have formed cohesive groups and have been able to fully take advantage of their power; all have remained to some degree dependent on Putin. This applies also to hawkish silovarchs like Patrushev Sr and Bortnikov, who have heavily contributed to spreading conspiratorial views of American, European and Ukrainian plots against Russia. Nikolai Patrushev was a friend of Putin's in Leningrad; he subsequently became Director of the FSB (1999–2008) and Secretary of the Security

Council of Russia (2008–24). His reputation is that of a powerful and influential hard-liner, capable of swaying Putin himself (Galeotti 2023). Bortnikov, another hard-liner, has replaced Patrushev as FSB Director in 2008. Having said that, despite the growing media and political narrative of an 'FSB state' or a 'silovarchy', Russia remains a state ruled by a leader who still negotiates among several different factions. While the *siloviki* have grown in importance and the Soviet legacy is strong (like in other Eurasian states such as Belarus, Kazakhstan and Uzbekistan), Putin has also relied on a discourse of imperial Russia and its return to a position of world power (McNabb 2016), a fact which has led to the rise of more ideological nationalists, traditionalists and Eurasianists. Economic technocrats in the bureaucracy have not disappeared either.

Over time, Putin has also become increasingly reliant on the informal ties and loyalties of his own family and personal friends. Also in this case, there are many overlaps with other 'groups'. One key person in Putin's inner circle is the billionaire, Arkady Rotenberg. A constructor, including of pipelines, and a beneficiary of Putin's policies (especially on the occasion of the building of the Russia-China 'Power of Siberia' mega pipeline from 2012), Rotenberg is a long-time friend of Putin's, with whom he apparently shares a passion for judo (Forbes 2025b). Another long-time friend and collaborator is the already mentioned Sergey Chemezov, the CEO of the giant military-industrial complex, Rostec. A similar case is that of Nikolay Tokarev, a collaborator of Putin's in the KGB days in East Germany and the President of Transneft, which transports some 90% of Russia's oil and has provided Tokarev with the opportunity to build up his own business empire (Shleynov 2016; Brancaleone 2021). The wealthiest and most important member of Putin's 'inner circle' remains anyway Gennady Timchenko, a multibillionaire who is active as an international investor and became a friend of Putin's in the 1990s in St Petersburg. He has mostly invested in fossil fuels companies such as Novatek (a gas giant) and SIBUR (a firm in the petrochemical industry). With an estimated net worth of $23.2 billions, he is among the world's 100 richest people (Forbes 2025c).

Friends, *siloviki* and even family members have gained more prominence during years of growing authoritarian repression and economic stalemate, especially in the wake of the pandemic's inception. Alexey Navalny, Putin's most vocal and charismatic opponent, was apparently poisoned whilst in Russia (Harding and Roth 2020). In July 2020, the constitutional amendments which handed further power to Putin were approved with a referendum. Repression of NGOs continued. The slope towards hard authoritarianism, which draws on fear (Treisman 2008) rather than a modicum of consent or spin, became ever more slippery.

In January 2021, Navalny was arrested and detained, a fact which sparked new mass protests. Until 2007 a member of Yabloko, later Navalny became a blogger and a leader of the National Democrats (ND), a movement in which he often expressed xenophobic and anti-immigration positions, despite its commitment to liberalism and democracy. Although Navalny would later regret those positions, his trajectory remained contradictory (Laruelle 2014). Most of his efforts would then be directed against Putin and his corrupt *sistema*. Due to his charisma and popularity, he became Putin's main challenger, even if his populist rhetoric did not translate into a strong and well-articulated narrative and a powerful protest movement.

Navalny's judicial ordeal continued throughout 2021 and 2022. In September 2021, towards the end of the pandemic, new Duma elections took place. Economic problems, Covid-19's mismanagement, the effect of protests, and the emergence of new forces led to a slight decline in United Russia's performance. The party ended with 49.8% of the votes, amidst allegations of fraud and vote-rigging. Zyuganov's Communists regained some support and obtained 18.9%. The LDPR, by contrast, sank to 7.6%. Mironov's 'A Just Russia' went up to 7.5% and a new moderate party, New People (*Novyye Lyudi*), garnered a surprising 5.3% (BBC 2021). The Communists and the LDPR, however, never posed a real threat to Putin, who was able to use parts of their ideologies; at the same time the emergence of some opposition, if broadly liberal, never really materialised, in part because of conflicts between different forces and in part because of the absence of possible key actors (Yavlinsky and especially Navalny).

The second half of 2021 was already haunted by worldwide debates on Russia-Ukraine tensions and by Russia's propaganda on the issue, including the threat of a military invasion of Ukraine. A much-discussed essay on the unity of Russians and Ukrainians was written by Putin and published on the Kremlin's website on 12 July 2021 (President of Russia 2021). What did eventually lead to the conflict that started on 24 February 2022, after being creeping under the surface since the Crimean annexation (2014)? How did Russia's political economy contribute to the invasion and how did it change in its aftermath?

There have been many and controversial debates (several of them in the media, though, and not yet in the academia) on the invasion's causes. Some authors, including in the USA, have pointed their fingers at the West's (and especially the USA's) responsibilities in pushing towards the conflict (Mearsheimer 2022). Russia would have reacted to the USA's pressure to have Ukraine into the NATO since at least the late 2000s and especially after 2021; Ukraine's NATO accession was and is seen in Moscow as an existential threat and a 'red line' not to be crossed. After all, anti-Americanism in Russia has long been ripe, together with the sentiment that the USA (and its European allies) had damaged Russia's economy in the 1990s, expanded NATO despite promises, and 'contained' Russia with the aims of curbing its power, using its resources (the cheaper, the better) and opening new market opportunities. While there certainly had been external pressures, the latter found fertile ground in the transformations of Russian politics (and political economy) in the late 2010s.

As is clear from Navalny's (and his supporters') ordeal, since the late 2010s Russia had become more authoritarian. This was in part a response to long-term changes in a society which had developed as more 'modern', open, cosmopolitan, and not only in the largest cities like Moscow and St Petersburg. Protests had in fact continued (Treisman 2022) and the government's response, driven by fear, had evolved into a more violent one, with arrests, detentions, shutting down of associations, and other repressive measures. Such violent attitude combined with the political rise of the *siloviki* (Treisman 2022), their growing demand for political and economic capital and their increasing influence on Putin himself. Ideas of top security elites such as Nikolai Patrushev and Sergei Naryshkin, the Head of the Foreign Intelligence Service (SVR), certainly held sway on the President (Kragh and Umland 2023).

Knowing whether the decision to invade Ukraine was mostly Putin's brainchild (Seddon, Miller and Schwartz 2023) or pushed by some Rasputin-like advisers (such as Nikolai Patrushev, the banker, Yuri Kovalchuk, or other leading *siloviki*; Galeotti 2023) remains difficult. Probably there is some truth in both interpretations. Certainly, the paranoid anti-Americanism, the anti-Ukraine feelings and the attitude to violence of Putin's close advisers in early 2022 made the decision easier. While the President was still relying on economic and bureaucratic experts such as Mishustin or Siluanov, the rise in power of the *siloviki* contributed to the Kremlin's belligerent attitude and authoritarianism.

The invasion triggered a raft of sanctions, mostly from Western countries and their allies. Despite the sanctions, and the subsequent freezing of financial assets and barriers on trading oil, gas, and commodities, the Russian economy fell by just a modest 2.1% in 2022 and even recovered by a significant +3.6% in 2023. The recovery took place notwithstanding the destructions, horrors and uncertainties of the war (The World Bank 2025a). This was in part due to a spike in commodities' prices as well as to the growth of new markets, in Latin America, Africa, South Asia and of course China. Moreover, the Bank of Russia's management of the crisis, once again led by Elvira Nabiullina, was sound and effective (Demertzis et al 2022). Whatever the key reason, Russia has not experienced any financial or economic meltdown, its economy has stood on two legs and has even grown more than expected, also due to the rise of a strong military industry. Little has changed in politics: if anything, Russia's authoritarianism has predictably consolidated.

In early 2022 there were expectations that Russia might have quickly won the conflict and the West's efforts to support Ukraine were therefore strong, in terms of both sanctions and military aid. Yet, amidst the war's horrors, there were many shocks and surprises, and Russia's early win did not materialise. While its economy proved resilient, and Russia was able to claim some diplomatic leverage in several African, Asian, and Latin American countries, also thanks to spinning, on 24–25 June 2023 the ruthless and brutal warlord of the Wagner Group, Yevgeny Prigozhin, staged an insurrection against the Russian army and the state itself. His mercenary forces reached within 200 km from Moscow, when Belarus' President Lukashenko stepped in and brokered an agreement which avoided a bloodbath. Although Prigozhin died, probably killed, in a plane crash two months later, the humiliation for Putin had been huge (Roth and Sauer 2023). The President's traditional *sistema* of manual control of different power groups had been dealt a blow and looked faltering.

As a result, Putin attempted to further steer Russia into an even more authoritarian and repressive direction. He singled out companies for renationalisation, also with the aim of changing their leadership and forming younger and potentially more loyal generations of cadres and managers (Petrov 2023). Yet later in 2023, Siluanov hinted at the necessity to reinforce the private sector and increase its presence in state-controlled corporations, especially in order to collect funds and promote national domestic investments to sustain the war effort (Marrow and Korsunskaya 2023). Defense and security matters had become crucial to Russia's budget.

In the latest years Putin has become increasingly associated not only with stronger forms of authoritarianism but even with fascism, which was one political tendency of Putin's favourite writer, Ivan Ilyin (1883–1954). Ilyin had reactionary nostalgia for tsarist Russia and rejected Communism. He developed a strong form of Russian nationalism and expressed sympathy for some aspects of nazifascism as well (Snyder 2018, esp. chapters 1 and 2). It is though important to remember that Ilyin did not fully reject liberalism – an aspect which renders his thoughts more interesting in the context of authoritarian neoliberalism – and also that Putin's preferred ideologies have usually been pragmatic, flexible and eclectic (Laruelle 2024). References made by Putin to Ilyin, Eurasianism or ultra-nationalism are more tactical signals to the elites rather than guidelines for clear courses of action. Certainly, Putin's growing authoritarianism has manifested itself in the brutal conduct of the Ukraine war and its tragical developments as well as in the personal and political tragedy of Navalny, who continued criticising the Kremlin, particularly because of and during the Ukraine war, and was found dead in prison on 16 February 2024 (Luscombe, Oladipo and Slawson 2024). The subsequent presidential elections (15–7 March) have been even more irregular and manipulated than in the past. No other candidate has dared to truly oppose Putin, who won with an unprecedented 87.8% of the votes. His senior Communist opponent, Kharitonov, did not even reach 4%, while Leonid Slutsky, heir to the late Zhirinovsky, stopped at around 3%, less than the moderate, Vladislav Davankov (Faulconbridge and Osborn 2024). Soon after the elections, Mishustin has formed a new cabinet, with another technocrat, the economist, Denis Manturov, as the only First Deputy PM. Siluanov and Lavrov maintained their positions, while Belousov moved to Defence.

In a context of war and fully-fledged authoritarianism, writing about economic policies or changes in Russia's political economy becomes extremely difficult. Especially in a war scenario, what role is played by technological innovation, particularly in sectors such as the digital economy and AI which, also according to Putin (Gigova 2017), can have a tremendous impact on power and international relations? Some authors (Dear 2019) claim that Russia's engagement with AI is modest, and the country is lagging far behind potential competitors, from the USA to China and other European states. In more recent times, however, it has been highlighted how, while Russia's strategy and resources are clearly less effective and more limited than China's or the US' (Saveliev and Zhurenkov 2021), the state sector, mostly through the Sber group, is supporting AI projects to the detriment of private companies (Yandex) and some state-controlled corporations (Rostec), which specialise in other products (Petrella, Miller and Cooper 2021).

As of 2024/25, Russia is far from isolated. Large economies such as China and South Africa are leaning towards it, while Brazil, Turkey and India have remained neutral. Iran is a moderate supporter and some African and Latin American countries (not to mention Hungary) have moved closer to the Kremlin. In light of worldwide political transformations, authoritarianism is becoming stronger, and not only in Russia. At the same time, Putin is cultivating neoliberal policies, which sometimes are more in favour of private enterprise and sometimes rely on a stronger state hand. Yet neoliberalism and authoritarianism, especially in Russia's context, share a ruthless, socially Darwinian and oppressive approach, by which little is left to any humanity. Authoritarianism found fertile ground in the wreckage of Russia's early 1990s and grew in parallel with neoliberal policies. The country's evolution will highly depend on its forthcoming relations with both Western and Eastern neighbours, which to different degrees seem to have remained trapped in the same quick sands of authoritarian neoliberalism. At the moment a more optimistic vision of Russia's future remains beyond any reasonable forecast.

CHAPTER 7

Conclusions

After reviewing the vicissitudes of authoritarian neoliberalism in three big economies, all of which are members of the G20 and with a total population of slightly less than 300 millions, we are left at the very least rather puzzled. Italy has witnessed no less than four fully-fledged technocratic executives and is now governed by a Prime Minister who in her youth was a member of the neo-fascist, Youth Front. Russia, after the economic abyss of the 1990s, has gradually shifted to a fully authoritarian regime steered by a fraction of its security services elite, past and present. Despite a recent return to a more inclusive form of neoliberalism, Britain risks falling to a fast-growing nationalist right, which is partly expressed by the re-emerging Farage's brainchild, Reform UK. We cannot of course forget the evolutions in the world's largest economy, which is witnessing the 'normalisation' of a rather unusual election win, whereby President Trump and some of his collaborators, notably Elon Musk, incarnate a new combination of nationalist, authoritarian and technocratic norms. Such combinations are not entirely new and seem to be represented also by other leaders in the same hemisphere, Nayib Bukele in El Salvador and Javier Milei in Argentina. We are clearly assisting at the re-emergence of authoritarianism in combination with neoliberal economic programs and perhaps at the rise of some form of new authoritarianism, whose contours are difficult to define and remain in a kind of cloudy region. Are even more dangerous mutations of authoritarianism likely to take place? How deep and entrenched would a type of 'new authoritarianism' be?

In *The 18th Brumaire of Louis Bonaparte*, Karl Marx famously wrote: "Hegel remarks somewhere that all great world-historic facts appear, so to speak, twice. He forgot to add: the first time as tragedy, the second time as farce" (Marx 1852 n.p.).

Several scholars and commentators are wondering if a return to some form of fascism or nazism is currently in the cards. It would not be a farce in any case. Fascism has recently been associated with Putin's Russia (Motyl 2016), Bolsonaro's Brazil (Lopes de Sousa 2020), Trump's USA (Connolly 2017), Modi's India (Sinha 2021) and a number of other states or parties. There is also a growing literature on neo-fascism (Cox and Skidmore-Hess 2022; Ayers 2024).

Yet this book claims that we are not risking a return to fascism or nazism, in their various socio-historical forms. Social and political phenomena have their historical specificities and do not resurface in the same forms as before. What looks possible, and even likely, is a turn to some form of fascism or authoritarianism whose features are not yet clear but may already find some incarnation (at least in a region of Europe) in Hungary under Viktor Orbán. After all, we have already discussed a literature on 'new authoritarianism' in Central and Eastern Europe (Wiatr, ed., 2019). Other states with elements of some new fascism (or authoritarianism) may be Putin's Russia, Modi's India, Bolsonaro's Brasil, and we are waiting for the unfolding of Trump's second administration. Once the judiciary, the media, the police (in some countries, the armed forces) and education are silenced or tamed, any opposition's room for manoeuvre becomes incredibly limited. And authoritarianism is then a possibility, even without the use of force and fraud as in Putin's Russia's rise.

In many aspects, the preconditions of authoritarianism or even fascism seem to be already there. Crises are usually the most important of them, as Gramsci taught us. The 21st century started with a massive crisis associated with transnational terrorism and the ensuing 'Global War On Terror', which was already following a range of financial and economic crises in the 1990s (in most of Latin America, culminating in Argentina's collapse; in Russia, East Asia, and the 'dotcom' bubble in the USA) and led to a first wave of authoritarian policies and neoconservative nationalism, especially (though not exclusively) in the USA. Then there appeared the 'Great recession' with its worldwide ramifications; in 2020, when a real recovery had not yet started, the Covid-19 pandemic kicked in. In the meantime, the climate crisis has never been stopped or even significantly mitigated. Some authors began writing about a 'polycrisis', borrowing an expression first used by the French sociologist, Edgar Morin (1999).

Any crisis, or polycrisis, unfolding in the early 21st century, is deeply rooted in neoliberal politics. The erosion of meaning of long-standing social and political institutions, from parties to states, the rise of digital technologies and economic technocracy, the dilemmas faced by traditional leftist forces, the apparent inability to address the climate crisis, have all contributed to democracy's emptying in the West and beyond. Disaffection and disillusion have become widespread. Insecurity, a crucial aspect of the neoliberal era, has emboldened the rise of anti-democratic forces and nurtured the emergence of vicious forms of scapegoating and discrimination, or outright racism. Additionally, substantial fractions of the capitalist class have re-orientated their strategies from globalisation to nationalism, protectionism and a return of the nation-state, as events in the USA, Britain, Brazil, the EU, Russia, India, Japan, South Korea, and other countries have clearly demonstrated.

To summarise, some elements of fascism and authoritarianism are already at play. But the elective affinities between neoliberalism and authoritarianism do not end here. Neoliberalism as an ideology, a practice and a process developed in the West and the world well before the success of populist leaders like Trump or Farage. Over the decades, neoliberalism nurtured a logic by which, almost *naturally*, humans are divided into 'winners' and 'losers' (Ayers 2024: 426). Such competitive *Weltanschauung*, according to which the human world is for the winners to take, is common to neoliberalism and fascism – let alone any type of authoritarianism. Furthermore, nationalism, fascism, and for that matter, Trumpism, incarnate *Ersatz* narratives which deliver to the frustrations, disillusions and desires of tens of millions of impoverished members of the middle and working classes, or ailing businesses (Walker 2021; Ayers 2024).

While neoliberalism, fascism, neo- and post fascism are different beasts, there are common ideological aspects, which are more visibly emerging under challenging socio-economic conditions and in the context of the rise of radical right groups, from the 'alt-right' to white nationalism, from the 'alt-lite' to the return of American paleoconservatism.

European radical right parties and governments share nativist and anti-immigration positions, social conservatism, ecological scepticism, economic neoliberalism (although some of them such as France's National Rally are also protectionist), and in some cases (the faction *Der Flügel* in AfD, *Alternative für Deutschland* is allegedly one of them) proximity to 'extreme right' groups. The similarities between on the one hand Modi's and BJP's ideology of *Hindutva* and on the other hand fascism have been debated and highlighted for a long time, despite *Hindutva*'s emphasis on religion rather than race (Desai 2016; Das 2020). Even stronger (and partly better-documented) ideological forms have been rising in the USA and, thanks to availability of capital and organisational tools, have already impacted politics well beyond Trump's White House, especially in Europe and the Americas. Paleoconservatism, traditionally expressed by the long-time campaigner, Pat Buchanan, and now to some extent by the influential journalist, Tucker Carlson, emphasises strong nationalism, traditional values, economic protectionism, and a rejection of both immigrants and international engagements (Kiely 2019). Such ideas are a part of Trumpism's complex ideological blend, which also includes the white nationalist 'alt-right' (Hawley 2017) and the no less reassuring 'alt-lite', spearheaded by the sinister ideologue, Steve Bannon. How will some fascist elements, which form a part of Trumpism (Paxton 2021), unfold in the tycoon's second administration? What role will also be played by Christian nationalism, which is growing in Latin America as well?

One extremely worrying aspect of authoritarian neoliberalism is the return of militia formations. A key case is that of the USA, where the militia movement has gained prominence since the 1990s and has been involved in episodes of violence in the latest three decades, including in the events of the 6 January 2021 Capitol insurrection (The Southern Poverty Law Centre n.d.). Militias are generally supporting Trump and many often express far-right, white nationalist views. Not only are these groups training to combat; they also espouse anti-immigration and at times racist views. In the meantime, in Brazil there are strong links between the Bolsonaro family and militia groups (Hernandez 2019), while the existence of far-right militias is well-documented in Hungary (Varga 2014) and of course in India, where Narendra Modi himself is a member of the controversial, RSS. But even in the case of the EU, its border managing agency, Frontex, has a historically problematic relationship with human rights (Kalkman 2021), further highlighting a dark side of authoritarian, technocratic neoliberalism.

While overall these new forms of authoritarianism look ideologically thin, it is also possible that some more structured ideology may be in-the-making. After all, fascism remained for a long time mostly 'action', without any concern for ideas, ideologies or doctrines. In Mussolini's words (1932: 3–4):

> I had in mind no specific doctrinal program. ... [...].... My doctrine during that period had been the doctrine of action. ... [...].... Fascism was not the nursling of a doctrine previously drafted at a desk; it was born of a need of action, and was action. ... [...].... There were discussions but ... [...].... there was something more sacred and more important. ...[...].... death. ... [...].... Fascists knew how to die. A doctrine, fully elaborated, divided up into chapters and paragraphs with annotations, may have been lacking, but it was replaced by something far more decisive, – by a faith.

These short and crude sentences are sufficient to realise how ideologies are always somehow in-the-making, and how intellectual labour is often despised in the name of 'action' or even some form of blind 'faith'. What strikes in Mussolini's rapid sketch is a flavour of anti-intellectualism, which has become so visible in the current anti-intellectualism of populist, nationalist, authoritarian movements.

In a sense, this may be the case also because the intellectual dimension is left to experts, technocrats, problem-solvers, with their specialist, 'objective', 'neutral', form of knowledge. Even more impressively, the technocrat is giving way to a machine-like technocracy or to fully-fledged AI. Intellectual efforts would be wasted time; the AI would make decisions and leave more time to 'action'. A new technocracy, perhaps a technocracy 2.0, seems to merge authoritarian, fascist, nationalist elements. While overall tangential to the Silicon Valley, neoreactionary thinking (NRx) has been influencing billionaires such as Peter

Thiel, the founder of PayPal and Palantir, an AI investor, an arch-conservative and an indirect supporter of technocratic authors whose ideas include that of creating a world of thousands of corporations ('gov-corps') as a replacement for states (Smith and Burrows 2021), with unelected managers and executives in the place of elected politicians. In broader terms, the whole ethics of the new Silicon Valley seems to be inspired by a 'techno-authoritarianism' (LaFrance 2024). From Zuckerberg to Musk, Thiel to Alex Karp (Palantir's other founder), they would all have expressed elitist and non-democratic views.

The likes of Facebook and newer social media have morphed into a kind of global parliament, except for the fact that nobody is elected and control takes precedence over debate (see LaFrance's 2024 reflections). At the same time, images and speed take precedence over any kind of rational or egalitarian deliberation. In a nutshell, the social media's main benefit is for the plutocratic owners. Precisely the combination of plutocracy, impatience with democracy, emphasis on speed and technology, nationalism and new forms of authoritarianism could prove decisive in bringing the planet towards a neo-authoritarian abyss. However, before any easy pessimism, it is important to remember that we as humans can still think, and not in soundbites. And of course we can act, be our agents.

Bibliography

Abe, Shinzo (2015) *Policy Speech by Prime Minister Shinzo Abe to the 189th Session of the Diet.* Prime Minister of Japan and his Cabinet. Speeches and Statements by the Prime Minister. Available (consulted 29 January 2025) at: https://japan.kantei.go.jp/97_abe/statement/201502/policy.html.

Abrahamsen, R. and Williams, M. (2024) How not to counter the radical right. *The Conversation*, 28, April. Available (consulted 10 May 2024) at: https://theconversation.com/how-not-to-counter-the-radical-right-228640.

Addison, Paul (1975) *The Road to 1945*. London: Jonathan Cape.

Adler, E. and Pouliot, V. (2011) International practices. *International Theory* 3(1): 1–36.

Adorno, T.W., Frenkel-Brunswik, E., Levinson, D. and Sanford, N. (1950) *The Authoritarian Personality*. New York City, NY: Harper.

Agerholm, Harriet (2016) Theresa May: the new Prime Minister's five most controversial moments. *The Independent*, 19, July. Available (consulted 13 January 2024) at: https://www.independent.co.uk/news/uk/home-news/theresa-may-the-new-prime-minister-s-5-most-controversial-moments-a7142321.html.

AGI (2018) Politica. "Il premier tecnico di un governo politico". Cosa dicono i giornali. 22, May. Available (consulted 26 July 2023) at: https://www.agi.it/politica/giuseppe_conte_rassegna_stampa-3931524/news/2018-05-22/.

Airaudo, G. and Marcon, G. (2016) Le slide che Renzi non vi farà vedere. *Sbilanciamoci*, 22, February. Available (consulted 24 July 2022) at: https://sbilanciamoci.info/le-slide-che-renzi-non-vi-fara-vedere/.

Akin, William E. (1977) *Technocracy and the American Dream. The Technocrat Movement, 1900–1941*. Berkeley, CA: University of California Press.

Albertazzi, D. and McDonnell, D. (2008) *Twenty-First Century Populism*. Houndmills and New York: Palgrave Macmillan.

Albertazzi, D., Giovannini, A. and Seddone, A. (2018) No regionalism please, we are *Leghisti*! The transformation of the Italian Lega Nord under the leadership of Matteo Salvini. *Regional and Federal Studies* 28(5): 645–71.

Albertazzi, D., McDonnell, D. and Newell, J.L. (2011) Di lotta e di governo: The Lega Nord and Rifondazione Comunista in office. *Party Politics* 17(4): 471–87.

Albertson, K. and Stepney, P. (2020) 1979 and all that: a 40-year reassessment of Margaret Thatcher's legacy on her own terms. *Cambridge Journal of Economics* 44(2): 319–42.

Allegretti, Aubrey (2023) Sunak offers at least 6% pay rise to millions of public sector workers. *The Guardian*, 13, July. Available (consulted 13 May 2024) at: https://www.theguardian.com/society/2023/jul/13/rishi-sunak-agrees-to-public-sector-pay-rises-of-6-plus-without-raising-budgets.

Al-Rasheed, Madawi (2018) *Salman's Legacy: The Dilemmas of a New Era in Saudi Arabia*. Oxford: Oxford University Press.

Al Jazeera Staff (2012) Zyuganov and Mironov: Back to the Future. *Al Jazeera*, 26, February. Available (consulted 27 June 2024) at: https://www.aljazeera.com/news/2012/2/26/zyuganov-and-mironov-back-to-the-future.

Amable, B., Guillaud, E. and Palombarini, S. 2011. "The political economy of neoliberalism in Italy and France." CES Working Papers. Paris. https://centredeconomiesorbonne.univ-paris1.fr/bandeau-haut/documents-de-travail/.

Ambrosio, Thomas (2010) Constructing a Framework of Authoritarian Diffusion. *International Studies Perspectives* 11(4): 375–92.

Ambrosio, Thomas (2012) The rise of the 'China Model' and 'Beijing Consensus': evidence of authoritarian diffusion? *Contemporary Politics* 18(4): 381–99.

Amyot, G.G. (2003) *Business, The State and Economic Policy, The Case of Italy*. London: Routledge.

Anceschi, Luca (2021) After Personalism: Rethinking Power Transfers in Turkmenistan and Uzbekistan. *Journal of Contemporary Asia* 51(4): 660–80.

Anders, Günther (1956) *Die Antiquiertheit des Menschen. Band I: Über die Seele im Zeitalter der zweiter industriellen Revolution*. München: Beck.

Anderson, Perry (2014) The Italian Disaster. *London Review of Books*, 22, May. Available (consulted 23 July 2023) at: https://www.lrb.co.uk/the-paper/v36/n10/perry-anderson/the-italian-disaster.

Anishchuk, Alexei (2011) Russia's Medvedev raps Putin's Libya "crusade" jibe. *Reuters*, 21, March. Available (consulted 25 June 2024) at: https://www.reuters.com/article/us-libya-russia-idUSTRE72K5AJ20110321/.

Aon (2023) "Fulvio Conti". https://www.aon.com/about-aon/corporate-governance/corporate/board-directors/fulvio-conti.jsp.

Armijo, Leslie (2007) The BRICS countries (Brazil, Russia, India, and China) as analytical category: mirage or insight? *Asian perspective* 31(4): 7–42.

Artoni, Roberto (ed.) (2014) *Storia dell'IRI. Crisi e privatizzazione*. Roma-Bari: Laterza.

Artoni, Roberto (2021) Il "modello" dietro la legge di bilancio del governo Draghi. *Sbilanciamoci*, 3, November. Available (consulted 1 August 2023) at: https://sbilanciamoci.info/il-modello-che-traspare-dalla-legge-di-bilancio-del-governo-draghi/.

Avci, Akif (2022) The New Regime of Free Trade and Transnational Capital in Turkey. *Journal of Balkan and Near Eastern Studies* 24(1): 78–96.

Ayers, A.J. (2024) 'The Fire This Time': The Long Crisis of Neoliberal Capitalist Accumulation and Spectre of Neofascism. *Critical Sociology* 50(3): 413–35.

Bagehot (2016) An optimistic Eurosceptic. *The Economist*, 21, January. Available (consulted 4 January 2024) at: https://www.economist.com/britain/2016/01/21/an-optimistic-eurosceptic.

Bagnai, Alberto (2013) Introduction to the Symposium: The euro, manage it or leave it! *Comparative Economic Studies* 55: 381–86.

Balcet, Giovanni (1997) *L'economia italiana. Evoluzione, problemi e paradossi.* Milano: Feltrinelli.

Baldini, G., Tronconi, F. and Angelucci, D. (2022) Yet Another Populist Party? Understanding the Rise of Brothers of Italy. *South European Society and Politics* 27(3): 385–405.

Bale, Tim (2023) *The Conservative Party After Brexit: Turmoil and Transformation.* Cambridge: Polity Press.

Ban, Cornel (2016) *Ruling Ideas. How Global Neoliberalism Goes Local.* Oxford: Oxford University Press.

Ban, C., Scheiring, G. and Vasile, M. (2023) The political economy of national-neoliberalism. *European Politics & Society* 24(1): 96–114.

Banca d'Italia (2019) "Media. News. Fabrizio Saccomanni (1942–2019)". https://www.bancaditalia.it/media/notizia/fabrizio-saccomanni-1942-2019/?com.dotmarketing.htmlpage.language=1&dotcache=refresh.

Barrenechea, R. and Dargent, E. (2020) Populists and Technocrats in Latin America: Conflict, Cohabitation, and Cooperation. *Politics and Governance* 8(4): 509–19.

Bartle, J. and King, A. (eds.) (2005) *Britain at the Polls 2005.* London: CQ Press.

BBC (1997a) Politics 97. 3 May 1979. *BBC*. Available (consulted 8 July 2024) at: https://www.bbc.co.uk/news/special/politics97/background/pastelec/ge79.shtml.

BBC (1997b) Politics 97. 9 June 1983. *BBC*. Available (consulted 6 March 2024) at: https://www.bbc.co.uk/news/special/politics97/background/pastelec/ge83.shtml.

BBC (1997c) Politics 97. 11 June 1987. *BBC*. Available (consulted 6 March 2024) at: https://www.bbc.co.uk/news/special/politics97/background/pastelec/ge87.shtml.

BBC (1997d) Politics 97. 1 May 1997. *BBC*. Available (consulted 26 September 2023) at: https://www.bbc.co.uk/news/special/politics97/background/pastelec/ge97.shtml.

BBC (2000) Zyuganov: compromising with communism. *BBC*, 27, March. Available (consulted 10 June 2024) at: http://news.bbc.co.uk/2/hi/europe/667747.stm.

BBC (2001) Vote 2001. *BBC News*, 14, August. Available (consulted 2 October 2023) at: http://news.bbc.co.uk/news/vote2001/.

BBC (2007a) Brown is UK's new prime minister. *BBC News*, 27, June. Available (consulted 8 October 2023) at: http://news.bbc.co.uk/1/hi/uk_politics/6245682.stm.

BBC (2007b) Northern Rock gets bank bailout. *BBC News*, 13, September. Available (consulted 13 October 2023) at: http://news.bbc.co.uk/1/hi/business/6994099.stm.

BBC (2009a) RBS reports record corporate loss. 26, February. Available (consulted 14 October 2023) at: http://news.bbc.co.uk/1/hi/business/7911722.stm.

BBC (2009b) UK in recession as economy slides. *BBC News*, 23, January. Available (consulted 14 October 2023) at: http://news.bbc.co.uk/1/hi/business/7846266.stm.

BBC (2009c) UKIP beats Labour to second place. *BBC News*, 8, June. Available (consulted 25 September 2023) at: http://news.bbc.co.uk/1/hi/uk_politics/8088343.stm.

BBC (2010a) Benefits system overhaul 'to make work pay'. *BBC News*, 11, November. Available (consulted 17 October 2023) at: https://www.bbc.co.uk/news/uk-politics-11728546.

BBC (2010b) Election 2010. Results. Available (consulted 16 October 2023) at: http://news.bbc.co.uk/1/shared/election2010/results/.

BBC (2011) Boris Johnson adds to Tory EU referendum pressure on MP. 7, December. Available (consulted 23 October 2023) at: https://www.bbc.co.uk/news/uk-politics-16063911.

BBC (2012) Budget 2012: Tracking the UK economy. *BBC News*, 15, March. Available (consulted 22 October 2023) at: https://www.bbc.co.uk/news/business-17379243.

BBC (2014a) Scottish referendum: Scotland votes 'No' to independence. *BBC News*, 19, September. Available (consulted 16 December 2023) at: https://www.bbc.co.uk/news/uk-scotland-29270441.

BBC (2014b) Vote 2014. *BBC News*. Available (consulted 30 October 2023) at: https://www.bbc.co.uk/news/events/vote2014/eu-uk-results.

BBC (2015a) Election results: Conservatives win majority. *BBC News*, 8, May. Available (consulted 18 December 2023) at: https://www.bbc.co.uk/news/election-2015-32633099.

BBC (2015b) Russia's former PM Yevgeni Primakov dies aged 85. *BBC News*, 26, June. Available (consulted 06 May 2024) at: https://www.bbc.com/news/world-europe-33290421.

BBC (2016) EU Referendum. Results. *BBC News*. Available (consulted 6 May 2024) at: https://www.bbc.co.uk/news/politics/eu_referendum/results.

BBC (2019a) Election 2019. Results. *BBC News*. Available (consulted 11 January 2024) at: https://www.bbc.com/news/election/2019/results.

BBC (2019b) The UK's European elections 2019. *BBC News*. Available (consulted 13 January 2024) at: https://www.bbc.co.uk/news/topics/crjeqkdevwvt/the-uks-european-elections-2019.

BBC (2020a) Coronavirus: Italy extends emergency measures nationwide. *BBC News*, 10, March. Available (consulted 25 May 2024) at: https://www.bbc.com/news/world-europe-51810673.

BBC (2020b) Dominic Cummings: Did he break lockdown rules? *BBC News. Politics*, 28, May. Available (consulted 10 March 2024) at: https://www.bbc.co.uk/news/uk-politics-52784290.

BBC (2021) Russia election: Putin's party wins election marred by fraud claims. *BBC News*, 20, September. Available (consulted 20 July 2024) at: https://www.bbc.co.uk/news/world-europe-58614227.

BBC (2022a) Autumn Statement 2022: Key points at-a-glance. *BBC News. Business*, 17, November. Available (consulted 2 April 2024) at: https://www.bbc.co.uk/news/business-63555313.

BBC (2022b) First UK coal mine in decades approved despite climate concerns. *BBC News,* 7, December. Available (consulted 2 April 2024) at: https://www.bbc.co.uk/news/uk-politics-63892381.

BBC (2022c) UK strikes revised deal with France on Channel migrants. *BBC News,* 14, November. Available (consulted 2 April 2024) at: https://www.bbc.co.uk/news/uk-politics-63615653.

BBC News (2009) Nations seek currency rule change. 16, June. Available (consulted 24 June 2024) at: http://news.bbc.co.uk/1/hi/business/8102216.stm.

BBC News (2013) Q&A: Mikhail Khodorkovsky and Russia. 22, December. Available (consulted 14 June 2024) at: https://www.bbc.com/news/world-europe-25467275.

BBC News (2024) General election 2024 in maps and charts. 4, July. Available (consulted 10 July 2024) at: https://www.bbc.co.uk/news/articles/c4nglegege1o.

Becker, G.S. 1997. "What Latin America Owes to the 'Chicago Boys'". Hoover Institution. Hoover Digest. Stanford, CA. https://web.archive.org/web/20100724040917/http://www.hoover.org/publications/hoover-digest/article/7743.

Behuria, Pritish (2018) Learning from Role Models in Rwanda: Incoherent Emulation in the Construction of a Neoliberal Developmental State. *New Political Economy* 23(4): 422–40.

Bel, Germà (2011) The first privatisation: selling SOEs and privatising public monopolies in Fascist Italy (1922–1925). *Cambridge Journal of Economics* 35(5): 937–56.

Bell, Daniel A. (2015) *The China Model: Political Meritocracy and the Limits of Democracy.* Princeton, NJ: Princeton University Press.

Benvenuti, Andrea (2016) Italy, the Monti government and the Euro crisis (2011–12). *Australia and New Zealand Journal of European Studies* 8(2): 80–95.

Bergmann, M. and Clark, S. 2021. "By Engaging Italy, Biden Can Strengthen Both The United States and The EU." Center for American Progress. Washington, DC. https://www.americanprogress.org/article/engaging-italy-biden-can-strengthen-united-states-eu/.

Berlin, Isaiah (1969) *Four Essays on Liberty.* Oxford: Oxford University Press.

Bermeo, Nancy (2016) On Democratic Backsliding. *Journal of Democracy* 27(1): 5–19.

Berteloot, Tristan (2018) Portrait. Jordan Bardella, poupée de Front pour les européennes. *Liberation,* 26, December. Available (consulted 5 July 2024) at: https://www.liberation.fr/les-pouvoirs/2018/12/26/jordan-bardella-poupee-de-front-pour-les-europeennes_1699848/.

Bhambra, Gurminder K. (2017a) Brexit, Trump, and 'methodological whiteness': on the misrecognition of race and class. *The British Journal of Sociology* 68(1): 214–32.

Bhambra, Gurminder K. (2017b) "'Our island story': the dangerous story of belonging in austere times" In *Austere Histories in European Societies. Social Exclusion and the Contest of Colonial Memories,* edited by Stefan Jonsson and Julia Willén. London: Routledge, 2017, 21–37.

Bhambra, Gurminder K. (2022) Relations of extraction, relations of redistribution: Empire, nation and the construction of the British welfare state. *The British Journal of Sociology* 73: 4–15.

Bhatty, K. and Sundar, N. (2020) Sliding from majoritarianism towards fascism: Educating India under the Modi regime. *International Sociology* 35(6): 632–50.

Bickerton, C. and Invernizzi Accetti, C. (2017) Populism and technocracy: opposites or complements? *Critical Review of International Social and Political Philosophy* 20(2): 186–206.

Bickerton, C. and Invernizzi Accetti, C. (2018) Techno-populism as a new party family: The case of the Five Star Movement and Podemos. *Contemporary Italian Politics* 10(2): 132–50.

Biorcio, Roberto (2015) *Il populismo nella politica italiana: da Bossi a Berlusconi, da Grillo a Renzi.* Milano-Udine: Mimesis.

Blackburn, Dean (2017) Reassessing Britain's 'Post-war consensus': the politics of reason 1945–1979. *British Politics* 13(2): 195–214.

Blair, Tony (1997) *Leader's speech.* Brighton 1997. Available (consulted 6 December 2023) at: http://www.britishpoliticalspeech.org/speech-archive.htm?speech=203.

Blim, Michael (2000) What is still left for the Left in Italy? Piecing together a post-communist position on labor and employment. *Journal of Modern Italian Studies* 5(2): 169–85.

Blondel, J. and Segatti, P. (eds.) (2004) The Second Berlusconi Government. *Italian Politics* 18. New York, NY: Berghahn.

Bloom, Peter (2016) *Authoritarian Capitalism in the Age of Globalization.* Cheltenham: Elgar.

Blyth, Mark (2013) *Austerity: The history of a dangerous idea.* Oxford: Oxford University Press.

Blyth, M. and Hopkin, J. (2018) The global economics of European populism: Growth regimes and party system change in Europe. *Government and Opposition* 54(2): 193–225.

Boas, T.C. and Gans-Morse, J. (2009) Neoliberalism: From New Liberal Philosophy to Anti-Liberal Slogan. *Studies in Comparative International Development* 44: 137–61.

Bobbio, Norberto (1997) *Verso la seconda Repubblica.* Torino: La Stampa.

Boffey, D. and O'Carroll, L. (2020) UK and EU agree Brexit trade deal. *The Guardian*, 24, December. Available (consulted 16 January 2024) at: https://www.theguardian.com/politics/2020/dec/24/uk-eu-agree-brexit-trade-deal-agreement.

Boycko, M., Shleifer, A. and Vishny, R.W. 1993. "Privatizing Russia." Brookings Papers on Economic Activities. Cambridge, MA. https://www.jstor.org/stable/2534566.

Brancaleone, Marie. 2021. "The Russian Elite in the post-Putin Era." CECRI. Louvain-la-Neuve. https://cecrilouvain.be/wp-content/uploads/2021/03/The-Russian-Elite-in-the-post-Putin-era.pdf.

Brenner, N., Peck, J. and Theodore, N. (2010) Variegated neoliberalization: geographies, modalities, pathways. *Global networks* 10(2): 182–222.

Breslin, Shaun (2011) The 'China model' and the global crisis: from Friedrich List to a Chinese mode of governance? *International Affairs* 87(6): 1323–43.

Bronzini, Giuseppe (2014) Il reddito di cittadinanza, tra aspetti definitori ed esperienze applicative. *Rivista del Diritto della Sicurezza Sociale* XIV(1): 1–32.

Broomfield, Matt (2017) How Theresa May's "hostile environment" created an underworld. *The New Statesman*, 19, December. Available (consulted 3 May 2024) at: https://www.newstatesman.com/long-reads/2017/12/how-theresa-may-s-hostile-environment-created-underworld.

Brown, M. and Stewart, H. (2022) Starmer says he won't be 'ideological' amid renationalisation row. *The Guardian*, 25, July. Available (consulted 14 May 2024) at: https://www.theguardian.com/politics/2022/jul/25/starmer-says-he-wont-be-ideological-labour-renationalisation-row.

Brubaker, Rogers (2019) Populism and nationalism. *Nations and Nationalism* 26(1): 1–23.

Brudny, Y.M. "Ruslan Khasbulatov, Alexander Rutskoi, and Intraelite Conflict in Postcommunist Russia, 1991–1994". In *Patterns In Post-soviet Leadership*, edited by Timothy Colton and Robert C. Tucker. New York: Routledge, 1995, 74–100.

Brudny, Y.M. (1996) In Pursuit of the Russian Presidency: Why and How Yeltsin Won the 1996 Presidential Election. *Communist and Post-Communist Studies* 30(3): 255–75.

Bruff, Ian (2012) Authoritarian neoliberalism, the Occupy movements, and IPE. *Journal of Critical Globalisation Studies* 1(5): 114–16.

Bruff, Ian (2014) The rise of authoritarian neoliberalism. *Rethinking Marxism* 26(1): 113–29.

Bruff, I. and Tansel, C.B. (2019) Authoritarian neoliberalism: Trajectories of knowledge production and praxis. *Globalizations* 16(3): 233–44.

Buchanan, J.M. (1960) *Fiscal Theory and Political Economy. Selected Papers*. Chapel Hill, NC: The University of North Carolina Press.

Bufacchi, V. and Burgess, S. (1997) *Italy since 1989. Events and Interpretations*. London: Palgrave Macmillan.

Burgin, Angus (2012) *The Great Persuasion: Reinventing Free Markets Since the Depression*. Cambridge, MA: Harvard University Press.

Burke Foundation (2024) https://burke.foundation/.

Burnham, Peter (1999) The politics of economic management in the 1990s. *New Political Economy* 4(1): 37–54.

Burnham, Peter (2001) New Labour and the politics of depoliticisation. *British Journal of Politics and International Relations* 3(2): 127–49.

Burnham, Peter (2014) Depoliticisation: economic crisis and political management. *Policy & Politics* 42(2): 189–206.

Busch, A. and Manow, P. (2001) "The SPD and the Neue Mitte in Germany". In *New Labour. The Progressive Future?*, edited by Stuart White. London: Palgrave Macmillan, 2001, 1715–89.

Buštíková, L. and Guasti, P. (2018) The State as a Firm: Understanding the Autocratic Roots of Technocratic Populism. *East European Politics and Societies and Cultures* 33(2): 302–30.

Butler, D. and Kavanagh, D. (1980) *The British General Election of 1979*. London: Macmillan.

Butler, Sarah (2022) Igor Shuvalov: the former Russian deputy PM with an £11m flat in Whitehall. *The Guardian*, 2, March. Available (consulted 29 June 2024) at: https://www.theguardian.com/uk-news/2022/mar/02/keir-starmer-calls-uk-blacklist-russian-crony-igor-shuvalov.

Caciagli, M. and Kertzer, D.I. (eds.) (1996) The Stalled Transition. *Italian Politics* 11. New York, NY: Berghahn.

Calise, Mauro (1994) The Italian Particracy: Beyond President and Parliament. *Political Science Quarterly* 109(3): 441–60.

Callahan, William A. (2016) China's "Asia Dream": The Belt Road Initiative and the new regional order. *Asian Journal of Comparative Politics* 1(3): 226–43.

Callison, W. and Manfredi, Z. (eds.) (2020) *Mutant Neoliberalism: Market Rule and Political Rupture*. New York, NY: Fordham University Press.

Cameron, David (2011a) *PM's speech at Munich Security Conference*. Available (consulted 10 December 2023) at: https://www.gov.uk/government/speeches/pms-speech-at-munich-security-conference.

Cameron, David (2011b) *Speech on the fightback after the riots*. Available (consulted 10 December 2023) at: https://www.gov.uk/government/speeches/pms-speech-on-the-fightback-after-the-riots.

Cameron, David (2013) *EU speech at Bloomberg*. Available (consulted 14 December 2023) at: https://www.gov.uk/government/speeches/eu-speech-at-bloomberg.

Cameron, David (2014) David Cameron's EU speech: full text. *BBC News*, 28, November. Available (consulted 18 December 2023) at: https://www.bbc.co.uk/news/uk-politics-30250299.

Cannon, Lou (2000) *President Reagan: The Role Of A Lifetime*. New York, NY: Public Affairs.

Capano, G. and Sandri, G. (2022) The political leadership of Mario Draghi: an historical watershed or an inevitable bump in the road? *Contemporary Italian Politics* 14(2): 118–32.

Caramani, Daniele (2017) Will vs. reason: The populist and technocratic forms of political representation and their critique to party government. *American Political Science Review* 111(1): 54–67.

Carter, Neil (2009) Vote Blue, Go Green? Cameron's Conservatives and the Environment. *The Political Quarterly* 80(2): 233–42.

Castaldo, A. and Verzichelli, L. (2020) Technocratic Populism in Italy after Berlusconi: The Trendsetter and his Disciples. *Politics and Governance* 8(4): 485–95.

Castellina, Luciana (2021) Le lacune di Draghi. *Sbilanciamoci*, 24, February. Available (consulted 1 August 2023) at: https://sbilanciamoci.info/le-lacune-di-draghi/.

Cavallo, Domingo (2004) Commentary. Argentina and the IMF During the Two Bush Administrations. *International Finance* 7(1): 137–50.

Cazzullo, Aldo (2023) Cairo: "Berlusconi? Lo incontrai a 24 anni, fu una specie di magia." *Corriere della Sera*, 12, June. Available (consulted 12 July 2023) at: https://www.corriere.it/politica/23_giugno_12/cairo-berlusconi-intervista-63fc5042-092d-11ee-9252-2eef801783fd.shtml.

Centeno, Miguel A. (1993) The New Leviathan: The Dynamics and Limits of Technocracy. *Theory and Society* 22(3): 307–35.

Centeno, Miguel A. (2010) *Democracy within reason: technocratic revolution in Mexico*. University Park, PA: The Pennsylvania State University Press.

Cesaratto, Sergio (2014) Il ministro Padoan oltre Keynes. Nel '75. *Il Manifesto*. Available (consulted 22 July 2023) at: https://ilmanifesto.it/il-ministro-padoan-oltre-keynes-nel-75.

Cesaratto, S. and Zezza, G. (2018) "Farsi male da soli. Disciplina esterna, domanda aggregata e il declino economico italiano." Quaderni del Dipartimento di Economia Politica e Statistica. https://www.deps.unisi.it/it/ricerca/pubblicazioni-deps/quaderni-deps/anno-2018-da-n771-n/793-farsi-male-da-soli-disciplina.

Chacko, Priya (2018) The Right Turn in India: Authoritarianism, Populism and Neoliberalisation. *Journal of Contemporary Asia* 48(4): 541–65.

Chacko, Priya (2019) Marketising Hindutva: The state, society and markets in Hindu Nationalism. *Modern Asian Studies* 53(2): 377–410.

Chakraborty, Aditya (2011) UK riots: political classes see what they want to see. *The Guardian*, 10, August. Available (consulted 21 October 2023) at: https://www.theguardian.com/uk/2011/aug/10/uk-riots-political-classes.

Chamedes, Giuliana (2021) Will Mario Draghi's Center Hold? *Dissent*, 17, March. Available (consulted 1 August 2023) at: https://www.dissentmagazine.org/online_articles/will-mario-draghis-center-hold/.

Chatham House. 2013. "Italy and the UK in an Evolving EU." Transcript Q&A. https://www.chathamhouse.org/sites/default/files/public/Meetings/Meeting%20Transcripts/160713LettaQA.pdf.

Cheibub, José A., Gandhi, J. and Vreeland, J.R. (2010) Democracy and dictatorship revisited. *Public Choice* 143 (1–2): 67–101.

Chiaramonte, A., Emanuele, V., Maggini, N. and Paparo, A. (2018) Populist Success in a Hung Parliament: The 2018 General Election in Italy. *South European Society and Politics* 23(4): 479–501.

Ciampi, Carlo A. (1992) Scienza e arte del banchiere centrale. *Il Mulino*. XLI(1): 5–17.

Ciampi, Carlo A. (2011) In ricordo di Tommaso Padoa-Schioppa. *Moneta e Credito* 64(253): 3–8.

Ciccarelli, Roberto (2023) Mario Pianta: « Non lasciare a Meloni la critica dell'austerità ». *Sbilanciamoci*, 29, June. Available (consulted 7 August 2023) at: https://sbilanciamoci.info/mario-pianta-non-lasciare-a-meloni-la-critica-dellausterita/.

Claeys, G., Leandro, A. and Mandra, A. 2015. "European Central Bank Quantitative Easing: The Detailed Manual." Bruegel Policy Contribution. YPSF Documents. 112. https://elischolar.library.yale.edu/cgi/viewcontent.cgi?article=1160&context=ypfs-documents.

Clark, Timothy D. (2017) Rethinking Chile's 'Chicago Boys': neoliberal technocrats or revolutionary vanguard? *Third World Quarterly* 38(6): 1350–65.

Clem, R.S. and Craumer, P.R. (1993) The Geography of the April 25 (1993) Russian Referendum. *Post-Soviet Geography* 34(8): 481–96.

Clift, Ben (2022) *The OBR and the politics of technocratic economic governance*. Oxford: Oxford University Press.

Clift, Ben (2023) Technocratic economic governance and the politics of UK fiscal rules. *British Politics* 18: 254–78.

Clift, Ben (2024) The OBR and the fragilities, complexities and promise of technocratic economic governance. *British Politics*. Available (consulted 24 August 2024) at: file:///Users/ernestogallo/Downloads/s41293-024-00261-6%20(2).pdf.

Clift, B. and Tomlinson, J. (2008) Negotiating Credibility: Britain and the International Monetary Fund, 1956–1976. *Contemporary European History* 17(4): 545–66.

Clua-Losada, M. and Ribera-Almandoz, O. "Authoritarian Neoliberalism and the Disciplining of Labour". In *State of Discipline: Authoritarian Neoliberalism and the Contested Reproduction of Capitalist Order*, edited by Cemal Burak Tansel. London: Rowman & Littlefield, 2017, 29–46.

Colton, T.J. and Hale, H.E. 2013. "Putin's Uneasy Return: The 2012 Russian Election Studies Survey." NCEEER Working Paper. University of Washington, WA. https://www.ucis.pitt.edu/nceeer/2013_827-15_Hale.pdf.

Columbia University (2007). "Yegor Gaidar". https://worldleaders.columbia.edu/directory/yegor-gaidar.

Commanding Heights (2000). Anatoly Chubais. *PBS*, 12, December. Available (consulted 24 May 2024) at: https://www.pbs.org/wgbh/commandingheights/shared/minitext/int_anatoliichubais.html.

Connell, R. and Dados, N. (2014) Where in the world does neoliberalism come from? The market agenda in southern perspective. *Theory and Society: Renewal and Critique in Social Theory* 43(2): 117–38.

Connolly, Richard (2016) The Empire Strikes Back: Economic Statecraft and the Securitisation of Political Economy in Russia. *Europe-Asia Studies* 68(4): 750–73.

Connolly, W.E. (2017) Trump, the Working Class, and Fascist Rhetoric. *Theory & Event* 20(1): 23–37.

Conservative Party Manifesto (2010) https://general-election-2010.co.uk/2010-general-election-manifestos/Conservative-Party-Manifesto-2010.pdf.

Conservative Party Manifesto (2015) https://www.theresavilliers.co.uk/sites/www.theresavilliers.co.uk/files/conservativemanifesto2015.pdf.

Conservative Party Manifesto (2019) https://www.conservatives.com/our-plan/conservative-party-manifesto-2019.

Corriere della Sera (2011) Trichet e Draghi: un'azione pressante per ristabilire la fiducia degli investitori. 29, September. Available (consulted 17 July 2023) at: https://www.corriere.it/economia/11_settembre_29/trichet_draghi_inglese_304a5f1e-ea59-11e0-ae06-4da866778017.shtml?fr=correlati.

Cox, R.W. and Skidmore-Hess, D. (2024) How Neofascism Emerges from Neoliberal Capitalism. *New Political Science* 44(4): 590–606.

Cozzolino, Adriano (2018) Trumpism as *nationalist neoliberalism.* A critical enquiry into Donald Trump's political economy. *Interdisciplinary Political Studies* 4(1): 47–73.

Cozzolino, Adriano (2020) The Discursive Construction of Europe in Italy in the Age of Permanent Austerity. *Journal of Common Market Studies* 58(3): 580–98.

Craveri, Piero (2012) "MORO, Aldo". Dizionario biografico degli Italiani Treccani. https://www.treccani.it/enciclopedia/aldo-moro_%28Dizionario-Biografico%29/.

Crerar, P., Elgot, J. and Lawson, A. (2022) Liz Truss to appoint cabinet of loyalists as she becomes UK's next prime minister. *The Guardian*, 5, September. Available (consulted 26 March 2024) at: https://www.theguardian.com/politics/2022/sep/05/liz-truss-to-appoint-cabinet-of-loyalists-as-she-becomes-uks-next-pm.

Croce, Benedetto (1970) *History as the story of liberty*. Chicago, IL: Regnery.

Crouch, Colin (2011) *The strange non-death of neo-liberalism*. Cambridge: Polity Press.

Crouch, Colin (2017) Neoliberalism, Nationalism and the Decline of Political Traditions. *The Political Quarterly* 88(2): 221–29.

Culpepper, P.D. (2014) The political economy of unmediated democracy: Italian austerity under Mario Monti. *West European Politics* 37(6): 1264–81.

Cummings, Dominic (2017) Dominic Cummings: how the Brexit referendum was won. *The Spectator*, 9, January. Available (consulted 28 December 2023) at: https://web.archive.org/web/20181031033811/https://blogs.spectator.co.uk/2017/01/dominic-cummings-brexit-referendum-won/.

Curtice, John (2017) Why Leave Won the UK's EU Referendum. *JCMS: Journal of Common Market Studies* 55: 19–37.

D'Alema, Massimo (1995) *Un paese normale. La sinistra e il futuro dell'Italia*. Arnoldo Mondadori: Milano.

Da Costa Vieira, Thomas (2023) 'In time, every worker a capitalist': Accumulation by legitimation and authoritarian neoliberalism in Thatcher's Britain. *Competition & Change* 27(5): 729–47.

Dale, Gareth (ed.) (2011) *First the Transition, then the Crash. Eastern Europe in the 2000s.* London: Pluto Press.

Daly, Patrick (2022) UK's Rwanda asylum plan breaches international law, says UN refugee agency. *Independent*, 22, April. Available (consulted 23 January 2024) at: https://www.independent.co.uk/news/uk/politics/rwanda-asylum-seekers-uk-priti-patel-b2059064.html.

Dardot, P. and Laval, C. (2019) *Never-Ending Nightmare: The Neoliberal Assault on Democracy.* London: Verso.

Das, R.J. (2024) *Critical Reflections on Economy and Politics in India. A Class Theory Perspective.* Leiden: Brill.

Datablog (2012) Youth unemployment across the OECD: how does the UK compare? *The Guardian,* 16, May. Available (consulted 17 May 2025) at: https://www.theguardian.com/news/datablog/2012/may/16/youth-unemployment-europe-oecd.

Datta, Ayona (2015) A 100 smart cities, a 100 utopias. *Dialogues in Human Geography* 5(1): 49–53.

Davies, Will (2016) The new neoliberalism. *New Left Review* 101: 121–34.

Davis, A. and Walsh, C. (2017) Distinguishing Financialization from Neoliberalism. *Theory, Culture and Society* 34(5–6): 27–51.

Dear, Keith (2019) Will Russia Rule the World Through AI? *The RUSI Journal* 5–6: 36–60.

Dearden, Lizzie (2023) Bible verse, conspiracy and the 'cult of trans': The ultra-conservative Americans infiltrating the Tory party. *The Independent,* 19, May. Available (consulted 10 April 2024) at: https://www.independent.co.uk/news/uk/politics/conservative-party-conference-suella-braverman-michael-gove-b2341890.html.

De Felice, Franco (1999) *La questione della nazione repubblicana.* Roma-Bari: Laterza.

De La Torre, Carlos (2013) In the Name of the People: Democratizations, Popular Organizations, and Populism in Venezuela, Bolivia, and Ecuador. *European Review of Latin American and Caribbean Studies* 95: 27–48.

de Orellana, Pablo and Michelsen, Nicholas (2019) Reactionary Internationalism: the philosophy of the New Right. *Review of International Studies* 45(5): 748–67.

Del Corno, Mauro (2020) Benetton, "famiglia apolitica" che ha fatto affari con destra e sinistra: profitti miliardari con Autostrade, Autogrill e Aeroporti Roma. *Il Fatto Quotidiano,* 13, July. Available (consulted 30 June 2023) at: https://www.ilfattoquotidiano.it/2020/07/13/benetton-famiglia-apolitica-che-ha-fatto-affari-con-destra-e-sinistra-profitti-miliardari-con-autostrade-autogrill-e-aeroporti-roma/5866441/.

Della Sala, Vincent. "D'Alema's Dilemmas: Third Way, Italian Style." In *The Third Way Transformation of Social Democracy*, edited by Oliver Schmidtke, Aldershot, Ashgate, 2002.

Demertzis, M., Hilgenstock, B., McWilliams, B., Ribakova, E. and Tagliapietra, S. 2022. "How have sanctions impacted Russia?" Policy contribution 18/2022. Bruegel. Brussels. https://hdl.handle.net/10419/274172.

Denham, A. and Garnett, M. (2002) Sir Keith Joseph and the undoing of British conservatism. *Journal of Political Ideologies* 7(1): 57–75.

Denisova, Anastasia (2017) Democracy, protest and public sphere in Russia after the 2011–2012 anti-government protests: digital media at stake. *Media, Culture & Society* 39(7): 976–94.

Dennison, J. and Geddes, A. (2023) The centre no longer holds: the Lega, Matteo Salvini and the remaking of Italian immigration politics. *Journal of Ethnic and Migration Studies* 48(2): 441–60.

Desai, Radhika (2016) Hindutva and Fascism. *Economic and Political Weekly* 51(53): 20–4.

Deseriis, Marco (2017) Technopopulism: The emergence of a discursive formation. tripleC 15(2): 441–58.

Diamond, Larry (1999) *Developing democracy: toward consolidation.* Baltimore, MD: Johns Hopkins University Press.

Di Quirico, Roberto (2023) Economic reform strategies and recovery policies from Conte to Draghi. *Italian Political Science* 17(1): 105–20.

Dobson, Hugo (2017) Is Japan Really Back? The "Abe Doctrine" and Global Governance. *Journal of Contemporary Asia* 47(2): 199–224.

Dorey, Peter (2017) Jeremy Corbyn confounds his critics: explaining the Labour party's remarkable resurgence in the 2017 election. *British Politics* 12(3): 308–34.

Dorling, Danny (2016) Brexit: the decision of a divided country. *The British Medical Journal* 354.

Dornbusch, Ruediger. 1984. "Argentina Since Martinez De Hoz." NBER Working Paper No. 1466. Cambridge, MA. https://www.nber.org/system/files/working_papers/w1466/w1466.pdf.

Dosi, G. and Roventini, A. (2022) The Leopard: How a Post-Fascist Party Rose to Power in Italy. *Intereconomics* 57(5): 270–71.

Draghi, Mario (2020) Draghi: we face a war against coronavirus and must mobilise accordingly. *Financial Times*, 25, March. Available (consulted 28 July 2023) at: https://www.ft.com/content/c6d2de3a-6ec5-11ea-89df-41bea055720b.

Duckett, Jane (2020) Neoliberalism, Authoritarian Politics and Social Policy in China. *Development and Change*. 51(2): 523–39.

Duménil, G. and Lévy, D. (2004) *Capital Resurgent. Roots of the Neoliberal Revolution.* Cambridge, MA: Harvard University Press.

Duncan, P.J.S. 2007. "'Oligarchs', Business and Russian Foreign Policy: From El'tsin to Putin." Economics Working Paper No. 83. UCL SSEES. Centre for Economic and Social Change in Europe. London. https://discovery.ucl.ac.uk/id/eprint/12932/.

Dyson, K. and Featherstone, K. (2006) Italy and EMU as a 'Vincolo Esterno': Empowering the Technocrats, Transforming the State. *South European Society & Politics*. 1(2): 272–99.

Eatwell, Roger (2003) *Fascism. A History*. London: Penguin.

Eatwell, R. and Goodwin, M. (2018) *National Populism: The Revolt against Liberal Democracy*. London: Penguin.

ECB (2012) "Verbatim of the remarks made by Mario Draghi. Speech by Mario Draghi, President of the European Central Bank, at the Global Investment Conference in London, 26 July 2012". https://www.ecb.europa.eu/press/key/date/2012/html/sp120726.en.html.

Economy, Elizabeth C. (2018) *The Third Revolution. Xi Jinping and the New Chinese State*. Oxford: Oxford University Press.

Einaudi, Luigi (1986) *La guerra e l'unità europea*. Milano: Comunità.

Einaudi, L. and Croce, B. (1988) *Carteggio (1902–1953)*, a cura di Luigi Firpo. Torino: Fondazione Luigi Einaudi.

Einzenberger, R. and Schaffar, W. (2018) The political economy of new authoritarianism in Southeast Asia. *Austrian Journal of South-East Asian Studies*. 11(1): 1–12.

Elder, Miriam (2013a) Boris Berezovsky: kingmaker reduced to a shadow in exile. *The Guardian*, 23, March. Available (consulted 12 June 2024) at: https://www.theguardian.com/world/2013/mar/23/boris-berezovsky-kingmaker-vladimir-putin.

Elder, Miriam (2013b) Russia raids human rights groups in crackdown on 'foreign agents'. *The Guardian*, 27, March. Available (consulted 1 July 2024) at: https://www.theguardian.com/world/2013/mar/27/russia-raids-human-rights-crackdown.

Elgie, Robert (2011) Core executive studies two decades on. *Public Administration* 89(1): 64–77.

Elgot, Jessica (2023) Why Rishi Sunak may be the most socially conservative PM of his generation. *The Guardian*, 18, April. Available (consulted 13 May 2024) at: https://www.theguardian.com/politics/2023/apr/18/why-rishi-sunak-is-perhaps-the-most-socially-conservative-pm-of-his-generation.

Eligendo (1996a) "L'Archivio. Camera 21/04/1996. Area ITALIA". https://elezionistorico.interno.gov.it/index.php?tpel=C&dtel=21/04/1996&eso=S&tpa=I&levo=0&levsuto=0&ms=S&tpe=A.

Eligendo (1996b) "L'Archivio. Senato 21/04/1996. Area ITALIA". https://elezionistorico.interno.gov.it/index.php?tpel=S&dtel=21/04/1996&eso=S&tpa=I&levo=0&levsuto=0&ms=S&tpe=A.

Eligendo (2001a) "L'Archivio. Camera 13/05/2001. Area ITALIA". https://elezionistorico.interno.gov.it/index.php?tpel=C&dtel=13/05/2001&eso=S&tpa=I&levo=0&levsuto=0&ms=S&tpe=A.

Eligendo (2001b) "L'Archivio. Senato 13/05/2001. Area ITALIA". https://elezionistorico.interno.gov.it/index.php?tpel=S&dtel=13/05/2001&eso=S&tpa=I&levo=0&levsuto=0&ms=S&tpe=A.

Eligendo (2008a) "L'Archivio. Camera 13/04/2008. Area ITALIA". https://elezionistorico.interno.gov.it/index.php?tpel=C&dtel=13/04/2008&eso=S&tpa=I&levo=0&levsuto=0&ms=S&tpe=A.

Eligendo (2008b) "L'Archivio. Senato 13/04/2008. Area ITALIA". https://elezionistorico.interno.gov.it/index.php?tpel=S&dtel=13/04/2008&eso=S&tpa=I&levo=0&levsuto=0&ms=S&tpe=A.

Eligendo (2013) "L'Archivio. Camera 24/02/2013. Area ITALIA (escl. Valle d'Aosta)". https://elezionistorico.interno.gov.it/index.php?tpel=C&dtel=24/02/2013&eso=S&tpa=I&levo=0&levsuto=0&ms=S&tpe=A.

Eligendo (2018a) "L'Archivio. Camera 04/03/2018. Area ITALIA (escl. Valle d'Aosta)". https://elezionistorico.interno.gov.it/index.php?tpel=C&dtel=04/03/2018&eso=S&tpa=I&levo=0&levsuto=0&ms=S&tpe=A.

Eligendo (2018b) "L'Archivio. Senato 04/03/2018. Area ITALIA (escl. Valle d'Aosta)". https://elezionistorico.interno.gov.it/index.php?tpel=S&dtel=04/03/2018&eso=S&tpa=I&levo=0&levsuto=0&ms=S&tpe=A.

Eligendo (2022a) "L'Archivio. Camera 25/09/2022. Area ITALIA (escl. Valle d'Aosta)". https://elezionistorico.interno.gov.it/index.php?tpel=C&dtel=25/09/2022&eso=S&tpa=I&levo=0&levsuto=0&ms=S&tpe=A.

Eligendo (2022b) "L'Archivio. Senato 25/09/2022. Area ITALIA (escl. Valle d'Aosta e Trentino-Alto Adige)".

Elliott, Larry (2022) UK inflation jumps to 11.1% on back of energy and food price rises. *The Guardian*, 16, November. Available (consulted 2 April 2024) at: https://www.theguardian.com/business/2022/nov/16/uk-inflation-rate-energy-price-rises.

Ellul, Jacques (1964) *The Technological Society*. Translated by John Wilkinson. New York, NY: Vintage Books. https://archive.org/details/technologicalsoc00ellu/page/n3/mode/2up.

ENEL (2023) "Azionisti". https://www.enel.com/it/investitori/investimenti/azionisti.

England, K. and Ward, K. (eds.) (2007) *Neoliberalization: States, networks, peoples*. Malden, MA: Blackwell.

ENI (2009) "L'Azienda. Paolo Scaroni, Amministratore Delegato". https://web.archive.org/web/20100407065036/http://www.eni.com/it_IT/azienda/organigramma/amministratore-delegato/paolo-scaroni-amm-delegato.shtml.

ENI (2024) "Azionisti". https://www.eni.com/it-IT/governance/azionariato.

Erlanger, Steven (1992) Man in the News; Kremlin's Technocrat: Viktor Stepanovich Chernomyrdin. *The New York Times*, 15, December. Available (consulted 28 May 2024) at: https://www.nytimes.com/1992/12/15/world/man-in-the-news-kremlin-s-technocrat-viktor-stepanovich-chernomyrdin.html.

Fabry, Adam (2018) The origins of neoliberalism in late 'socialist' Hungary: The case of the Financial Research Institute and 'Turnabout and Reform'. *Capital & Class* 42(1): 77–107.

Fabry, Adam (2019) *The Political Economy of Hungary*. London: Palgrave Macmillan.

Faucci, Riccardo (2012) "Luigi Einaudi". Enciclopedia Treccani. Il Contributo italiano alla storia del Pensiero: Economia. https://www.treccani.it/enciclopedia/luigi-einaudi_%28Il-Contributo-italiano-alla-storia-del-Pensiero:-Economia%29/.

Faulconbridge, G. and Osborn, A. (2024) Putin wins Russia election in landslide with no serious competition. *Reuters*, 17, March. Available (consulted 24 July 2024) at: https://www.reuters.com/world/europe/russias-presidential-vote-starts-final-day-with-accusations-kyiv-sabotage-2024-03-17/.

FdI (2022) "Il Programma. Pronti a risollevare l'Italia". https://www.programmafdi2022.it.

Federici, Silvia (2012) *Revolution at Point Zero: Housework, Reproduction, and Feminist Struggle*. Brooklyn, MA: Common Notions.

Fekete, Liz (2016) Flying the flag for neoliberalism. *Race & Class* 58(3): 3–22.

Fekete, Liz (2023) The hurricane from the Right. *Race & Class* 65(3): 92–103.

Feldmann, M. and Morgan, G. (2021a) Brexit and British Business Elites: Business Power and Noisy Politics. *Politics & Society* 49(1): 107–31.

Feldmann, M. and Morgan, G. (2021b) *Business has been a bystander to Brexit*. LSE Brexit Blog, 15, March. Available (consulted 26 December 2023) at: https://blogs.lse.ac.uk/brexit/2021/03/15/business-has-been-a-bystander-to-brexit/.

Ferdinand, Peter (1992) Russia and Russians after Communism: Western or Eurasian? *The World Today* 48(12): 225–29.

Fifi, Gianmarco (2023) From social protection to 'progressive neoliberalism': writing the Left into the rise and resilience of neoliberal policies (1968–2019). *Review of International Political Economy* 30(4): 1436–58.

Fitoussi, J.-P. and Saraceno, F. (2013) European economic governance: the Berlin-Washington Consensus. *Cambridge Journal of Economics* 37(3): 479–96.

Foley, James (2023) Race, nation, empire? Historicising outward and inward-facing British nationalism. *International Relations*. Available (consulted 23 August 2024) at: https://journals.sagepub.com/doi/10.1177/00471178231196073.

Fomin, I. and Nadskakula-Kamarczuk, O. (2022) Against Putin and Corruption, for Navalny and the "Revolution"? The Dynamics of Framing and Mobilization in the Russian Political Protests of 2017–18. *Communist and Post-Communist Studies* 55(1): 99–130.

Forbes (2025a) *Profile. Arkady Rotenberg*. Available (consulted 2 May 2025) at: https://www.forbes.com/billionaires/.

Forbes (2025b) *Profile. Gennady Timchenko*. Available (consulted 2 May 2025) at: https://www.forbes.com/billionaires/.

Forbes (2025c) *World's Billionaires List. The Richest in 2025*. Available (consulted 2 May 2025) at: https://www.forbes.com/billionaires/.

Ford, Rob (2016) Older 'left-behind' voters turned against a political class with values opposed to theirs. *The Observer*, 25, June. Available (consulted 23 December 2023) at: https://www.theguardian.com/politics/2016/jun/25/left-behind-eu-referendum-vote-ukip-revolt-brexit.

Ford, R. and Goodwin, M. (2014) *Revolt on the Right: Explaining Support for the Radical Right in Britain*. London: Routledge.

Ford, R. and Goodwin, M. (2017) Britain After Brexit: A Nation Divided. *Journal of Democracy* 28(1): 17–30.

Forgnone, Valeria (a cura di, 2023) Silvio Berlusconi è morto. Folla ad Arcore per il feretro, mercoledì i funerali di Stato in Duomo con Mattarella e lutto nazionale. Putin: "Amico vero". *La Repubblica*, 12, June. Available (consulted 19 August 2023) at: https://www.repubblica.it/politica/2023/06/12/diretta/silvio_berlusconi_san_raffaele_news-404165204/.

Formigoni, L. and Forni, M. (eds.) (2018) "Elezioni Politiche 2018. Il post-voto". Ipsos. https://www.ipsos.com/sites/default/files/ct/news/documents/2018-03/elezioni_politiche_2018_-_analisi_post-voto_ipsos-twig.pdf.

Forti, Steven (2024) Extreme Right 2.0, A Big Global Family. *NACLA Report on the Americas* 56(1): 20–7.

Foucault, Michel (2008) *The birth of biopolitics: lectures at the Collège de France, 1978–1979*. Translated by Graham Burchell. New York, NY: Palgrave Macmillan.

Francis, Sam (2024) Starmer confirms Rwanda deportation plan 'dead'. *BBC News*, 6, July. Available (consulted 11 July 2024) at: https://www.bbc.co.uk/news/articles/cz9dn8erg3zo.

Francis, S. and Seddon, P. (2024) Keir Starmer vows to scrap Rwanda asylum scheme 'straightaway'. *BBC*, 10, May. Available (consulted 14 May 2024) at: https://www.bbc.co.uk/news/uk-politics-68984778#:~:text=Sir%20Keir%20Starmer%20has%20pledged,%22smash%22%20people%20smuggling%20gangs.

Fraser, Nancy (2017) The End of Progressive Neoliberalism. *Dissent*, 2, January. Available (consulted 4 April 2023) at: https://www.bresserpereira.org.br/terceiros/2017/fevereiro/17.02-End-of-Progressive-Neoliberalism.pdf.

Fraser, Nancy (2019) *The Old is Dying and the New Cannot be Born: From Progressive Neoliberalism to Trump and Beyond*. London: Verso.

Freedland, Jonathan (2017) The Road to Somewhere by David Goodhart – a liberal's right wing turn on immigration. *The Guardian*, 22, March. Available (consulted 9 May 2024) at: https://www.theguardian.com/books/2017/mar/22/the-road-to-somewhere-david-goodhart-populist-revolt-future-politics.

Freedland, Jonathan (2021) Don't call it sleaze, call it corruption – why scandal haunts Boris Johnson's government. *The Guardian*, 16, December. Available (consulted

4 May 2023) at: https://www.theguardian.com/politics/2021/dec/16/dont-call-it-sleaze-call-it-corruption-why-scandal-haunts-boris-johnsons-government.

Freedom House (2023a) "Freedom in the World 2023. Russia". https://freedomhouse.org/country/russia/freedom-world/2023.

Freedom House (2023b) "Freedom in the World 2023. United Kingdom". https://freedomhouse.org/country/united-kingdom/freedom-world/2023.

Freedom House (2024a) "Freedom in the World 2024. United Kingdom". Available https://freedomhouse.org/country/united-kingdom/freedom-world/2024.

Freedom House (2024b) "Freedom in the World 2024. United States". https://freedom-house.org/country/united-states/freedom-world/2024.

Freedom House (2025) "Freedom in the World 2025. United States". https://freedom-house.org/country/united-states/freedom-world/2025.

Fry, G. K. (2008) *The Politics of the Thatcher Revolution. An Interpretation of British Politics 1979–1990*. London: Macmillan.

Fuchs, Christian (2016) Neoliberalism in Britain: From Thatcherism to Cameronism. *triple C* 14(1): 163–88.

Fuchs, Christian (2017) Donald trump: a critical theory-perspective on authoritarian capitalism. *triple C* 15(1): 1–72.

Fukuyama, Francis (1989) The End of History? *The National Interest* 16: 3–18.

Gagliardi, Andrea (2022) Nasce il governo Meloni: ecco chi sono tutti i ministri. *Il Sole-24 Ore*, 21, October. Available (consulted 2 August 2023) at: https://www.ilsole24ore.com/art/nasce-governo-meloni-ecco-chi-sono-tutti-ministri-AEDBkTAC.

Gaidar, Y.T. (1999) *Days of Defeat and Victory*. Seattle, WA: University of Washington Press.

Galasso, Giuseppe (2002) *Croce e lo spirito del suo tempo*. Milano: Il Saggiatore.

Galbraith, J.K. (1967) *The New Industrial State*. Boston, MA: Houghton Mifflin.

Galeotti, Mark. 2016. "Putin's hydra: inside Russia's intelligence services." European Council on Foreign Relations. London. https://www.jstor.org/stable/pdf/resrep21577.pdf.

Galeotti, Mark (2018) *The Vory: Russia's Super Mafia*. New Haven, CT: Yale University Press.

Galeotti, Mark (2023) Nikolai Patrushev, the man dripping poison into Putin's ear. *The Spectator*, 28, March. Available (consulted 21 July 2024) at: https://www.spectator.co.uk/article/nikolai-patrushev-the-man-dripping-poison-into-putins-ear/.

Gallo, Ernesto (2021) Globalisation, Authoritarianism and the Post-Soviet State in Kazakhstan and Uzbekistan. *Europe-Asia Studies* 73(2): 340–63.

Gallo, Ernesto (2022) Three varieties of Authoritarian Neoliberalism: Rule by the experts, the people, the leader. *Competition & Change* 26(5): 554–74.

Gallo, E., Wu, Z. and Sergi, B.S. (2020) China's Power in Its Strategic Energy Partnership with the Eurasian Economic Union. *Communist and Post-Communist Studies* 53(4): 200–19.

Gamble, Andrew (1979) The Free Economy and the Strong State: The Rise of the Social Market Economy. *The Socialist Register* 16: 1–25.

Gamble, Andrew (1988) *The Free Economy and the Strong State: The Politics of Thatcherism*. London: Macmillan.

Gamble, Andrew (1996) *Hayek. The Iron Cage of Liberty*. New York, NY: Routledge.

Gamble, Andrew (2021a) Making Sense of Populist Nationalism. *New Political Economy* 26(2): 283–90.

Gamble, Andrew (2021b) The remaking of conservatism: Boris Johnson and the politics of Brexit. *The Political Quarterly* 92(3): 461–68.

Garcia-Navarro, Lulu (2024) Inside the Heritage Foundation's Plans for 'Institutionalizing Trumpism', *The New York Times*, 21, January. Available at (consulted 4 July 2024): https://www.nytimes.com/2024/01/21/magazine/heritage-foundation-kevin-roberts.html.

Garzia, D. and Karremans, J. (2021) Super Mario 2: Comparing the technocrat-led Monti and Draghi governments in Italy. *Contemporary Italian Politics* 13(1): 105–15.

Gasiorowski, Mark J. "The Political Regime Project". In *On Measuring Democracy: Its Consequences and Concomitants*, edited by Axel Inkeles. New Brunswick, NJ: Transactions, 2006, 110–11.

Gasseau, G. and Maccarrone, V. (2023) How business interests and fiscal constraints shaped the economic policies of the Italian populist government. *Global Political Economy* 2(2): 185–200.

Geddes, B., Wright, J., and Frantz, E. (2014) Autocratic Breakdown and Regime Transitions: A New Data Set. *Perspectives on Politics* 12(2): 313–31.

Geiger, Chas (2024) Kemi Badenoch: who is new Tory leader and what does she stand for? *BBC news*, 17, November. Available (consulted 24 December 2024) at: https://www.bbc.com/news/articles/c1d59k513qgo.

Gel'man, Vladimir (2018) Politics versus Policy: Technocratic Traps of Russia's Policy Reforms. *Russian Politics* 3(2): 282–304.

Gemma, Alessio (2022) Fratelli d'Italia, dirigenti al ristorante di Milano tra le effigie del Duce. *La Repubblica Napoli*, 2, May. Available (consulted 2 August 2023) at: https://napoli.repubblica.it/cronaca/2022/05/02/news/fratelli_ditalia_dirigenti_duce_mussolini_ristorante_di_milano-347798805/.

Gentleman, Amelia (2018) 'I felt like dirt': disabled Canadian woman told to leave UK after 44 years. *The Guardian*, 24, April. Available (consulted 7 May 2024) at: https://www.theguardian.com/uk-news/2018/apr/24/canadian-woman-told-to-leave-uk-margaret-obrien.

Gentleman, Amelia (2021) A 975-day nightmare: how the Home Office forced a British citizen into destitution abroad. *The Guardian*, 2, December. Available (consulted 7 May 2024) at: https://www.theguardian.com/uk-news/2021/dec/02/home-office-forced-british-citizen-into-destitution-abroad-windrush-compensation-scheme.

Gervasoni, Marco (2004) Metamorfosi della cultura socialista? Il PSI e gli intellettuali. *Italianieuropei*, 1, November. Available (consulted 3 June 2023) at: https://www.italianieuropei.it/it/la-rivista/archivio-della-rivista/item/801-metamorfosi-della-cultura-socialista?-il-psi-e-gli-intellettuali.html.

Gessen, Masha (2012) The Wrath of Putin. *Vanity Fair*, 2, March. Available (consulted 13 June 2024) at: https://www.vanityfair.com/news/politics/2012/04/vladimir-putin-mikhail-khodorkovsky-russia.

Ghodsee, K. and Orenstein, M.A. (2021) *Taking Stock of Shock: Social Consequences of the 1989 Revolutions*. New York, NY: Oxford University Press.

Giannini, Massimo (2010) La vittoria dell'asse Berlusconi-Geronzi. *La Repubblica*, 22, September. Available (consulted 12 July 2023) at: https://www.repubblica.it/economia/2010/09/22/news/profumo_giannini-7301261/.

Giannone, Diego (2010) Political and ideological aspects in the measurement of democracy: the Freedom House case. *Democratization* 17(1): 68–97.

Giannone, D. and Cozzolino, A. (2023) *La democrazia dei tecnocrati. Discorsi e Politiche dei tecnici al governo in Italia*. Milano: Mimesis.

Gigliobianco, Alfredo (2006) *Via Nazionale. Banca d'Italia e classe dirigente. Cento anni di storia*. Roma: Donzelli.

Gigova, Radina (2017) Who Vladimir Putin thinks will rule the world. *CNN World*, 1, September. Available (consulted 24 July 2024) at: https://edition.cnn.com/2017/09/01/world/putin-artificial-intelligence-will-rule-world/index.html.

Gilbert, Mark (1998) In search of normality, the political strategy of Massimo D'Alema. *Journal of Modern Italian Studies* 3(3): 307–17.

Gingrich, Newt (1994) *Contract with America: the bold plan by Rep. Newt Gingrich, Rep. Dick Armey, and the House Republicans to Change The Nation*. New York, NY: Time Books.

Ginsborg, Paul (2003a) *A History of Contemporary Italy. Society and Politics 1943–1988*. London: Penguin.

Ginsborg, Paul (2003b) *Italy and Its Discontents. 1980–2001*. London: Penguin.

Giovannini, A., Vampa, D. and Valbruzzi, M. (2022) Special Issue Introduction – The 2022 Italian general election: a political shock or the new normal? *Italian Journal of Electoral Studies* 86(1): 3–11.

Giroux, H.A. (2017) *The Public in Peril: Trump and the Menace of American Authoritarianism*. London: Routledge.

Giroux, H.A. (2018) *The terror of neoliberalism*. London: Routledge.

Giuffrida, Angela (2022a) Italy's far right celebrate Draghi's downfall and look poised to take power. *The Guardian*, 21, July. Available (consulted 26 May 2024) at: https://www.theguardian.com/world/2022/jul/21/italy-far-right-brothers-of-italy-mario-draghi.

Giuffrida, Angela (2022b) Scepticism over Giorgia Meloni's claim 'fascism is history' in Italian far right. *The Guardian*, 11, August. Available (consulted 4 August 2023) at:

https://www.theguardian.com/world/2022/aug/11/scepticism-over-giorgia-melonis-claims-fascism-is-history-in-italian-far-right.

Glasius, Marliese (2018a) Extraterritorial authoritarian practices: a framework. *Globalizations* 15(2): 179–97.

Glasius, Marliese (2018b) What authoritarianism is ... and is not: a practice perspective. *International Affairs* 94(3): 515–33.

Glasius, M. and Michaelsen, M. (2018) Illiberal and Authoritarian Practices in the Digital Sphere. Prologue. *International Journal of Communication* 12: 3795–813.

Glencross, Andrew (2015) Why a British referendum on EU membership will not solve the Europe question. *International Affairs* 91(2): 303–17.

Götz, Elias (2017) Putin, the State, and War: The Causes of Russia's Near Abroad Assertion Revisited. *International Studies Review* 19: 228–53.

Goldstein, Andrea. 2003. "Privatization in Italy 1993–2002: Goals, Institutions, Outcomes, and Outstanding Issues". CESIfo Working Paper, No. 912. https://www.cesifo.org/DocDL/cesifo_wp912.pdf.

Goncharenko, Roman (2018) Russia's 1993 crisis still shaping Kremlin. *Deutsche Welle*. 10, March. Available (consulted 29 May 2024) at: https://www.dw.com/en/russias-1993-crisis-still-shaping-kremlin-politics-25-years-on/a-45733546.

Goodfellow, Maya (2020) *Hostile Environment. How Immigrants Became Scapegoats*. London: Verso.

Goodwin, Matthew. 2014. "Explaining the Rise of the UK Independence Party". Heinrich-Böll-Stiftung. https://eu.boell.org/sites/default/files/uploads/2014/06/ukip_eu.pdf.

Goodwin, M. and Heath, O. 2016a. "Brexit vote explained: poverty, low skills and lack of opportunity". Joseph Rowntree Foundation. https://www.jrf.org.uk/political-mindsets/brexit-vote-explained-poverty-low-skills-and-lack-of-opportunities.

Goodwin, M. and Heath, O. (2016b) The 2016 Referendum, Brexit and the Left Behind: An Aggregate-level Analysis of the Result. *The Political Quarterly* 87(3): 323–32.

Goodwin, M. and Milazzo, C. (2017) Taking back control?: investigating the role of immigration in the 2016 vote for Brexit. *British Journal of Politics and International Relations* 19(3): 450–64.

Gorodnichenko, Y., Martinez-Vazquez, J., Sabirianova Peter K. 2008. "Myth and Reality of Flat Tax Reform: Micro Estimates of Tax Evasion Response and Welfare Effects in Russia". NBER Working Paper No. 13719. http://www.nber.org/papers/w13719.

Governo (2022) "Governo Draghi". https://www.governo.it/it/i-governi-dal-1943-ad-oggi/xviii-legislatura-dal-23-marzo-2018/governo-draghi/16211.

Gramsci, Antonio (1971) *Selection from the Prison Notebooks*. Translated by Quentin Hoare and Geoffrey Nowell-Smith. London: International Publishers.

Green, E.H.H. (2002) *Ideologies of Conservatism: Conservative Political Ideas in the Twentieth Century*. Oxford: Oxford University Press.

Griffiths, M. and Yeo, C. (2021) The UK's hostile environment: Deputising immigration control. *Critical Social Policy* 41(4): 521–44.

Gruin, Julian (2019) Financializing authoritarian capitalism: Chinese fintech and the institutional foundations of algorithmic governance. *Finance and Society* 5(2): 84–104.

Gualmini, E. and Hopkin, J. (2012) Liberalization within Diversity: Welfare and Labour Market Reforms in Italy and the UK. *Spanish Labour Law and Employment Relations Journal* 1(1–2): 64–81.

Guasti, P. and Buštíková, L. (2020) A Marriage of Convenience: Responsive Populists and Responsible Experts. *Politics and Governance* 8(4): 468–72.

Guidi, Sebastián (2024) Javier Milei, o el populismo cientifico. *El Pais*, 16, January. Available (consulted 1 July 2024) at: https://elpais.com/chile/2024-01-16/javier-milei-o-el-populismo-cientifico.html#.

Guriev, S. and Rachinsky, A. (2005) The Role of Oligarchs in Russian Capitalism. *Journal of Economic Perspectives* 19(1): 145–46.

Hahn, G.M. (2010) Medvedev, Putin, and Perestroika 2.0. *Demokratizatsiya* 18(3): 228–59.

Hale, Henry E. (2015) *Patronal Politics: Eurasian Regime Dynamics in Comparative Perspective*. New York, NY: Cambridge University Press.

Hall, Stuart (1979) The Great Moving Right Show. *Marxism Today* 14–20.

Hall, Stuart (2011) The neo-liberal revolution. *Cultural Studies* 25(6): 705–28.

Hanson, Philip (2007) The turn to statism in Russian economic policy. *The International Spectator* 42(1): 29–42.

Hanson, Philip (2009) The resistible rise of state control in the Russian oil industry. *Eurasian Geography and Economics* 50(1): 14–27.

Hanson, P. and Teague, E. 2013. "Liberal Insiders and Economic Reform in Russia". REP 2013/01. Chatham House. London https://www.chathamhouse.org/sites/default/files/public/Research/Russia%20and%20Eurasia/0113pr_hansonteague.pdf.

Harb, Ali (2022) Why Republicans are elated by 'triumph' of Italy's Giorgia Meloni. *Al Jazeera*, 27, September. Available (consulted 7 August 2023) at: https://www.aljazeera.com/news/2022/9/27/why-us-republicans-are-elated-by-triumph-of-italys-giorgia-meloni.

Harding, L. and Roth, A. (2020) A cup of tea, then screams of agony: how Alexei Navalny was left fighting for his life. *The Guardian*, 20, August. Available (consulted 19 July 2024) at: https://www.theguardian.com/world/2020/aug/20/a-cup-of-tea-then-screams-of-agony-how-alexei-navalny-was-left-fighting-for-his-life.

Harding, L. and Weaver, M. (2009) Barack Obama calls for 'reset' in US-Russia relations. *The Guardian*, 7, July. Available (consulted 22 June 2024) at: https://www.theguardian.com/world/2009/jul/07/barack-obama-russia-moscow-speech.

Harmes, Adam (2012) The rise of neoliberal nationalism. *Review of International Political Economy* 19(1): 59–86.

Harris, John (2013) Ukip: the battle for Britain. *The Guardian*, 17, May. Available (consulted 29 October 2023) at: https://www.theguardian.com/politics/2013/may/17/ukip-the-battle-for-britain.

Harrison, E., Casciani, D. and Sheils McNamee, M. (2023) Small boat arrivals to be swiftly removed. *BBC News*, 7, March. Available (consulted 3 April 2024) at: https://www.bbc.co.uk/news/uk-politics-64875591.

Harrison, Graham (2010) *Neoliberal Africa. The Impact of Global Social Engineering*. London & New York, NY: Zed Books.

Harrison, Graham (2019) Authoritarian neoliberalism and capitalist transformation in Africa: all pain, no gain. *Globalizations* 16(3): 274–88.

Hart, Gillian (2020) Why did it take so long? Trump-Bannonism in a global conjunctural frame. *Geografiska Annaler, Series B, Human Geography* 102(3): 239–66.

Harvey, David (2003) *The New Imperialism*. Oxford: Oxford University Press.

Harvey, David (2004) The 'new' imperialism: accumulation by dispossession. *Socialist Register* 40: 63–87.

Harvey, David (2005) *A Brief History of Neoliberalism*. Oxford: Oxford University Press.

Harvey, David (2006) Neo-liberalism as creative destruction. *Geografiska Annaler: Series B, Human Geography* 88(2): 145–58.

Harvey, David (2016) Neoliberalism is a Political Project. An Interview with David Harvey. *Jacobin*, 23, July. Available (consulted 2 July 2022) at: https://jacobin.com/2016/07/david-harvey-neoliberalism-capitalism-labor-crisis-resistance.

Hawley, George (2017) *Making Sense of the Alt-Right*. New York, NY: Columbia University Press.

Hay, Colin (2009) The Winter of Discontent Thirty Years On. *The Political Quarterly* 80(4): 545–52.

Hay, Colin (2010) Chronicles of a Death Foretold: the Winter of Discontent and Construction of the Crisis of British Keynesianism. *Parliamentary Affairs* 63(3): 446–70.

Hayek, Friedrich A. von (1944) *The Road to Serfdom*. Chicago, IL: University of Chicago Press.

Hayek, Friedrich A. von (2012) *Hayek on Hayek. An Autobiographical Dialogue*. Chicago, IL: University of Chicago Press.

Hayton, Richard (2021) Conservative Party Statecraft and the Johnson Government. *The Political Quarterly* 92(3): 412–19.

Hazony, Yoram (2022) *Conservatism: A Rediscovery*. New York, NY: Simon & Schuster.

Heath, A., Jowell, R., Taylor, B. and Thomson, K. (1998) Euroscepticism and the referendum party. *British Elections and Parties Review* 8(1): 95–110.

Heidegger, Martin. 1953. "Die Frage nach der Technik". In *Gesamtausgabe. I Abteilung: Veröffentlichte Schriften 1910–1976. Band 7. Vorträge und Aufsätze*. Frankfurt am Main: Klostermann, 5–63. https://monoskop.org/images/2/27/Heidegger_Martin_1953_2000_Die_Frage_nach_der_Technik.pdf.

Hellier, D., Inman, P., and Butler, S. (2016) EU referendum: Top firms back pro-EU letter, but supermarkets refuse to sign. *The Guardian*, 22, February. Available (consulted 14 April 2023) at: https://www.theguardian.com/politics/2016/feb/22/brexit-eu-referendum-top-firms-sign-letter-times-pro-eu-shell-easyjet-bae-systems-supermarkets-sainsbury-morrisons-tesco.

Hendrikse, Reijer (2021) The Rise of Neo-Illiberalism. *Krisis* 41(1): 65–93.

Hennessy, Peter (2007) *Having it so good: Britain in the fifties*. London: Penguin.

Heppell, Timothy (2014) *The Tories. From Winston Churchill to David Cameron*. London: Bloomsbury.

Hernandez, Anabel (2019) Brazil's dangerous militias. *Deutsche Welle*, 9, April. Available (consulted 3 January 2025) at: https://www.dw.com/en/against-the-current-brazils-dangerous-militias/a-50288049.

Hickson, K. and Williams, B. (eds.) (2017) *John Major: An Unsuccessful Prime Minister? Reappraising John Major*. Hull: Biteback.

Hickson, K., Page, R. and Williams, B. (2020) Strangled at birth: the One Nation ideology of Theresa May. *Journal of Political Ideologies* 25(3): 334–50.

Hine, D. and Vassallo, S. (eds.) (1998) The Return of Politics. *Italian Politics* 14. New York, NY: Berghahn.

HM Government (2021) "New Plan for Immigration. Policy Statement". https://assets.publishing.service.gov.uk/government/uploads/system/uploads/attachment_data/file/972517/CCS207_CCS0820091708-001_Sovereign_Borders_Web_Accessible.pdf.

Hockstader, Lee (1996) Yeltsin, Communist Zyuganov Launch Presidential Bids. *Washington Post*, 16, February. Available (consulted 2 June 2024) at: https://www.washingtonpost.com/archive/politics/1996/02/16/yeltsin-communist-zyuganov-launch-presidential-bids/a56b04d0-bf9c-4295-a009-12ca1387774b/.

Holton, K. and James, W. (2023) Sunak delays UK petrol car ban, seeking voter support on climate. *Reuters*, 20, September. Available (consulted 13 May 2024) at: https://www.reuters.com/world/uk/uk-interior-minister-braverman-we-need-pragmatic-approach-net-zero-2023-09-20/.

Horesh, N. and Fan Lim, K. (2017) China: an East Asian alternative to neoliberalism? *The Pacific Review* 30(4): 425–42.

Huang, Yiping (2016) Understanding China's Belt & Road Initiative: Motivation, framework and assessment. *China Economic Review* 40: 314–21.

Humphrys, E. and Cahill, D. (2014) How Labour Made Neoliberalism. *Critical Sociology* 43(4–5): 669–84.

Huneeus, Carlos (2000) Technocrats and politicians in an authoritarian regime. The 'ODEPLAN Boys' and the 'Gremialists' in Pinochet's Chile. *Journal of Latin American Studies* 32: 461–501.

Huskey, Eugene (2010) Elite recruitment and state-society relations in technocratic-authoritarian regimes: The Russian case. *Communist and Post-Communist Studies* 43(4): 363–72.

Hutcheson, D.S. and McAllister, I. (2021) Consolidating the Putin Regime: The 2020 Referendum on Russia's Constitutional Amendments. *Russian Politics* 6: 355–76.

Iacobucci, Gareth (2023) Strikes are set to continue after government's "final offer" of 6% pay rise, say BMA. *British Medical Journal* 382: 16–24.

Iamamoto, S.A.S., Kubík Mano, M., and Summa, R. (2021) Brazilian far-right neoliberal nationalism: family, anti-communism and the myth of racial democracy. *Globalizations* 20(5): 782–98.

Ichino, A., Terlizzese, R. and Regini, M. (2012) Sulla riforma Gelmini. *Il Mulino*. 1/2012: 151–59.

IMF (2023) "Carlo Cottarelli". https://www.imf.org/external/np/bio/eng/ccot.htm.

IMF (2025) "World Economic Outlook Database". https://www.imf.org/en/Publications/WEO/weo-database/2025/april/.

INEOS (2016) "INEOS' vote of confidence after Brexit". https://www.ineos.com/inch-magazine/articles/issue-11/ineos-vote-of-confidence-after-brexit/.

Inglehart, R.F. and Norris, P. 2016. "Trump, Brexit, and the Rise of Populism: Economic Have-Nots and Cultural Backlash". HKS Working Paper RW P16–026. https://papers.ssrn.com/sol3/papers.cfm?abstract_id=2818659.

Inglehart, R.F. and Norris, P. (2019) *Cultural Backlash. Trump, Brexit and Authoritarian Populism*. Cambridge: Cambridge University Press.

Inman, Phillip (2012) Black Wednesday 20 years on: how the day unfolded. *The Guardian*, 13, September. Available (consulted 22 September 2023) at: https://www.theguardian.com/business/2012/sep/13/black-wednesday-20-years-pound-erm.

Inman, Phillip (2016) EU referendum: 250 business leaders sign up as backers of Vote Leave. *The Guardian*, 26, March. Available (consulted 26 December 2023) at: https://www.theguardian.com/politics/2016/mar/26/250-business-leaders-sign-up-as-backers-of-vote-leave.

Inozemtsev, Vladislav (2016) "Russia's Economic Modernization: The Causes of a failure". Russie. Nei. Visions. Ifri. https://www.ifri.org/sites/default/files/atoms/files/rnv96_inozemtsev_uk_protege.pdf.

Ipsos (2015) "How Britain voted in 2015". https://www.ipsos.com/en-uk/how-britain-voted-2015?view=wide.

Ipsos (2016) "How Britain voted in the 2016 EU referendum". https://www.ipsos.com/en-uk/how-britain-voted-2016-eu-referendum.

ISPI (2020) "#Med2020 Speaker. Luciana Lamorgese. Minister of the Interior, Italy". https://med.ispionline.it/speaker/luciana-lamorgese/.

Ivanova, A., Keen, M. and Klemm, A. (2005) The Russian 'flat tax' reform. *Economic policy* 20(43): 398–444.

Jackson, Ben (2016) Currents of Neo-Liberalism: British Political Ideologies and the New Right, c. 1955–1979. *The English Historical Review* 131(551): 823–50.

Jackson, B. and Saunders, R. (eds.) (2012) *Making Thatcher's Britain*. Cambridge: Cambridge University Press.

Jackson, D. and Thorsen, E. (eds.) (2015) *UK Election Analysis 2015: Media, Voters and the Campaign. Early reflections from leading UK academics*. Poole: Dorset Digital.

Jayasuriya, Kanishka (2018) Authoritarian Statism and the New Right in Asia's Conservative Democracies. *Journal of Contemporary Asia* 48(4): 584–604.

Jennings, W. and Lodge, M. (2019) Brexit, the tides and Canute: the fracturing politics of the British state. *Journal of European Public Policy* 26(5): 772–89.

Jenss, Alke (2019) Authoritarian neoliberal rescaling in Latin America: urban in/security and austerity in Oaxaca. *Globalizations* 16(3): 304–19.

Jessop, Bob. 2003. "From Thatcherism to New Labour: Neo-Liberalism, Workfarism, and Labour Market Regulation". Department of Sociology. Lancaster University. http://www.comp.lancs.ac.uk/sociology/soc131rj.pdf.

Jessop, Bob (2007) New labour or the normalization of neo-liberalism. *British Politics* 2(3): 282–88.

Jessop, Bob (2014) Repoliticising depoliticisation: Theoretical preliminaries on some responses to the American fiscal and Eurozone debt crises. *Policy & Politics* 42(2): 293–311.

Jessop, Bob (2015) Margaret Thatcher and Thatcherism: Dead but not buried. *British Politics* 10(1): 16–30.

Jessop, Bob (2019) Authoritarian neoliberalism: Periodization and critique. *South Atlantic Quarterly* 118(2): 343–61.

Jessop, B., Bonnett, K., Bromley, S. and Ling, T. (1988) *Thatcherism: A Tale of Two Nations*. Cambridge: Polity.

Johnson, J.M., Thomas, O.D. and Basham, V.M. (2024) 'Mr Rules': Keir Starmer and the juridification of politics. *British Politics*. Available (consulted 30 August 2024) at: https://doi.org/10.1057/s41293-024-00258-1.

Johnson, M., Ghiglione, D. and Fleming, S. (2020) Giuseppe Conte calls on EU to use full financial firepower. *Financial Times*, 19, March. Available (consulted 28 July 2023) at: https://www.ft.com/content/2038c7cc-69fe-11ea-a3c9-1fe6fedcca75.

Jones, Alistair (2016) *Britain and the European Union*. Edinburgh: Edinburgh University Press.

Jones, Erik (2012) Italy's Sovereign Debt Crisis. *Survival* 54(1): 83–110.

Jones, Erik (2018) "Italy and the Completion of the Euro Area". Sieps. https://www.sipotra.it/old/wp-content/uploads/2018/03/Italy-and-the-Completion-of-the-Euro-Area.pdf.

Joppke, Christian (2021) Nationalism in the neoliberal order: Old wine in new bottles? *Nations and Nationalism* 27(4): 960–75.

Joseph, Keith (1974) "Speech at Edgbaston ("our human stock is threatened")". https://www.margaretthatcher.org/document/101830.

Joseph, Keith (2014) *Four Speeches that changed the world*. London: Centre for Policy Studies.

Kalkman, J.P. (2021) Frontex: A Literature Review. *International Migration* 59(1): 165–81.

Karasik, Theodore (2000) Putin and Shoigu: Reversing Russia's Decline. *Demokratizatsiya* 178–85.

Kazmin, Amy (2024) Giorgia Meloni bolsters ties with Trump world. *Financial Times*. Available (consulted 18 December 2024) at: https://www.ft.com/content/7df9fa4f-adf4-4af2-b6f7-a46211df828f.

Kaul, Nitasha (2019) The Political Project of Postcolonial Neoliberal Nationalism. *Indian Politics & Policy* 2(1): 3–30.

Kenkel, K.M. (2022) "Back from the Depths: Brazil, the World and the EU after Lula's Electoral Victory". https://www.ssoar.info/ssoar/bitstream/handle/document/83452/ssoar-2022-kenkel-Back_from_the_Depths_Brazil.pdf?sequence=1&isAllowed=y&lnkname=ssoar-2022-kenkel-Back_from_the_Depths_Brazil.pdf.

Khasbulatov, Ruslan (1993) *The Struggle for Russia. Power and Change in the Democratic Revolution*. London: Routledge.

Khmelnitskaya, Marina (2021) Socio-economic Development and the Politics of Expertise in Putin's Russia: The 'Hollow Paradigm' Perspective. *Europe-Asia Studies* 73(4): 625–46.

Kiely, Raymond (2019) Locating Trump: Paleoconservatism, Neoliberalism, and Anti-Globalization. *Socialist Register* 55: 126–49.

Kiely, R. and Saull, R. (2017) Neoliberalism and the far-right: An introduction. *Critical Sociology* 43(6): 821–29.

King, Lawrence (2002) Postcommunist Divergence: A Comparative Analysis of the Transition to Capitalism in Poland and Russia. *Studies in Comparative International Development* 37(3): 3–34.

Kipnis, Andrew (2007) Neoliberalism reified: *suzhi* discourse and tropes of neoliberalism in the People's Republic of China. *Journal of the Royal Anthropological Institute* (N.S.) 13: 383–400.

Kipp, J.W. (1994) The Zhirinovsky Threat. *Foreign Affairs* 73(3): 72–86.

Koff, S.P. (2002) *Italy: From the 1st to the 2nd Republic*. London: Routledge.

Konings, Martijn (2012) Neoliberalism & the State. *Alternate Routes: A Journal of Critical Social Research* 23: 85–98.

Konings, Martijn (2018) From Hayek to Trump: The Logic of Neoliberal Democracy. *Socialist Register* 54: 48–73.

Kotz, D.M. (1999) Russia's Financial Crisis: The Failure of Neoliberalism? *Z Magazine* 28–32.

Kozyrev, Andrei (1991) Russia: A Chance for Survival. *Foreign Affairs* 71(2): 1–16.

Kragh, M. and Umland, A. (2023) Putinism beyond Putin: the political ideas of Nikolai Patrushev and Sergei Naryshkin in 2006–20. *Post-Soviet Affairs* 39(5): 366–89.

Krastev, Nikola (2007) Russia: Youthful Billionaires Storm 'Forbes' List. *Rferl*, 9, March. Available (consulted 20 June 2024) at: https://www.rferl.org/a/1075155.html.

Krugman, Paul (2008) Gordon Does Good. *The New York Times*, 13, October. Available (consulted 13 October 2023) at: https://www.nytimes.com/2008/10/13/opinion/13krugman.html?_r=0.

Kubicek, Paul (1999) Russian foreign policy and the West. *Political Science Quarterly* 114(4): 547–68.

Kwarteng, K., Patel, P., Raab, D., Skidmore, C. and Truss, L. (2012) *Britannia Unchained: Global Lessons for Growth and Prosperity*. London: Palgrave Macmillan.

Kwarteng, Kwasi (2011) *Ghosts of empire: Britain's legacy in the modern world*. London: Bloomsbury.

La France, Adrienne (2024) The Rise of Techno-Authoritarianism. *The Atlantic*, 30, January. Available (consulted 4 January 2025) at: https://www.theatlantic.com/magazine/archive/2024/03/facebook-meta-silicon-valley-politics/677168/.

La Repubblica (2006) Elezioni Politiche 2006: Camera. Riepilogo Nazionale. Available (consulted 8 July 2023) at: https://www.repubblica.it/speciale/2006/elezioni/camera/riepilogo_nazionale.html.

La Repubblica (2019) Roberto Gualtieri, ministro dell'Economia del governo Conte bis, 4, September. Available (consulted 28 July 2023) at: https://www.repubblica.it/politica/2019/09/04/news/roberto_gualtieri_ministro_dell_economia-235148821/.

Labour Party Manifesto (1997) http://www.labour-party.org.uk/manifestos/1997/1997-labour-manifesto.shtml.

Lagna, Andrea (2016) Derivatives and the financialisation of the Italian state. *New Political Economy* 21(2): 167–86.

Lane, David (2013) *The Capitalist Transformation of State Socialism: The making and breaking of state socialist society, and what followed*. London: Routledge.

Lankina, Tomila. 2014. "Daring to protest: when, why, and how Russia's citizens engage in street protest." PONARS Eurasia Policy Memo. https://eprints.lse.ac.uk/63846/1/Lankina%20_daring_to_protest.pdf.

Lardy, N.R. 2008. "Financial Repression in China". Policy Brief 08-8. Peterson Institute for International Economics. https://www.piie.com/sites/default/files/publications/pb/pb08-8.pdf.

Larner, Wendy (2003) Neoliberalism? *Environment and Planning D: Society and Space* 21(5): 509–12.

Laruelle, Marlene (2014) Alexei Navalny and challenges in reconciling "nationalism" and "liberalism". *Post-Soviet Affairs* 30(4): 276–97.

Laruelle, Marlene. 2024. "Russia's Ideological Construction in the Context of the War in Ukraine". Russie. Eurasie. Reports. No. 46. IFRI. https://www.ifri.org/sites/default/files/atoms/files/ifri_laruelle_russia_ideology_march2024.pdf.

Laurell, Asa C. (2015) Three Decades of Neoliberalism in Mexico: The Destruction of Society. *International Journal of Health Services* 45(2): 246–64.

Ledeneva, A.V. (2012) Cronies, economic crime and capitalism in Putin's *sistema. International Affairs* 88(1): 149–57.

Ledeneva, A.V. (2013) *Can Russia Modernise?: Sistema, Power Networks and Informal Governance.* Cambridge: Cambridge University Press.

Lendvai-Bainton, N. and Szelewa, D. (2021) Governing new authoritarianism: Populism, nationalism and radical welfare reforms in Hungary and Poland. *Social Policy & Administration* 55: 559–72.

Lentini, Peter (1995) *Elections and Political Order in Russia.* Budapest: Central European University Press.

Leonardo (2024) "Composizione dell'azionariato". https://www.leonardo.com/documents/15646808/0/AGM+2024_Leonardo_ITA.pdf?t=1714665260170.

Leoni, Bruno (1961) *Freedom and the Law.* New York, NY: Nostrand.

Lester, Jeremy (1997) Overdosing on nationalism: Gennadii Zyuganov and the communist party of the Russian Federation. *New Left Review* I/221.

Levitsky, S. and Way, L. (2010) The Rise of Competitive Authoritarianism. *Journal of Democracy* 13(2): 51–65.

Levitsky, S. and Ziblatt, D. (2018) *How Democracies Die. What History Reveals About Our Future.* London: Penguin.

Lewis, Aidan (2008) Italy's Northern League resurgent. *BBC News*, 17, April. Available (consulted 9 August 2023) at: http://news.bbc.co.uk/1/hi/world/europe/7350691.stm.

Lieberthal, Kenneth G. and Lampton, David M. (eds.) (1992) *Bureaucracy, Politics and Decision Making in Post-Mao China.* Berkeley, CA: University of California Press.

Linz, Juan J. "An Authoritarian Regime: The Case of Spain". In *Cleavages, Ideologies and Party Systems*, edited by Eric Allard and Yrjo Littunen. Helsinki: Academic Bookstore, 1964, 291–341.

Linz, Juan J. (1978) Una interpretación de los regímenes autoritarios. *Papers: Revista de Sociología* 8: 11–26.

Linz, Juan J. (2000) *Totalitarian and Authoritarian Regimes.* Boulder, CO: Lynne Rienner.

Lopes de Sousa, Marcelo (2020) The land of the past? Neo-populism, neo-fascism, and the failure of the left in Brazil. *Political Geography* 83. Available (consulted 20 December 2024) at: https://pmc.ncbi.nlm.nih.gov/articles/PMC7139254/.

Logvinenko, Igor (2020) Authoritarian Welfare State, Regime Stability, and the 2018 Pension Reform in Russia. *Communist and Post-Communist Studies* 53(1): 100–16.

Luscombe, R., Oladipo, G. and Slawson, N. (2024) Alexei Navalny death: dozens reportedly arrested in Russia protests as Biden blames Putin 'and his thugs': as it happened. *The Guardian*, 16, February. Available (consulted 24 July 2024) at: https://www.theguardian.com/world/live/2024/feb/16/ukraine-war-live-russia-avdiivka-assault-continues-as-zelenskiy-set-to-visit-europe.

Lynch, P., Whitaker, R. and Loomes, G. (2012) The UK Independence Party: Understanding a Niche Party's Strategy, Candidates and Supporters. *Parliamentary Affairs* 65(4): 733–57.

McAllister, I. and White, S. (2008) It's the economy, Comrade! Parties and voters in the 2007 Russian Duma elections. *Europe-Asia Studies* 60(6): 931–57.

McDonnell, D. and Valbruzzi, M. (2014) Defining and Classifying Technocrat-led and Technocratic Governments. *European Journal of Political Research* 53(4): 654–71.

McFaul, Michael (1997) *Russia's 1996 presidential election: the end of polarized politics*. Stanford, CA: Hoover Institution Press, Stanford University.

McFaul, Michael (1999) Russia's 1999 Parliamentary Elections: Party Consolidation and Fragmentation. *Demokratizatsiya* 8(1): 5–23.

McKee, Martin (2024) The Safety of Rwanda Act: a pointless exercise in performative cruelty. *The British Medical Journal* 385: q947.

McMichael, Philip (1990) Incorporating Comparison within a World-Historical Perspective: An Alternative Comparative Method. *American Sociological Review* 55(3): 385–97.

McNabb, David E. (2016), *Vladimir Putin and Russia's Imperial Revival*. New York, NY: Routledge.

McSmith, A., Chu, B. and Garner, R. (2013) Margaret Thatcher's legacy: Spilt milk, New Labour, and the Big Bang – she changed everything. *The Independent*, 8 April. Available (consulted 9 July 2024) at: https://www.independent.co.uk/news/uk/politics/margaret-thatcher-s-legacy-spilt-milk-new-labour-and-the-big-bang-she-changed-everything-8564541.html.

Madariaga, Aldo (2020) *Neoliberal Resilience: Lessons in Democracy and Development from Latin America and Eastern Europe*. Princeton, NJ: Princeton University Press.

Maerz, S.F., Lührmann, A., Lachapelle, J. and Edgell, A.B. (2020) "Worth the Sacrifice? Illiberal and Authoritarian Practices during Covid-19". https://papers.ssrn.com/sol3/papers.cfm?abstract_id=3701720.

Magness, P.W. (2019) "The Fairytale of Hegemonic Neoliberalism". https://www.aier.org/article/the-fairytale-of-hegemonic-neoliberalism/.

Magyar, Bálint (2016) *Post-Communist Mafia State: The Case of Hungary*. Budapest: Central European University Press.

Maher, Henry (2023) Neoliberalism versus the market? Liz Truss, neoliberal resilience, and Lacan's theory of the four discourses. *The British Journal of Politics and International Relations* 26(2): 325–42.

Majone, Giandomenico (1996) *Regulating Europe*. London: Routledge.

Makortoff, K. and Kollewe, J. (2024) Rachel Reeves launches £7.3bn national wealth fund. *The Guardian*, 9, July. Available (consulted 11 July 2024) at: https://www.theguardian.com/business/article/2024/jul/09/rachel-reeves-national-wealth-fund-labour.

Malagutti, Vittorio (2018) Il j'accuse dell'economista M5S: « L'alleanza con la Lega? Un tradimento ». *L'Espresso*, 14, June. Available (consulted 26 July 2023) at: https://espresso.repubblica.it/palazzo/2018/06/14/news/l-alleanza-con-la-lega-un-tradimento-spero-che-i-cinque-stelle-in-parlamento-si-ribellino-1.323788?refresh_ce.

Mancini, Paolo. 2011. "Between Commodification and Lifestyle Politics. Does Silvio Berlusconi Provide a New Model of Politics for the Twenty-First Century?" Reuters Institute for the Study of Journalism. University of Oxford. https://ora.ox.ac.uk/objects/uuid:db47a434-d41f-41aa-a379-285779d8e14a.

Mann, Michael (1984) The autonomous power of the state: its origins, mechanisms and results. *European Journal of Sociology* 25(2): 185–213.

Manwaring, R., Duncan, G. and Lees, C. (2024) 'Thin labourism': ideological and policy comparisons between the Australian, British, and New Zealand labour parties. *The British Journal of Politics and International Relations* 26(1): 39–61.

Marangoni, Francesco (2012) Technocrats in Government: The Composition and Legislative Initiatives of the Monti Government Eight Months into its Term of Office. *Bulletin of Italian Politics* 4(1): 135–49.

Marangoni, F. and Kreppel, A. (2022) From the 'yellow-red' to the technocratic government in the pandemic era. The formation and activity of the Draghi government during its first nine months in charge. *Contemporary Italian Politics* 14(2): 133–50.

Marangos, John (2004) Was Shock Therapy Consistent with Democracy? *Review of Social Economy* LII(2): 221–43.

Marcon, Giulio (2014) Berlusconi, Grillo, Renzi. I tre populismi italiani. *Sbilanciamoci*, 11, April. Available (consulted 24 July 2023) at: https://sbilanciamoci.info/berlusconi-grillo-renzi-i-tre-populismi-italiani-23790/.

Markus, Stanislav (2017) The Atlas That has Not Shrugged: Why Russia's Oligarchs are an Unlikely Force for Change. *Daedalus* 146(2): 101–12.

Marois, Thomas (2011) Emerging markets bank rescues in an era of finance-led neoliberalism: A comparison of Mexico and Turkey. *Review of International Political Economy* 18(2): 168–96.

Marrow, A. and Korsunskaya, D. (2023) Russia lists around 30 state companies for possible privatisation. *Reuters*, 21, December. Available (consulted 23 July 2024) at: https://www.reuters.com/business/russia-lists-around-30-state-companies-possible-privatisation-2023-12-21/.

Martino, Antonio (2005) *Milton Friedman: una biografia intellettuale*. Soveria Mannelli: Rubbettino.

Marx, Karl (1852) "The Eighteenth Brumaire of Louis Bonaparte". https://www.marxists.org/archive/marx/works/1852/18th-brumaire/ch01.htm.

Marx, K. and Engels, F. (1848) "Manifesto of the Communist Party". https://www.marxists.org/archive/marx/works/download/pdf/Manifesto.pdf.

Mascitelli, B. and Zucchi, E. (2007) Expectations and Reality: The Italian Economy under Berlusconi. *Journal of Contemporary European Studies*. 15(2): 129–48.

Masini, Fabio (2019) Tracing neoliberalism in Italy: intellectual and political connections. *The European Journal of the History of Economic Thought* 26(2): 327–51.

Mason, Rowena (2014a) Tory rightwinger Priti Patel promoted to Treasury. *The Guardian*, 15, July. Available (consulted 8 May 2024) at: https://www.theguardian.com/politics/2014/jul/15/priti-patel-tory-rightwinger-promoted-to-treasury.

Mason, Rowena (2014b) Nigel Farage asked former Conservative MP Enoch Powell to back Ukip. *The Guardian*, 13, December. Available (consulted 1 May 2024) at: https://www.theguardian.com/politics/2014/dec/13/nigel-farage-enoch-powell-endorsement-russell-brand.

Mason, Rowena and agencies (2014) Nigel Farage backs 'basic principle' of Enoch Powell's immigration warning. *The Guardian*, 5, January. Available (consulted 25 September 2023) at: https://www.theguardian.com/politics/2014/jan/05/nigel-farage-enoch-powell-immigration.

Mattei, C.E. (2017) The Guardians of Capitalism: International Consensus and Fascist Technocratic Implementation of Austerity. *Journal of Law and Society* 44(1): 10–31.

Mattei, C.E. (2022a) *The Capital Order: How Economists Invented Austerity and Paved the Way to Fascism*. Chicago, IL: The University of Chicago Press.

Mattei, C.E. (2022b) When Liberals Fell in Love With Benito Mussolini. *Jacobin*, 28, October. Available (consulted 31 May 2023) at: https://jacobin.com/2022/10/mussolini-fascism-liberalism-austerity.

Matthijs, Matthias (2017) Integration at What Price? The Erosion of National Democracy in the Euro Periphery. *Government and Opposition* 52(2): 266–94.

Matveev, Ilya (2019) State, Capital, and the Transformation of the Neoliberal Policy Paradigm in Putin's Russia. *International Review of Modern Sociology* 45(1): 29–51.

Mazzocco, Ilaria. 2022. "How Inequality Is Undermining China's Prosperity". https://www.csis.org/analysis/how-inequality-undermining-chinas-prosperity.

Mearsheimer, John J. (2022) The Causes and Consequences of the Ukraine War. *Horizons: Journal of International Relations and Sustainable Development* 21: 12–27.

Medvedev, Dmitry (2008). *Dmitry Medvedev. Presidential Inaugural Address*. American Rhetoric. Available (consulted 28 May 2024) at: https://www.americanrhetoric.com/speeches/dmitrymedvedev.htm.

Melhuish, Francesca (2024) Powellite nostalgia and racialised nationalist narratives: Connecting Global Britain and Little England. *The British Journal of Politics and International Relations* 26(2): 466–86.

Merrick, Rob (2018) Theresa May vows her 'hostile environment' on illegal immigration will continue, despite the Windrush scandal. *Independent*, 25, April. Available (consulted 7 May 2024) at: https://www.independent.co.uk/news/uk/politics/theresa-may-windrush-scandal-illegal-immigration-rules-stay-uk-pmqs-a8321606.html.

Milanovic, Branko (1998) *Income, Inequality, and Poverty During the Transformation from Planned to Market Economy*. Washington, DC: The World Bank.

Miley, Thomas J. (2011) Franquism as Authoritarianism: Juan Linz and his Critics. *Politics, Religion & Ideology* 12(1): 27–50.

Mirowski, P. and Plehwe, D. (2009) *The Road from Mont Pelerin: The Making of the Neoliberal Thought Collective*. Cambridge, MA: Harvard University Press.

Mkandawire, Thandika (2014) The Spread of Economic Doctrines and Policymaking in Postcolonial Africa. *African Studies Review* 57(1): 171–98.

Modigliani, F. and Padoa-Schioppa, T. (1978) The management of an economy with 100% plus wage indexation. *Princeton Essays in International Finance* 130.

Monaco, Davide (2023) The rise of anti-establishment and far-right forces in Italy: Neoliberalisation in a new guise? *Competition & Change* 27(1): 224–43.

Monaghan, A.C. (2012a) "The End of the Putin Era?" The Carnegie Papers. Carnegie Europe. Carnegie Endowment for International Peace. https://ciaotest.cc.columbia.edu/wps/ceip/0026106/f_0026106_21392.pdf.

Monaghan, A.C. (2012b) The Vertikal: Power and Authority in Russia. *International Affairs* 88(1): 11–6.

Monbiot, George (2016) Neoliberalism – The 'Zombie Doctrine' at the Root of All Our Problems. *Common Dreams*, 15, April. Available (consulted 24 December 2024) at: https://www.commondreams.org/views/2016/04/15/neoliberalism-zombie-doctrine-root-all-our-problems.

Monbiot, George (2018) Dark money lurks at the heart of our political crisis. *The Guardian*, 18, July. Available (consulted 17 January 2024) at: https://www.theguardian.com/commentisfree/2018/jul/18/dark-money-democracy-political-crisis-institute-economic-affairs.

Monti, Mario (2011) Il podestà forestiero. *Corriere della Sera*, 7, August. Available (consulted 17 July 2023) at: https://www.corriere.it/editoriali/11_agosto_07/monti-podesta_1a5c6670-c0c4-11e0-a989-deff7adce857.shtml.

Monticelli, Elena (2018) Il reddito di cittadinanza del M5S: di che stiamo parlando? *Sbilanciamoci*, 10, March. Available (consulted 27 July 2023) at: https://sbilanciamoci.info/reddito-cittadinanza-del-m5s-stiamo-parlando/.

Moran, Joe (2005) The Strange Birth of Middle England. *The Political Quarterly* 76(2): 232–40.

Morgan, Kenneth O. (1948) *Labour in Power 1945–1951*. Oxford: Oxford University Press.

Morin, E. and Kern, A.B. (1999) *Homeland Earth: A Manifesto for the New Millennium*. New York, NY: Hampton Press.

Morris, Jeremy (2019a) Russia's Incoherent State. *Current History* 251–7.

Morris, Jeremy (2019b) The Informal Economy and Post-Socialism: Imbricated Perspectives on Labor, the State, and Social Embeddedness. *Demokratizatsiya* 27(1): 9–30.

Morris, Jeremy (2021) From prefix capitalism to neoliberal economism: Russia as a laboratory in capitalist realism. *Sociology of Power* 33(1): 193–221.

Mosca, L. and Tronconi, F. (2015) Beyond left and right: the eclectic populism of the Five Star Movement. *West European Politics* 42(6): 1258–83.

Motyl, A.J. (2016) Putin's Russia as a fascist political system. *Communist and Post-Communist Studies* 49(1): 25–36.

Mudde, Cas (2007) *Populist Radical Right Parties in Europe*. Cambridge: Cambridge University Press.

Mudde, C. and Rovira Kaltwasser, C. (2018) Studying Populism in Comparative Perspective: Reflections on the Contemporary and Future Research Agenda. *Comparative Political Studies* 51(13): 1667–93.

Müller, Jan-Werner (2016) *What Is Populism?* Pittsburgh, PA: University of Pennsylvania Press.

Murrell, Peter (1993) What is Shock Therapy? What Did it Do in Poland and Russia? *Post-Soviet Affairs* 9(2): 111–40.

Mussolini, Benito (1932) "'The Doctrine of Fascism' (1932)". https://sjsu.edu/faculty/wooda/2B-HUM/Readings/The-Doctrine-of-Fascism.pdf.

Musthaq, Fathimath (2021) Dependency in a financialised global economy. *Review of African Political Economy* 48(21): 15–31.

Napoleoni, Loretta (2014) *Democrazia vendesi. Dalla crisi economica alla politica delle schede bianche*. Milano: Rizzoli.

National Conservatism (2020) "A Conference in Rome, Italy. February 3–4, 2020. Giorgia Meloni". https://nationalconservatism.org/natcon-rome-2020/presenters/giorgia-meloni/.

National Conservatism (2023) "A Conference in London, UK. May 15–17, 2023". https://nationalconservatism.org/natcon-uk-2023/.

Naughton, Barry (2007) *The Chinese Economy. Transitions and Growth*. Cambridge, MA: The MIT Press.

Navarro, P. and Autry, G. (2011) *Death by China: Confronting the Dragon – A Global Call to Action*. Upper Saddle River, NJ: Prentice Hall.

Neate, Rupert (2013) Rosneft takes over TNK-BP in $55bn deal. *The Guardian*, 21, March. Available (consulted 2 July 2024) at: https://www.theguardian.com/business/2013/mar/21/rosneft-takes-over-tnk-bp.

Nelsson, Richard (2015) Archive: how the Guardian reported the 1975 EEC referendum. *The Guardian*, 5, June. Available (consulted 2 July 2024) at: https://www.theguardian.com/politics/from-the-archive-blog/2015/jun/05/referendum-eec-europe-1975.

Nemtsov, Boris (2000) Reform for Russia. Forging a New Domestic Policy. *Harvard International Review* 22(2): 16–21.

Nesvetailova, Anastasia. "Globalization and Post-Soviet Capitalism: Internalizing Neoliberalism in Russia." In *Internalizing Globalization. The Rise of Neoliberalism and the Decline of National Varieties of Capitalism*, edited by Susanne Soederberg, Georg Menz and Philip G. Cerny, Basingstoke, Palgrave, 2005.

Next Generation EU (2020) https://next-generation-eu.europa.eu/index_en.

New Statesman (2023) The new Tory tribes. *The New Statesman*, 19, April. Available (consulted 28 March 2024) at: https://www.newstatesman.com/new-statesman-view/2023/04/the-new-tory-tribes.

News Blog (2011) Russian election protests. *The Guardian*, 10, December. Available (consulted 26 June 2024) at: https://www.theguardian.com/global/2011/dec/10/russia-elections-putin-protest.

Nicholas, N.G. (1952) The British General Election of 1951. *American Political Science Review* 46(2): 398–405.

Nolan, Peter (1995) *China's Rise, Russia's Fall*. London: Macmillan.

Nonini, Donald (2008) Is China Becoming Neoliberal? *Critique of Anthropology* 28(2): 145–76.

Okonjo-Iweala, Ngozi (2012) *Reforming the Unreformable: Lessons from Nigeria*. Cambridge, MA: MIT Press.

Ong, Aihwa (2007) Neoliberalism as a Mobile Technology. *Transactions of the Institute of British Geographers* 32: 3–8.

ONS (2023) "PS: Net Debt (excluding public sector banks) as a % of GDP: NSA". https://www.ons.gov.uk/economy/governmentpublicsectorandtaxes/publicsectorfinance/timeseries/hf6.

OSCE (2003) "Parliamentary Elections, 7 December 2003". OSCE Office for Democratic Institutions and Human Rights. https://www.osce.org/odihr/elections/57864.

OSCE (2004) "Presidential Election. 14 March 2004". OSCE Office for Democratic Institutions and Human Rights. https://www.osce.org/odihr/elections/russia/eoms/presidential_2004.

Ó Beacháin, D. and Polese, A. (eds.) (2010) *The colour Revolutions in the Former Soviet Republics: Successes and Failures*. London: Routledge.

O'Donnell, Guillermo (1988) *Bureaucratic Authoritarianism. Argentina, 1966–1973 in Comparative Perspective*. Berkeley, CA: University of California Press.

O'Donovan, Nick (2021) Demand, dysfunction and distribution: The UK growth model from neoliberalism to the knowledge economy. *The British Journal of Politics and International Relations* 25(1): 178–96.

Padoa-Schioppa, Tommaso (2001) *Europa, forza gentile*. Bologna: Il Mulino.

Panara, Marco (2013) Gutgeld, da Israele a Montecitorio. "Ecco le ricette della Renzinomics." *La Repubblica*, 23, September. Available (consulted 23 July 2023) at: https://www.repubblica.it/economia/affari-e-finanza/2013/09/23/news/gutgeld_da_israele_a_montecitorio_ecco_le_ricette_della_renzinomics-67071395/.

Parlamento Europeo (2024) "Risultati delle elezioni". https://results.elections.europa.eu/it/italia/.

Partington, Richard (2018) Who are the British business leaders still backing Brexit? *The Guardian*, 1, September. Available (consulted 26 December 2023) at: https://www.theguardian.com/business/2018/sep/01/uk-business-figures-still-backing-brexit.

Pasquino, G. and Valbruzzi, M. (2012) Non-partisan governments Italian-style: decision-making and accountability. *Journal of Modern Italian Studies* 17(5): 612–29.

Pasquino, G. and Valbruzzi, M. (2023) The 2022 general Italian elections. The long-awaited victory of the right. *Journal of Modern Italian Studies* 28(1): 1–21.

Patomäki, Heikki (2020) Neoliberalism and nationalist-authoritarian populism: Explaining their constitutive and causal connections. *ProtoSociology* 37: 101–51.

Paxton, R.O. (2021) I've Hesitated to Call Donald Trump a Fascist. Until Now. *Newsweek*, 11, January. Available (consulted 1 January 2025) at: https://www.newsweek.com/robert-paxton-trump-fascist-1560652.

Peck, Jamie (2004) Geography and public policy: Constructions of neoliberalism. *Progress in Human Geography* 28(3): 392–405.

Peck, J. and Tickell, A. (2002) Neoliberalizing Space. *Antipode* 34(3): 380–404.

Peet, R. and Hartwick, E. (2009) *Theories of Development*. New York, NY: Guilford Press.

Peña Miguel, N. and Cuadrado-Ballesteros, B. (2019) Is privatization related to corruption? An empirical analysis of European countries. *Public Management Review* 21(1): 69–95.

Perottino, M. and Guasti, P. (2020) Technocratic populism à la française? The roots and mechanisms of Emmanuel Macron's success. *Politics and Governance* 8(4): 545–55.

Petrella, S., Miller, C. and Cooper, B. (2021) Russia's Artificial Intelligence Strategy: The Role of State-Owned Firms. *Orbis* 65(1): 75–100.

Petrov, Nikolai (2023) "Putin is using de-privatization to create a new generation of loyal oligarchs". Chatham House. London. https://www.chathamhouse.org/2023/10/putin-using-de-privatization-create-new-generation-loyal-oligarchs.

Peyrouse, Sebastien (2012) The Kazakh neopatrimonial regime: Balancing uncertainties among the "family", technocrats and oligarchs. *Demokratizatsiya* 20(4): 345–70.

Pezzino, Paolo (2002) *Senza Stato. Le radici storiche della crisi italiana*. Roma-Bari: Laterza.

Pianta, Mario (2019) Il governo e l'economia politica del declino. *Sbilanciamoci*, 5, February. Available (consulted 26 July 2023) at: https://sbilanciamoci.info/il-governo-gialloverde-e-leconomia-politica-del-declino/.

Pianta, Mario (2021) Italy's Political Turmoil and Mario Draghi's European Challenges. *Intereconomics* 56(2): 82–5.

Piattoni, Simona (2016) Lo stile di policy del governo Renzi. *Rivista Italiana di Politiche Pubbliche* 1: 5–22.

Pifer, Steven. "US-Russia Relations in the Obama Era: From Reset to Refreeze?". In *OSCE Yearbook 2014*, edited by IFSH. Baden-Baden, 2015, 111–23.

Piketty, Thomas (2017) *Capital in the Twenty-First Century*. Cambridge, MA: Belknap Press.

Pimlott, Ben (1989) Is The 'Postwar Consensus' A Myth'? *Contemporary Record* 2(6): 12–4.

PNRR (2021) "Piano Nazionale di Ripresa e Resilienza". https://www.governo.it/sites/new.governo.it/files/PNRR_2021_0.pdf.

Poll of Polls (2025) United Kingdom. *Politico*. Available (consulted 24 December 2024) at: https://www.politico.eu/europe-poll-of-polls/united-kingdom/.

Poguntke, T. and Webb, P. (eds.) (2005) *The Presidenzialization of Politics: A Comparative Study of Modern Democracies*. Oxford: Oxford University Press.

Poulantzas, Nikos (1978) *State, Power, Socialism*. London: Verso.

Pratley, Nils (2024) Rachel Reeves didn't scare the markets. But nor did she impress with a growth plan. *The Guardian*, 30, October. Available (consulted 23 December 2024) at: https://www.theguardian.com/uk-news/nils-pratley-on-finance/2024/oct/30/rachel-reeves-markets-growth-plan-autumn-budget.

President of Russia (2007) *Speech and the Following Discussion at the Munich Conference on Security Policy*. Available (consulted 25 May 2024) at: http://en.kremlin.ru/events/president/transcripts/24034.

President of Russia. Events (2021) "Article by Vladimir Putin 'On the Historical Unity of Russians and Ukrainians'". http://en.kremlin.ru/events/president/news/66181.

President of Russia. Official Web Portal (2010) "The Constitution of Russia". http://archive.kremlin.ru/eng/articles/ConstIntro01.shtml.

Preston, Paul (2006) *The Spanish Civil War: Reaction, Revolution and Revenge*. London: Collins.

Priego, Daniela (2016) *Positivism, Science and 'The Scientists' in Porfirian Mexico. A Reappraisal*. Liverpool: Liverpool University Press.

Primakov, Yevgeny (2013) Perceptions of Russia in the World. *Russia in Global Affairs* 1. Available (consulted 06 June 2024) at: https://eng.globalaffairs.ru/articles/perception-of-russia-in-the-world/.

Project 2025. 2022. "Mandate for Leadership. The Conservative Promise". Washington, DC: The Heritage Foundation. https://www.project2025.org/policy/.

Przeworski, Adam. "A Conceptual History of Political Regimes: Democracy, Dictatorship, and Authoritarianism". In *New Authoritarianism: Challenges to Democracy in the 21st century*, edited by Jerzy J. Wiatr. Opladen: Budrich, 2019, 17–36.

Puleo, L. and Piccolino, G. (2022) Back to the Post-Fascist Past or Landing in the Populist Radical Right? The Brothers of Italy Between Continuity and Change. *South European Society and Politics* 27(3): 359–83.

Purvis, J. (2013) What was Margaret Thatcher's legacy for women? *Women's History Review* 22(6): 1014–18.

Quaglia, Lucia (2004) Italy's policy towards European monetary integration: Bringing ideas back in? *Journal of European Public Policy* 11(6): 1096–111.

Quaglia, Lucia (2005) An integrative approach to the politics of central bank independence: Lessons from Britain, Germany and Italy. *West European Politics* 28(3): 549–68.

Radaelli, Claudio M. (1999) The public policy of the European Union: whither politics of expertise? *Journal of European Public Policy* 6(5): 757–74.

Radaelli, Claudio M. (2017) *Technocracy in the European Union*. London: Routledge.

Rankin, Jennifer (2023) Europe's far right praises UK's illegal migration bill. *The Guardian*, 9, March. Available (consulted 19 April 2023) at: https://www.theguardian.com/world/2023/mar/09/europes-far-right-praise-uks-migration-bill.

Refworld (2024) "Freedom in the World 2003 – Russia." https://www.refworld.org/reference/annualreport/freehou/2002/en/51077.

Reuters Staff (2013) Berlusconi, Guido Barilla smentisce ruolo in futura leadership. *Reuters*, 2, August. Available (consulted 11 July 2023) at: https://www.reuters.com/article/berlusconi-barilla-leadership-idITL6N0G31WR20130802.

Ricolfi, Luca (2001) *La frattura etica. Saggio sulle basi etiche dei poli elettorali*. Torino: Trauben.

Ricolfi, Luca (2005) *Dossier Italia. A che punto e' il "Contratto con gli Italiani."* Bologna: Il Mulino.

Ricolfi, Luca (2006) *Tempo scaduto. Il "Contratto con gli Italiani" alla prova dei fatti*. Bologna: Il Mulino.

Ricolfi, Luca (2018) L'agguato del 2011 contro Berlusconi. *Panorama*, 18, February. Available (consulted 16 July 2023) at: https://www.panorama.it/economia/lagguato-del-2011-contro-berlusconi.

Ritzer, George (1993) *The McDonaldization of Society*. Thousand Oaks, CA: Sage.

Roberts, Kenneth M. (1995) Neoliberalism and the Transformation of Populism in Latin America: The Peruvian Case. *World Politics* 48(1): 82–116.

Robinson, Neil (1999) The global economy, reform and crisis in Russia. *Review of International Political Economy* 6(4): 531–64.

Rofel, Lisa (2007) *Desiring China: Experiments in Neoliberalism, Sexuality, and Public Culture*. Durham, NC: Duke University Press.

Rosenberg, Steve (2019) The man who helped make ex-KGB officer Vladimir Putin a president. *BBC News*, 17, December. Available (consulted 26 July 2024) at: https://www.bbc.co.uk/news/world-europe-50807747#:~:text=The%20secret%20succession,surprise%20decision%20to%20go%20early.

Rossi, Norma (2023) Populism without a people: neoliberal populism and the rise of the Italian far right. *Journal of Political Ideologies* 1–21.

Rossi, Salvatore (2007) *La politica economica italiana, 1968–2007*. Roma-Bari: Laterza.

Roth, A. and Sauer, P. (2023) After Prigozhin humiliated Putin, the question was how he survived so long. *The Guardian*, 24, August. Available (consulted 23 July 2024) at: https://www.theguardian.com/world/2023/aug/24/after-yevgeny-prigozhins-death-many-ask-how-he-survived-for-so-long.

Rovelli, Riccardo (2009) Economic Policy in a Global Crisis: Did Italy Get It Right? *Italian politics* 25: 223–41.

Roy, Denny (1994) Singapore, China and the "Soft Authoritarian" Challenge. *Asian Survey* 34(3): 231–42.

Ruddick, Graham (2016) Sir James Dyson upbeat about Brexit as company invests in expansion. *The Guardian*, 14, September. Available (consulted 27 December 2023) at:https://www.theguardian.com/technology/2016/sep/14/sir-james-dyson-upbeat-about-brexit-as-company-invests-in-expansion.

Runciman, David (2018) *How Democracy Ends*. London: Profile.

Rupprecht, Tobias (2020) Global Varieties of Neoliberalism: Ideas on Free Markets and Strong States in Late Twentieth-century Chile and Russia. *Global Perspectives* 1(1): 13278.

Russell, Rachel (2022) Tax cuts: Kwasi Kwarteng's measures benefit richest, Labour says. *BBC*, 24, September. Available (consulted 27 March 2024) at: https://www.bbc.co.uk/news/uk-politics-63019307.

Rutland, Peter (2013) Neoliberalism in Russia. *Review of International Political Economy* 20(2): 332–62.

Ryan, Matthew D.J. (2019) Interrogating 'authoritarian neoliberalism': The problem of periodization. *Competition & Change* 23(2): 116–37.

Saad-Filho, Alfredo (2011) Crisis in Neoliberalism or Crisis of Neoliberalism? *Socialist Register* 47: 242–59.

Saad-Filho, Alfredo (2020) Varieties of Neoliberalism in Brazil (2003–2019). *Latin American Perspectives* 47(1): 9–27.

Saad-Filho, A. and Boffo, M. (2021) The corruption of democracy: Corruption scandals, class alliances, and political authoritarianism in Brazil. *Geoforum* 124: 300–9.

Sacchi, Stefano (2014) Conditionality by other means: EU's involvement in Italy's structural reforms in the sovereign debt crisis. *Comparative European Politics* 13(1): 77–92.

Sachs, J. D. (1994) "Shock Therapy in Poland: Perspectives of Five Years". The Tanner Lectures on Human Values. University of Utah. 6 and 7, April. https://tannerlectures.org/wp-content/uploads/sites/105/2024/07/sachs95.pdf.

Sachs, J. D. (2012) "What I did in Russia". https://static1.squarespace.com/static/5d59c0bdfff8290001f869d1/t/5ed7d8e248deea6dbee5d577/1591204091062/Sachs+%282012%29_What+I+did+in+Russia.pdf.

Safdar, Anealla (2024) UK riots raise the spectre of racism and evoke haunting memories. *Al Jazeera*, 6, August. Available (consulted 15 August 2024) at: https://www

.aljazeera.com/news/2024/8/6/uk-riots-raise-the-spectre-of-racism-and-evoke-haunting-memories.

Sakwa, Richard (1997) The regime system in Russia. *Contemporary Politics* 3(1): 7–25.

Sakwa, Richard (2010) The Dual State in Russia. *Post-Soviet Affairs* 26(3): 185–206.

Sakwa, Richard (2011) *The Crisis of Russian Democracy: The Dual State, Factionalism and the Medvedev Succession*. Cambridge: Cambridge University Press.

Sakwa, Richard (2014) *Putin and the Oligarch: The Khodorkovsky-Yukos Affair*. London-New York: Tauris.

Sakwa, Richard (2016) Sovereignty and Democracy: Constructions and Contradictions in Russia and Beyond. *Region* 1(1): 3–27.

Sakwa, Richard (2020a) *Russian Politics and Society*. London: Routledge.

Sakwa, Richard (2020b) *The Putin Paradox*. London-New York: Tauris.

Sakwa, Richard (2021) Heterarchy: Russian politics between chaos and control. *Post-Soviet Affairs* 37(3): 222–41.

Salsano, Fernando (2014) "ANDREATTA, Beniamino". Dizionario Biografico degli Italiani. Enciclopedia Treccani. https://www.treccani.it/enciclopedia/beniamino-andreatta_%28Dizionario-Biografico%29/.

Sánchez-Cuenca, Ignacio (2017) From a deficit of democracy to a technocratic order: The postcrisis debate on Europe. *Annual Review of Political Science* 20: 351–69.

Sanders, David (2023) One Man's Damage: The Consequences of Boris Johnson's Assault on the British Political System. *The Political Quarterly* 94(2): 166–74.

Sanderson, Rachel (2017) Davide Serra: 'I have an Italian heart but a British brain.' *Financial Times*, 24, November. Available (consulted 23 July 2023) at: https://www.ft.com/content/c0213e30-cea7-11e7-9dbb-291a884dd8c6.

Sandford, Daniel (2024) Reform UK election pledges: 11 key policies analysed. *BBC*, 17, June. Available (consulted 13 July 2024) at: https://www.bbc.com/news/articles/cqll1edxgw40.

Sartori, Giovanni (1970) Concept Misinformation in Comparative Politics. *American Political Science Review* LXIV(4): 1033–53.

Saull, R., Anievas, A., Davidson, N., et al. (eds.) (2014) *The Longue Durée of the Far-Right: An International Historical Sociology*. Abingdon: Routledge.

Savage, M. and Isaac, A. (2023) Nigel Farage launching new website to help people denied accounts by banks. *The Guardian*, 30, July. Available (consulted 18 August 2023) at: https://www.theguardian.com/politics/2023/jul/30/nigel-farage-coutts-planning-new-website-to-help-people-denied-accounts-by-banks.

Saveliev, A. and Zhurenkov, D. (2021) Artificial intelligence and social responsibility: the case of the artificial intelligence strategies in the United States, Russia, and China. *Kybernetes* 50(3): 656–75.

Schedler, Andreas (1998) What is Democratic Consolidation? *Journal of Democracy* 9(2): 91–107.

Schedler, Andreas (2006) *Electoral Authoritarianism: The Dynamics of Unfree Competition*. Boulder, CO: Lynne Rienner.

Schedler, Andreas (2015) "Electoral Authoritarianism". Emerging Trends in the Social and Behavioral Sciences: An Interdisciplinary, Searchable, and Linkable Resource. Wiley Online Library. https://onlinelibrary.wiley.com/doi/epdf/10.1002/9781118900772.etrds0098.

Scheiring, Gabor (2022) The national-populist mutation of neoliberalism in dependent economies: the case of Viktor Orbán's Hungary. *Socio-Economic Review* 20(4): 1597–623.

Schneider, E. and Sandbeck, S. (2019) Monetary integration in the Eurozone and the rise of transnational authoritarian statism. *Competition & Change* 23(2): 138–64.

Schumpeter, J.A. (1986) *History of Economic Analysis*. London: Routledge.

Scottish Government (2013) "Deprivation – Scottish Index of Multiple Deprivation". https://web.archive.org/web/20170804213749/http://www.gov.scot/Topics/Statistics/Browse/Social-Welfare/TrendSIMD.

Schmidt, V.A. "Economic Crisis Management in the EU: from past Eurozone mistakes to future promise beyond the COVID-19 pandemic." In *EU Crisis Management*, edited by Christian Kreuder-Sonnen, Vivien A. Schmidt, Astride Séville, Anna Wetter Ryde and Jonathan White. Stockholm: SIEPS, 2022, 19–39.

Scicluna, N. and Auer, S. (2019) From the rule of law to the rule of rules: technocracy and the crisis of EU governance. *West European Politics* 42(7): 1420–42.

Sciorilli Borrelli, Silvia (2023) Giorgia Meloni takes 'full responsibility' for controversial bank tax. *Financial Times*, 14, August. Available (consulted 18 August 2023) at: https://www.ft.com/content/64fa6138-91c7-46d8-b3aa-d90e7c66d9f5.

Scott, Matthew (2011) Reflections on 'The Big Society'. *Community Development Journal* 46(1): 132–37.

Seddon, M., Miller, C. and Schwartz, F. (2023) How Putin blundered into Ukraine – then doubled down. *Financial Times*, 23, February. Available (consulted 21 July 2024) at: https://www.ft.com/content/80002564-33e8-48fb-b734-44810afb7a49.

Shaw, Martin (2022) *Political Racism. Brexit and its Aftermath*. Newcastle upon Tyne: Agenda Publishing.

Shearmur, Jeremy (2006) Hayek, *The Road to Serfdom*, and the British Conservatives. *Journal of the History of Economic Thought* 28(3): 309–14.

Sherman, N. and Espiner, T. (2022) IMF openly criticises UK government tax plans. *BBC*, 28, September. Available (consulted 27 March 2024) at: https://www.bbc.co.uk/news/business-63051702.

Shields, Stuart (2015) Neoliberalism Redux: Poland's Recombinant Populism and its Alternatives. *Critical Sociology* 41(4–5): 659–78.

Shilliam, Robbie (2018) *Race and the undeserving poor: from abolition to Brexit*. Newcastle: Agenda Publishing.

Shilliam, Robbie (2021) *Enoch Powell: Britain's First Neoliberal Politician*. New Political Economy 26(2): 239–49.

Shirk, Susan L. (1993) *The Political Logic of Economic Reform in China*. Berkeley and Los Angeles, CA: California University Press.

Shleynov, Roman (2016) Pals Prosper from Proximity to Putin's Power. *OCCRP*, 22, December. Available (consulted 19 July 2024) at: https://www.occrp.org/en/28-ccwatch/cc-watch-indepth/5917-pals-prosper-from-proximity-to-putin-s-power.

Shushkevich, Stanislau (2013) The End of the Soviet Union: Stanislau Shushkevich's Eyewitness Account. *Demokratizatsiya* 21(3): 315–38.

Siddiqui, Kalim (2017) Hindutva, Neoliberalism and the Reinventing of India. *Journal of Economic & Social Thought* 4(2): 142–86.

Signorini, L.F. (2018) "Carlo Azeglio Ciampi. Scritti nella Nuova Antologia". Banca d'Italia. https://www.bancaditalia.it/pubblicazioni/interventi-direttorio/int-dir-2018/signorini-20180312.pdf.

Simone, G. and Pianta, M. (2023) Understanding Inflation: The Italian Case. *Intereconomics* 58(1): 17–21.

Sinha, Subir (2021) 'Strong leaders', authoritarian populism and Indian developmentalism: The Modi moment in historical context. *Geoforum* 124: 320–33.

Skidelsky, R. (2003) *John Maynard Keynes: 1883–1946: Economist, Philosopher, Statesman*. London: Pan MacMillan.

Skidmore, T.E., Smith, P.E. and Green, J.N. (2014) *Modern Latin America*. Oxford: Oxford University Press.

Slobodian, Quinn (2018) *Globalists: The End of Empire and the Birth of Neoliberalism*. Cambridge, MA: Harvard University Press.

Slobodian, Quinn (2021) The Backlash Against Neoliberal Globalization from Above: Elite Origins of the Crisis of the New Constitutionalism. *Theory, Culture & Society* 38(6): 51–69.

Slobodian, Q. and Plehwe, D. "Neoliberals Against Europe." In *Mutant Neoliberalism: Market Rule and Political Rupture*, edited by William Callison and Zachary Manfredi. New York, NY: Fordham University Press, 2019: 89–111.

Smith, H. and Burrows, R. (2021) Software, Sovereignty and the Post-Neoliberal Politics of Exit. *Theory, Culture & Society* 38(6): 143–66.

Smith, Neil (2008) Neoliberalism is dead, dominant, defeatable – then what? *Human Geography* 1(2): 1–3.

Snyder, Timothy (2018) *The Road to Unfreedom: Russia, Europe, America*. New York, NY: Tim Duggan Books.

von Soest, Christian (2015) Democracy prevention: The international collaboration of authoritarian regimes. *European Journal of Political Research* 54(4): 623–38.

Sondel-Cedarmas, Joanna. "Giorgia Meloni's new Europe. Europe of sovereign nations in Brothers of Italy's party manifestos." In *The Right-Wing Critique of Europe.*

Nationalist, Sovereigntist and Right-Wing Populist Attitudes to the EU, edited by J. Sondel-Cedarmas and F. Berti. London: Routledge, 2022, 60–75.

Springer, Simon (2012) Neoliberalism as discourse: between Foucauldian political economy and Marxian poststructuralism. *Critical Discourse Studies* 9(2): 133–47.

Springer, Simon. "Klepto-neoliberalism: Authoritarianism and Patronage in Cambodia." In *States of Discipline: Authoritarian Neoliberalism and the Contested Reproduction of Capitalist Order*, edited by Cemal Burak Tansel. London: Rowman & Littlefield, 2017, 235–54.

Staff and agencies (2008) Northern Rock to be nationalised. *The Guardian*, 17, February. Available (consulted 13 October 2023) at: https://www.theguardian.com/business/2008/feb/17/northernrock.nationalisation.

Standing, Guy (1998) Societal Impoverishment: the Challenge for Russian Social Policy. *Journal of European Social Policy* 8(1): 23–42.

Steele, Jonathan (1991) Yeltsin races to victory in Russian poll. *The Guardian*, 14, June. Available (consulted 22 May 2024) at: https://www.theguardian.com/world/1991/jun/14/russia.jonathansteele.

Stewart, Heather (2016) Theresa May appeals to centre ground but cabinet tilts to the right. *The Guardian*, 13, July. Available (consulted 10 January 2016) at: https://www.theguardian.com/politics/2016/jul/13/theresa-may-becomes-britains-prime-minister.

Stiglitz, Joseph E. (2009) Moving beyond market fundamentalism to a more balanced economy. *Annals of Public and Cooperative Economics* 80(3): 345–60.

Stiglitz, Joseph E. (2019) The End of Neoliberalism and the Rebirth of History. *Project Syndicate*, 19, November. Available (consulted 27 February 2023) at: http://www.bresserpereira.org.br/terceiros/2019/novembro/19.11-End-Neoliberalism-Rebirth-History.pdf.

Stubbs, P. and Lendvai-Bainton, N. (2020) Authoritarian neoliberalism, radical conservatism and social policy within the European Union: Croatia, Hungary and Poland. *Development and Change* 51(2): 540–60.

Stuckler, D., King, L. and McKee, M. (2009) Mass privatisation and the post-communist mortality crisis. *The Lancet* 373(9661): 399–407.

Syal, Rajeev (2022a) Tens of thousands of asylum seekers could be sent to Rwanda, says Johnson. *The Guardian*, 14, April. Available (consulted 8 May 2024) at: https://www.theguardian.com/uk-news/2022/apr/14/tens-of-thousands-of-asylum-seekers-could-be-sent-to-rwanda-says-boris-johnson.

Syal, Rajeev (2022b) Suella Braverman revives Tory pledge to cut net migration to 'tens of thousands'. *The Guardian*, 4, October. Available (consulted on 11 July 2024) at: https://web.archive.org/web/20221005213353/https://www.theguardian.com/politics/2022/oct/04/suella-braverman-revives-tory-pledge-to-cut-net-migration-to-tens-of-thousands.

Syrovátka, J. and Holzer, I. (2024) Russian Prime Minister Mikhail Mishustin: A Study of a Rank-and-File Actor in an Authoritarian Regime. *Europe-Asia Studies* 76(7): 1102–19.

Szaló, Csaba. "The Cultural Sociology of Hungarian National Conservatism". In *Central European culture wars: beyond post-communism and populism*, edited by P. Barša, Z. Hesová and O. Slacálek. Prague: Humanitas, 2021, 84–126.

Talani, L.S. and de Bellis, F. "A Tale of Two Crisis: The Impact of EU Response to the Pandemic – The Case of Italy". In *The Political Economy of Global Responses to COVID-19*, edited by A.W. Cafruny and L.S. Talani. Cham: Springer, 2023, 153–80.

Tansel, C.B. (2019) Reproducing authoritarian neoliberalism in Turkey: urban governance and state restructuring in the shadow of executive centralization. *Globalizations* 16(3): 320–35.

Tarchi, Marco (2018) *Italia populista. Dal qualunquismo a Beppe Grillo*. Bologna: Il Mulino.

Taylor, Diane (2023) Europe's human rights watchdog warns UK over illegal migration bill. *The Guardian*, 29, March. Available (consulted 4 May 2023) at: https://www.theguardian.com/world/2023/mar/29/europe-human-rights-watchdog-warns-uk-over-migration-bill.

Taylor, Graham (2017) *Understanding Brexit*. Bingley: Emerald.

Thatcher, Margaret (1995) *The path to power*. London: HarperCollins.

The Economist (2005a) Exit Siniscalco, scandalised. 2, September. Available (consulted 20 September 2023) at: https://www.economist.com/news/2005/09/22/exit-siniscalco-scandalised.

The Economist (2005b) Addio, Dolce Vita – a survey of Italy. 26, November. Available (consulted 20 September 2023) at: https://www.economist.com/special-report/2005/11/26/addio-dolce-vita.

The Economist (2008) No contest. 11, December. Available (consulted 17 October 2022) at: https://www.economist.com/europe/2008/12/11/no-contest.

The Economist (2022) Who are Russia's supporters? 4, April. Available (consulted 16 February 2024) at: https://www.economist.com/graphic-detail/2022/04/04/who-are-russias-supporters.

The Economist (2023) Rishi Sunak, a very Tory kind of technocrat. 13, April. Available (consulted 7 June 2023) at: https://www.economist.com/britain/2023/04/13/rishi-sunak-a-very-tory-kind-of-technocrat.

The Growth Plan (2022) https://assets.publishing.service.gov.uk/government/uploads/system/uploads/attachment_data/file/1105985/HMT_Autumn_Statement_2022_PRINT.pdf.

The New European (2022) Farage remains in high spirits. 12, October. Available (consulted 27 March 2024) at: https://www.theneweuropean.co.uk/farage-remains-in-high-spirits/.

The Southern Poverty Law Centre. "Militia movement". https://www.splcenter.org/fighting-hate/extremist-files/ideology/militia-movement.

The Supreme Court (2023) "R (on the application of AAA and others) (Respondents/Cross Appellants) v Secretary of State for the Home Department (Appellant/Cross Respondent)". https://www.supremecourt.uk/cases/uksc-2023-0093.html.

The World Bank (No date a). "Data. Gini index – Russia". https://data.worldbank.org/indicator/SI.POV.GINI?locations=RU.

The World Bank (No date b). "Data. Gini index – United Kingdom, United States". https://data.worldbank.org/indicator/SI.POV.GINI?locations=GB-US.

The World Bank (2022) "Life expectancy at birth, male (years) – Russian Federation". https://data.worldbank.org/indicator/SP.DYN.LE00.MA.IN?locations=RU.

The World Bank (2023) "Data. GDP growth (annual % – Italy)" https://data.worldbank.org/indicator/NY.GDP.MKTP.KD.ZG?locations=IT.

The World Bank (2024a) "Data. GDP growth (annual % – United Kingdom)" https://data.worldbank.org/indicator/NY.GDP.MKTP.KD.ZG.

The World Bank (2024b) "Data. Inflation, GDP deflator (annual % – Russian Federation)" https://data.worldbank.org/indicator/NY.GDP.DEFL.KD.ZG?locations=RU.

The World Bank (2025a) "Data. GDP growth (annual % – Russian Federation)" https://data.worldbank.org/indicator/NY.GDP.MKTP.KD.ZG?locations=RU.

The World Bank (2025b) "Share of youth not in education, employment or training, total (% of youth population) – Italy" https://data.worldbank.org/indicator/SL.UEM.NEET.FE.ZS?locations=IT.

The World Bank (2025c) "Unemployment, female (% of female labor force) (modeled ILO estimate) – Italy" https://data.worldbank.org/indicator/SL.UEM.TOTL.FE.ZS?locations=IT.

The World Bank (2025d) "Unemployment, total (% of total labor force) (modeled ILO estimate) – Italy" https://data.worldbank.org/indicator/SL.UEM.TOTL.ZS?locations=IT.

The World Bank (2025e) "Unemployment, total (% of total labour force) (modeled ILO estimate) – Poland" https://data.worldbank.org/indicator/SL.UEM.TOTL.ZS?locations=PL.

Thomas, D. and Nanji, N. (2022) Bank of England steps in to calm markets. *BBC*, 12, October. Available (consulted 27 March 2024) at: https://www.bbc.co.uk/news/business-63061614.

Thompson, Mark R. (2002) Totalitarian and Post-Totalitarian Regimes in Transitions and Non-Transitions from Communism. *Totalitarian Movements and Political Religions* 3(1): 79–106.

Thurston, Alexander (2018) The Politics of Technocracy in Fourth Republic Nigeria. *African Studies Review* 61(1): 215–38.

Tognini, Giacomo (2023) Viaggio dentro Mediobanca, la banca d'affari dei miliardari italiani. *Forbes*, 6, March. Available (consulted 8 July 2023) at: https://forbes.it/2023/03/06/mediobanca-banca-affari-miliardari-italiani/.

Tompson, William. "Putin and the 'Oligarchs': A Two-Sided Commitment Problem?" In *Leading Russia: Putin in Perspective: Essays in Honour of Archie Brown*, edited by Alex Pravda. Oxford: Oxford University Press, 2005, 179–203.

Torrisi, Claudia (2022) The anti-women agenda of the woman set to be the next Italian prime minister. *Open Democracy*, 26, September. Available (consulted 4 August 2023) at: https://www.opendemocracy.net/en/5050/giorgia-meloni-far-right-brothers-of-italy-election-prime-minister-racism-gender/.

Tournier-Sol, Karine. "The ambivalence of UKIP towards Enoch Powell's legacy". In *The Lives and Afterlives of Enoch Powell*, edited by O. Esteves and S. Porion. London: Routledge, 2019, 162–75.

Traynor, Ian (2000a) Putin wins landslide victory in Russian presidency vote. *The Guardian*,27, March. Available (consulted 10 June 2024) at: https://www.theguardian.com/world/2000/mar/27/russia.iantraynor1.

Traynor, Ian (2000b) Vote gives Putin chance of life-long criminal immunity. *The Guardian*, 30, November. Available (consulted 17 June 2024) at: https://www.theguardian.com/world/2000/nov/30/russia.iantraynor.

Treanor, Jill (2006) Revolution hailed but City warned of a looming fight for supremacy. *The Guardian*, 27, October. Available (consulted 18 September 2023) at: https://www.theguardian.com/business/2006/oct/27/politics.economicpolicy.

Treisman, Daniel (2008) Putin's *Silovarchs*. *Orbis* 51(1): 141–53.

Treisman, Daniel (2013) Can Putin Keep His Grip on Power? *Current History* 112(756): 251–58.

Tremonti, Giulio (2008) *La paura e la speranza. Europa: la crisi globale che si avvicina e la via per superarla*. Milano: Mondadori.

Tremonti, Giulio (2025) giuliotremonti.it.

Tribe, Keith. "Liberalism and Neoliberalism in Britain, 1930–1980." In *The Road From Mont Pèlerin. The Making of the Neoliberal Thought Collective*, edited by P. Mirowski and D. Plehwe. Cambridge: MA, Harvard University Press, 2015, 68–97.

Tribune (2021) From Enoch Powell to Margaret Thatcher. An interview with Robbie Shilliam. 20, April. Available (consulted 13 December 2023) at: https://tribunemag.co.uk/2021/04/from-enoch-powell-to-margaret-thatcher.

Trilling, Daniel (2013) Thatcher: the PM who brought racism in from the cold. Verso blog post, 10, April. Available (consulted 15 December 2023) at: https://www.versobooks.com/en-gb/blogs/news/1282-thatcher-the-pm-who-brought-racism-in-from-the-cold.

Tronconi, Filippo (ed.) (2015) *Beppe Grillo's Five Star Movement: Organisation, Communication and Ideology*. Farnham: Ashgate.

UK Government. (2015) "Summer budget 2015: key announcements". https://www.gov.uk/government/news/summer-budget-2015-key-announcements.

UK Government (2022) "The Rt Hon Elizabeth Truss MP". https://www.gov.uk/government/people/elizabeth-truss.

UK Government (2024) "Autumn Budget 2024". https://www.gov.uk/government/publications/autumn-budget-2024.

UK Parliament (2019) "General Election 2017: full results and analysis". https://commonslibrary.parliament.uk/research-briefings/cbp-7979/.

Urban, Jordan (2024) "Donald Trump's America will be a different type of partner for the UK". Institute for Government. https://www.instituteforgovernment.org.uk/comment/donald-trump-partner-uk.

Vail, Mark (2015) Between One-Nation Toryism and Neoliberalism: The Dilemmas of British Conservatism and Britain's Evolving Place in Europe. *Journal of Common Market Studies* 53(1): 106–22.

Valdés, Juan G. (1995) *Pinochet's Economists: The Chicago School of Economics in Chile.* Cambridge: Cambridge University Press.

Vampa, Davide (2023) *Brothers of Italy. A New Populist Wave in an Unstable Party System.* London: Palgrave Macmillan.

Varga, Mihai (2014) Hungary's "anti-capitalist" far-right: Jobbik and the Hungarian Guard. *Nationalities Papers* 42(5): 791–807.

Varga, M. and Buzogány, A. (2022) The Two Faces of the 'Global Right': Revolutionary Conservatives and National-Conservatives. *Critical Sociology* 48(6): 1089–107.

Ventresca, Roberto (2023) Anti-inflationary commitment in the post-Bretton Woods era. Italy's road to stability-oriented monetary policies, 1975–1981. *Journal of Contemporary History* 58(1): 177–99.

Verdun, Amy (1999) The role of the Delors Committee in the creation of EMU: an epistemic community? *Journal of European Public Policy* 6(2): 308–28.

Verney, S. and Bosco, A. (2013) Living Parallel Lives: Italy and Greece in an Age of Austerity. *South European Society and Politics* 18(4): 397–426.

Viesti, Gianfranco (2023) La revisione del Pnrr del governo Meloni. *Sbilanciamoci*, 7, August. Available (consulted 7 August 2023) at: https://sbilanciamoci.info/la-revisione-del-pnrr-del-governo-meloni/.

Virdee, Satnam (2013) The lines of descent of the present crisis. *The Sociological Review* 71(2): 458–76.

Vujacic, Veljko (1996) Gennady Zyuganov and the 'Third Road'. *Post-Soviet Affairs* 12(2): 118–54.

Walker, Gavin (2021) Fascism and the Metapolitics of Imperialism. *Historical Materialism*. Blog. 8, May. Available (consulted 26 December 2024) at: https://www.historicalmaterialism.org/fascism-and-the-metapolitics-of-imperialism/.

Walker, Peter (2023) Ten things we learned from the UK NatCon Conference. *The Guardian*, 17, May. Available (consulted 13 April 2024) at: https://www.theguardian.com/politics/2023/may/17/10-things-we-learned-from-the-uk-natcon-conference.

Walker, Shaun (2017) Ex-minister's harsh jail sentence sends shockwaves through Russian elite. *The Guardian*, 15, December. Available (consulted 22 June 2024) at: https://www.theguardian.com/world/2017/dec/15/russia-jails-former-economy-minister-alexei-ulyukayev-for-corruption.

Wamsley, Dillon (2023) Crisis management, new constitutionalism, and depoliticisation: recasting the politics of austerity in the US and UK, 2010–16. *New Political Economy* 28(4): 646–61.

Ward, J. and Ward, B. (2021) From Brexit to COVID-19: The Johnson Government, Executive Centralisation and Authoritarian Populism. *Political Studies* 71(4): 1171–89.

Watkins, Heather (2016) Brexit And The British Establishment. *Progress in Political Economy*, 29, August. Available (consulted 3 February 2023) at: https://www.ppesydney.net/brexit-british-establishment/.

Watkins, H. and Urbina-Montana, M. (2022) Obstinate memory: Working-class politics and neoliberal forgetting in the United Kingdom and Chile. *Memory Studies* 15(5): 1127–41.

Watson, George (ed.) (2016) *The Unservile State: Essays in Liberty and Welfare*. London: Routledge.

Watt, Nicholas (2013) Ukip will change face of British politics like SDP, says Nigel Farage. *The Guardian*, 3, May. Available (consulted 29 October 2023) at: https://www.theguardian.com/politics/2013/may/03/nigel-farage-ukip-change-british-politics.

Wattnem, Tamara A. (2023) Neoliberal Resource Nationalism. The Scramble for Mexico's Hydrocarbons. *Latin American Perspectives* 30(20): 1–21.

Wearden, Graeme (2008) Government to spend £50bn to part-nationalise UK's banks. *The Guardian*, 8, October. Available (consulted on 13 October 2023) at: https://www.theguardian.com/business/2008/oct/08/creditcrunch.banking.

Webber, Jeffery R. (2020) A Great Little Man: The Shadow of Jair Bolsonaro. *Historical Materialism* 28(1): 3–49.

Weber, Isabella M. "China and neoliberalism: Moving beyond the China is/is not neoliberal dichotomy". In *SAGE Handbook of Neoliberalism*, edited by D. Cahill, M. Cooper, M. Konings, D. Primrose. London: SAGE, 2018, 219–33.

Weitz, Richard (2007) The Shanghai Cooperation Organization: The Primakov Vision and Central Asian Realities. *The Fletcher Forum of World Affairs* 31(1): 103–18.

Weyland, Kurt (1999) Neoliberal Populism in Latin America and Eastern Europe. *Comparative Politics* 31(4): 379–401.

White, S., Wyman, M. and Oates, S. (1997) Parties and Voters in the 1995 Russian Duma Election. *Europe-Asia Studies* 49(5): 767–98.

Wiatr, Jerzy J. "New and Old Authoritarianism in a Comparative Perspective". In *New Authoritarianism: Challenges to Democracy in the 21st century*, edited by Jerzy J. Wiatr. Opladen: Budrich, 2019, 17–36.

Wilkinson, Cai (2014) Putting "Traditional Values" Into Practice: The Rise and Contestation of Anti-Homopropaganda Laws in Russia. *Journal of Human Rights* 13(3): 363–79.

Wintour, Patrick (2014) Ukip's manifesto: immigration, Europe – and that's it. *The Guardian*, 20, May. Available (consulted 30 October 2023) at: https://www.theguardian.com/politics/2014/may/20/ukip-manifesto-europe-immigration.

WITS (2024) "GDP By Country, in current US$. 1988–2021". https://wits.worldbank.org/CountryProfile/en/country/bycountry/startyear/ltst/endyear/ltst/indicator/NY-GDP-MKTP-CD.

Worth, Owen (2022) The great moving Boris show: Brexit and the mainstreaming of the far right in Britain. *Globalizations* 20(5): 814–28.

Wraight, Tom (2019) From Reagan to Trump: The origins of US neoliberal protectionism. *The Political Quarterly* 90(4): 735–42.

Yale News. 2007. "Yale University President Levin Announces Selection of 2007 Yale World Fellows". https://news.yale.edu/2007/05/03/yale-university-president-levin-announces-selection-2007-yale-world-fellows.

Yin, Robert K. (2018) *Case Study Research and Applications*. London: SAGE.

Young, Hugo (1989) *One of Us: A Biography of Mrs Thatcher*. London: Pan.

Zagrebelsky, G. and Pallante, F. (2016) *Loro diranno, noi diciamo – Vademecum sulle riforme istituzionali*. Roma-Bari: Laterza.

Zakaria, Fareed (1997) The Rise of Illiberal Democracy. *Foreign Affairs* 76(6): 22–43.

Zamagni, Vera (1993) *The economic history of Italy 1860–1990*. Oxford: Oxford University Press.

Zeffman, H. and Whannel, K. (2023) The facts have changed, says Rishi Sunak, as he scraps HS2 leg. *BBC*, 4, October. Available (consulted 13 May 2024) at: https://www.bbc.co.uk/news/uk-politics-67005544.

Zhang, Aihua (2018) New Findings on Key Factors Influencing the UK's Referendum on Leaving the EU. *World Development* 102: 304–14.

Zhang, Chenchen (2018) Governing neoliberal authoritarian citizenship: theorizing *hukou* and the changing mobility regime in China. *Citizenship Studies* 22(8): 855–81.

Index

www.ingramcontent.com/pod-product-compliance
Lightning Source LLC
LaVergne TN
LVHW012050160826
845678LV00014B/2767

* 9 7 9 8 8 8 8 9 0 9 3 5 5 *